STATE ✦ FAIRS

GROWING
AMERICAN
CRAFT

Published by Smithsonian Books
PO Box 37012, MRC 513
Washington, DC 20013
smithsonianbooks.com

Director: Carolyn Gleason
Senior Editor: Jaime Schwender
Production Editor: Julie Huggins
Digital Imaging Technician: Bill Whitcher

Edited by Erika Bűky
Front and back cover artwork: Handmade seed art by Liz Schreiber
Designed by Christina Newhard

This book may be purchased for educational, business, or sales promotional use. For information please write the Special Markets Department at the address or website above.

Library of Congress Cataloging-in-Publication Data available.

Hardcover ISBN: 978-1-58834-800-5
Friends of the Smithsonian Edition ISBN: 978-1-58834-819-7

Printed in China, not at government expense
29 28 27 26 25   1 2 3 4 5

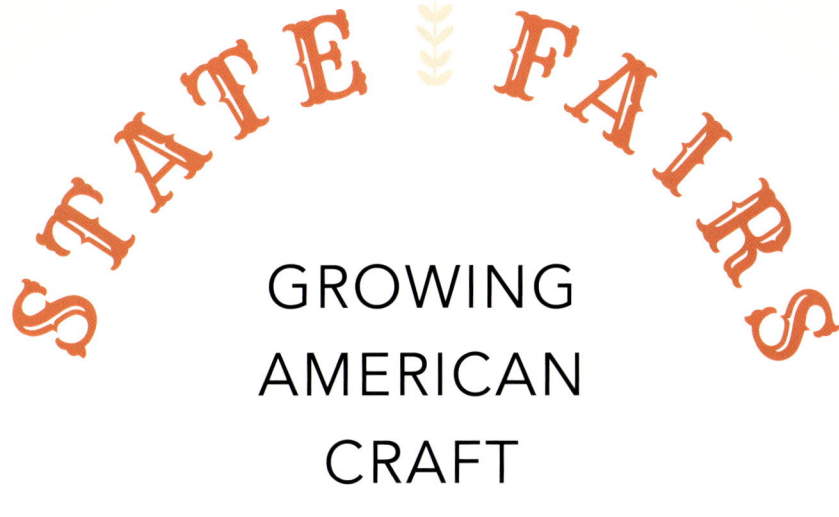

STATE FAIRS

GROWING AMERICAN CRAFT

EDITED BY Mary Savig

FOREWORD BY Wanda M. Corn

SMITHSONIAN BOOKS | WASHINGTON, DC

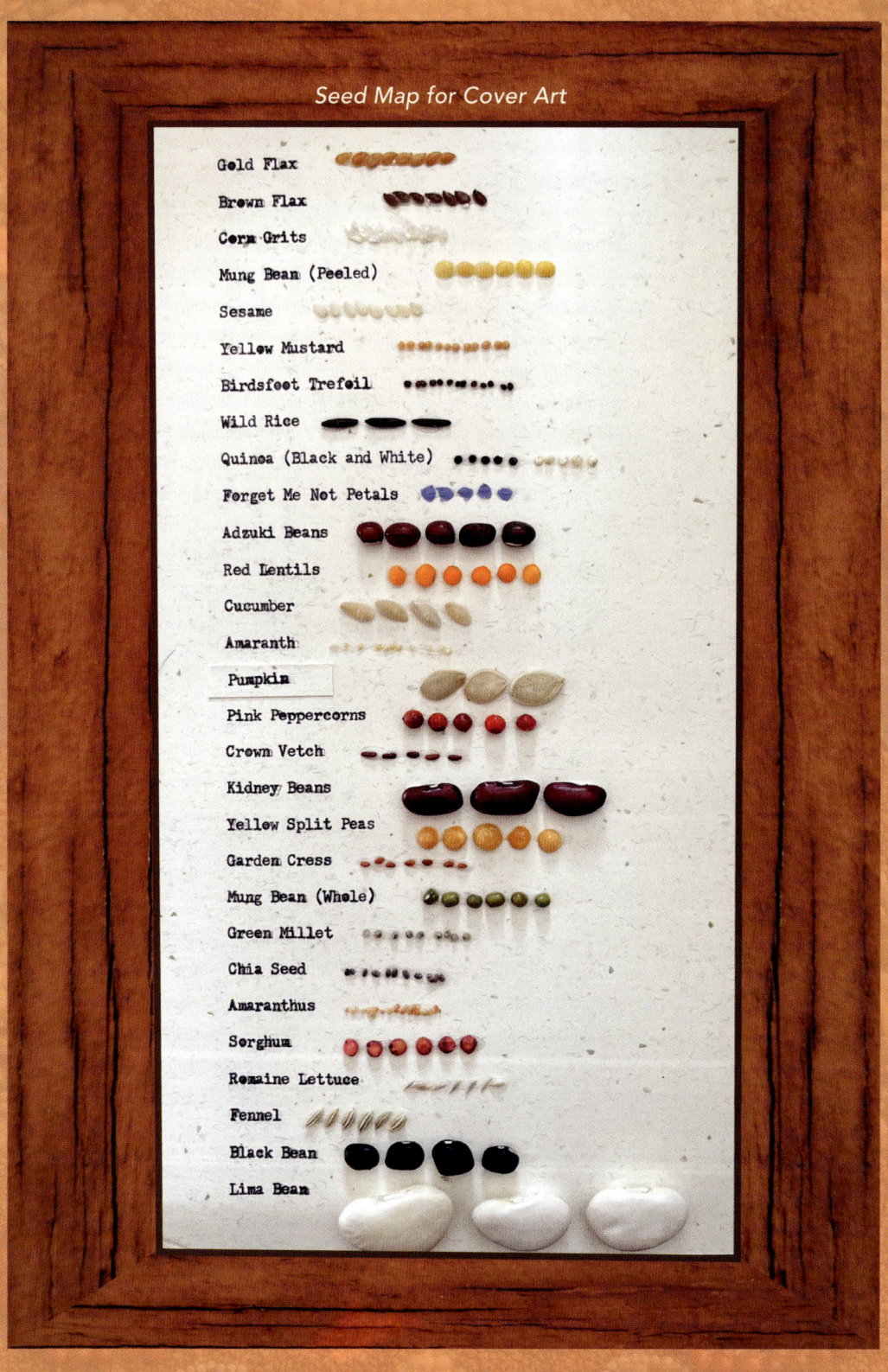

Seed Map for Cover Art

Gold Flax
Brown Flax
Corn Grits
Mung Bean (Peeled)
Sesame
Yellow Mustard
Birdsfoot Trefoil
Wild Rice
Quinoa (Black and White)
Forget Me Not Petals
Adzuki Beans
Red Lentils
Cucumber
Amaranth
Pumpkin
Pink Peppercorns
Crown Vetch
Kidney Beans
Yellow Split Peas
Garden Cress
Mung Bean (Whole)
Green Millet
Chia Seed
Amaranthus
Sorghum
Romaine Lettuce
Fennel
Black Bean
Lima Bean

CONTENTS

Foreword

WANDA M. CORN

I f the Midwestern painter Grant Wood could be asked today about the origins of his famous 1930 painting *American Gothic,* he would without a doubt mention the importance of the Iowa State Fair to his career. From its inception in 1854, the fair had showcased and given prizes for the best cattle, hogs, and farm equipment and the finest canned, baked, and fresh produce. But it also became a showcase for anything crafted by skilled hands: jewelry, needlepoint, quilts, wood carvings, ceramics, paintings—and even sculptures in butter, famous in Iowa since 1911. As the historian Chris Rasmussen explains in his book *Carnival in the Countryside,* the Iowa State Fair embraces low and high culture, products from farms and barns as well as from kitchens, parlors, and artists' studios. It functions as a rich source of information about agriculture and machinery and simultaneously as a people-pleasing carnival with pie-eating contests and midway rides.[1] The fair also shows off skills and talents in the arts in a friendly, supportive environment.

When Wood first submitted a work to the Art Salon at the fair in 1929, it was the biggest showcase for contemporary art in a young state that had not yet built an arts infrastructure of museums, galleries, and art schools. The attendance for the fair that year was 432,617.[2] Experimenting with a new style in painting, Wood was anxious about whether his work would be accepted. To his delight, the juror for the arts not only selected it for the exhibition but awarded it a cash prize. When he won three prizes at the fair the following year, including "Best of Show," Wood was so encouraged and inspired that he began to compose the work that would bring him worldwide recognition, depicting the solemn-faced farmer with the pitchfork and his wife. When *American Gothic*

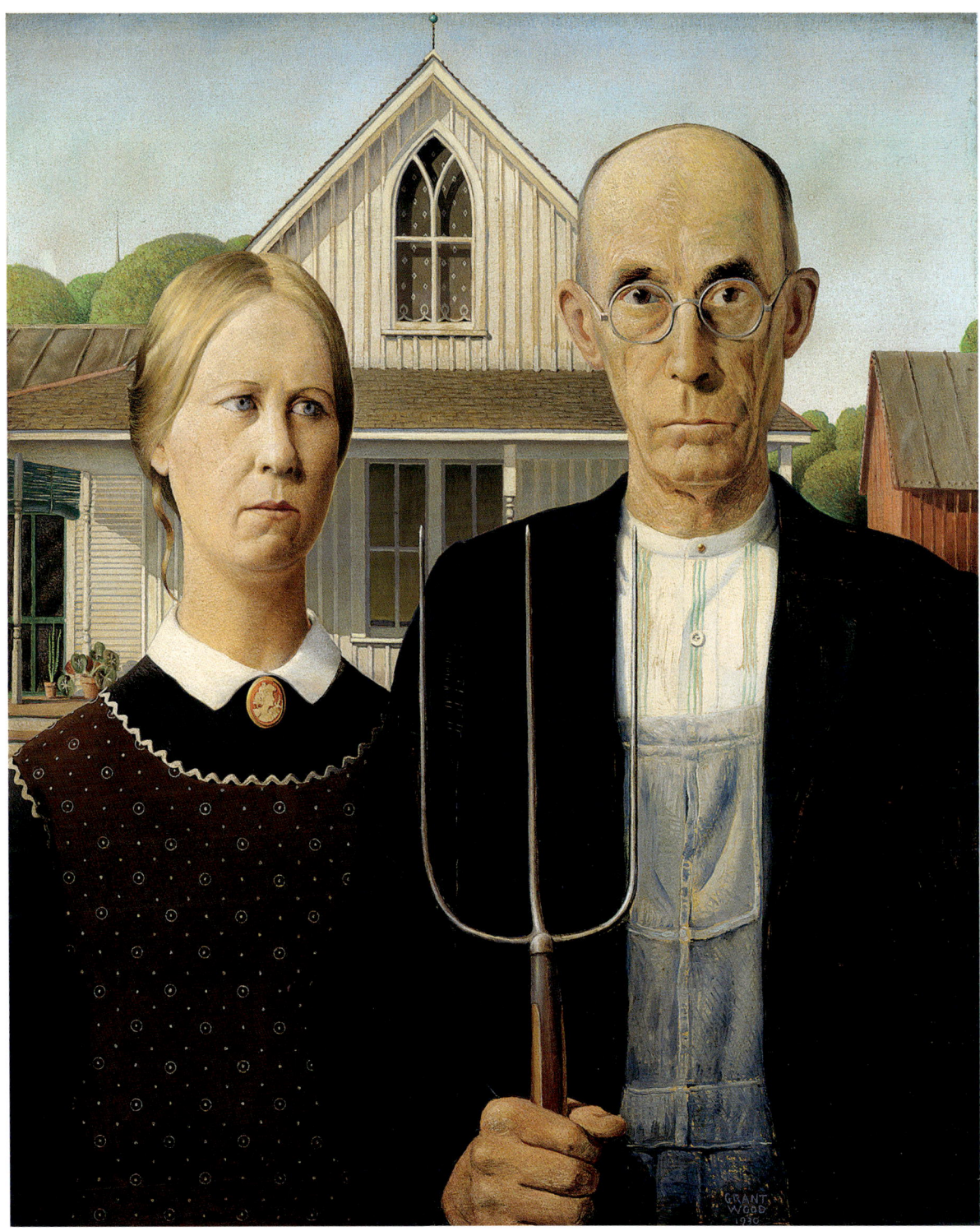

Grant Wood, American Gothic, 1930, oil on beaver board, 30¾ × 25¾ in.

gave him a national reputation, he credited the fair with his success. In turn, the fair has recognized Wood's imprint on the cultural identity of Iowa: in 1996, Norma "Duffy" Lyon, famous for her butter sculptures at the Iowa Fair, carved a rendition of *American Gothic* in celebration of the state's sesquicentennial.

This publication and its related exhibition in the Renwick Gallery celebrate the bounty of finely crafted artworks submitted to state fairs over the years. Many of these works have made their way into museum and private collections, while others are cherished as family heirlooms. The first nationwide survey of the presence and significance of craft at state fairs nationwide, this catalog introduces us to the diversity of voices, the variety of expression, the unusual materials, the amazing talent, and the endless surprises visitors look forward to seeing year after year. Contributions from Mary Savig, Sara Morris, Elana Hain, Jon Kay, and Amber-Dawn Bear Robe trace a journey through fairground sites, from the art galleries and pageant stages to the 4-H buildings and dairy barns. We experience the dazzling fairgrounds and the broad range of artists who show their art and craft each year at these unique crossroads and marketplaces.

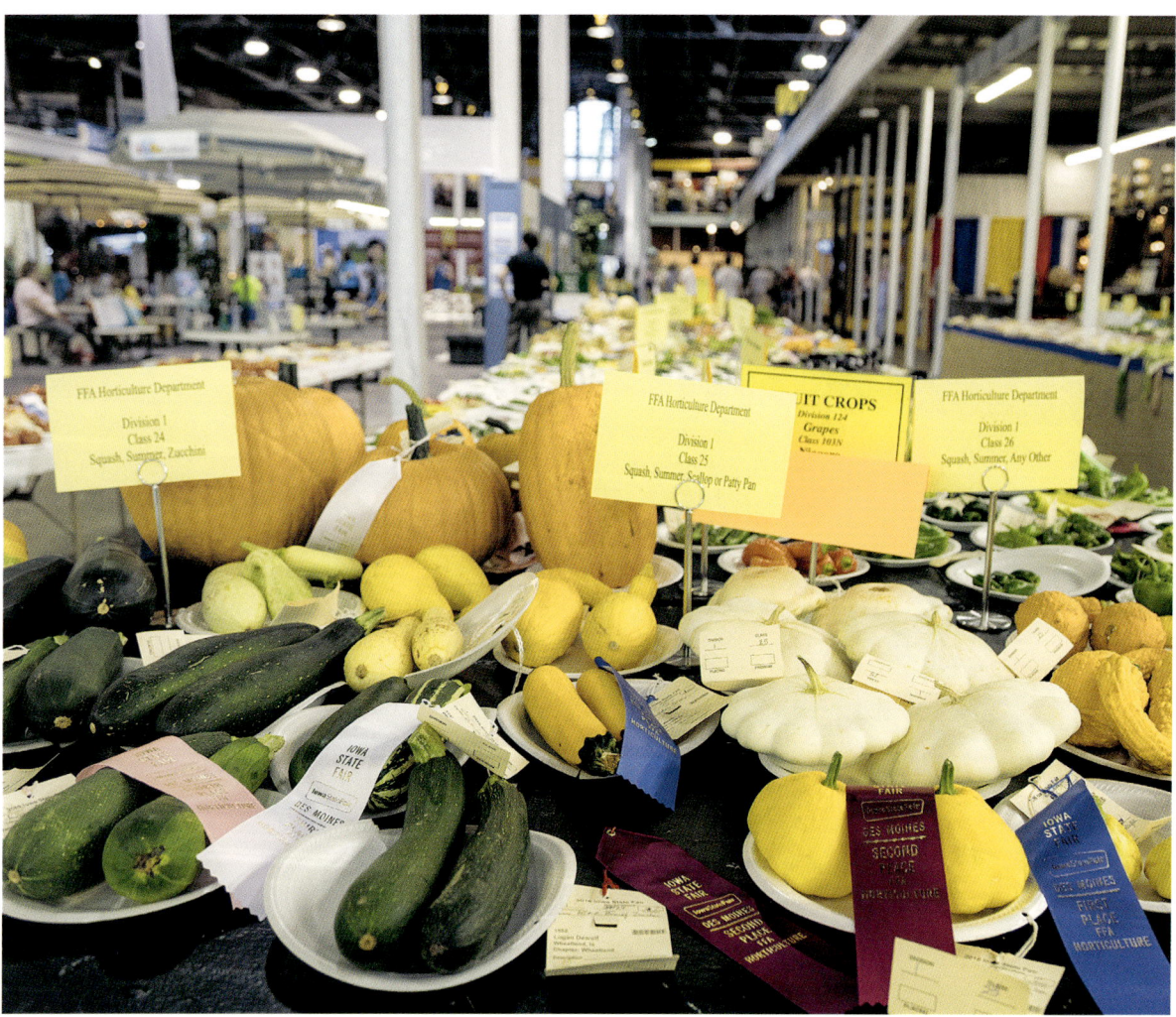

Prize-winning gourds inside the 4-H pavilion at the 2016 Iowa State Fair.

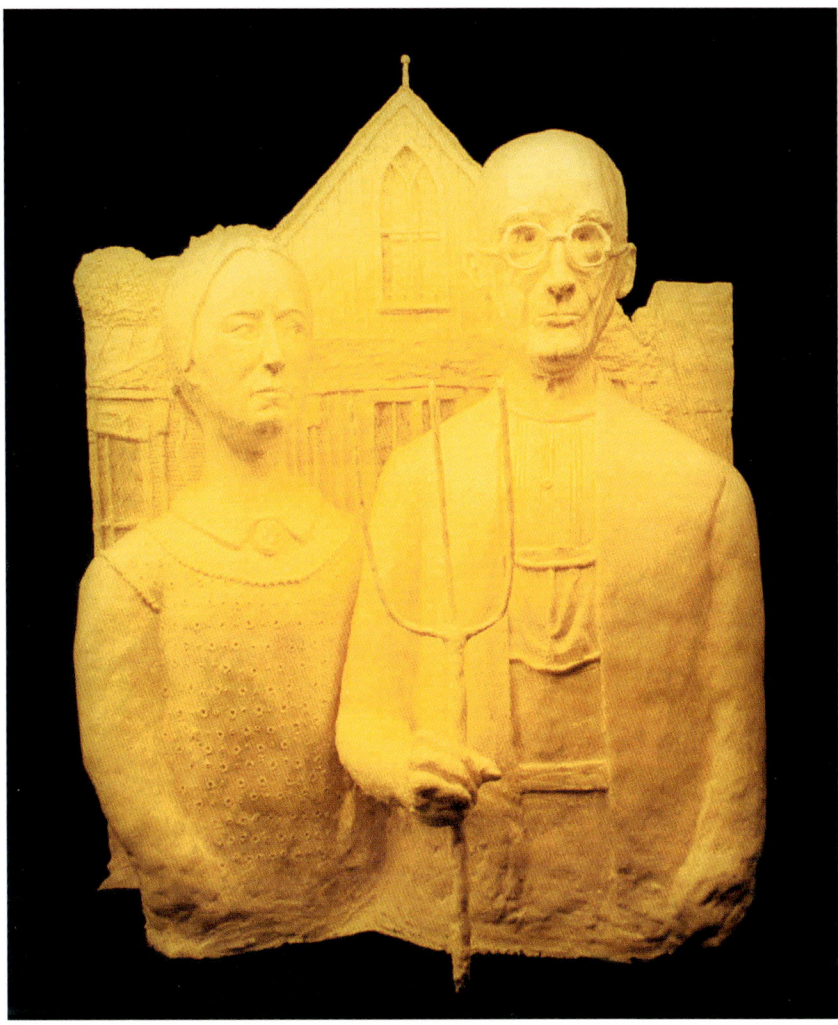

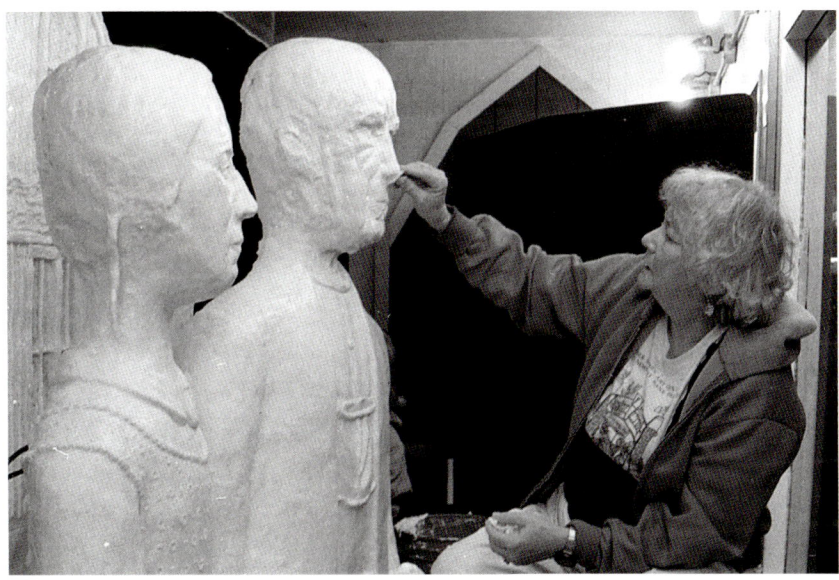

Introduction: Growing American Craft

MARY SAVIG

It all began with sheep. As the story goes, in May 1808 two Merino sheep excited local attention under the great elm tree in the public square in Pittsfield, Massachusetts. The owner of the sheep, Elkanah Watson, organized an exhibition to promote the Merino breed, newly imported from Spain. Soon after, Watson worked with Shaker weavers to fabricate samples of cloth from the fine Merino fleece to distribute to manufacturers. Together, these demonstrations of animals and craft became the building blocks of agricultural fairs in the United States. Today, for a few days each year, the permanent barns and display buildings of state fairgrounds across the nation are enlivened by people, animals, and spectacles, from displays of painstaking skill and prime

F. E. Fox, Spanish Merino Buck, ca. 1834–65, wood engraving. Merino sheep were introduced to the United States in the early nineteenth century.

livestock to the gaudiest of temporary amusements.

Craft has become an essential element of the state fair, demonstrating the creative and practical values of handmade goods in American culture. In turn, state fairs have altered the way artists exhibit their work and engage with the public. Though art in all forms (painting, photography, music, and dance, to name a few) abounds at state fairs, this project centers on craft.

What exactly is craft? That is a prize-winning question. Generally, craft involves making an item by hand and with skill. A handknit merino sweater, a forged horseshoe, a carved bird decoy, and a coil-built ceramic pot are just a few examples of craft. Craft is also about process: the way a maker refines creativity and skill over a lifetime, incorporating knowledge and experience gained into each new piece. Craft tells us how items were made and for what purpose, stretching through time and diverse cultural traditions. At a state fair, crafts on exhibit can range from a sculpted butter cow to a portrait made of seeds to a jar of deep red strawberry-rhubarb jam, and even to a sheep or cow patiently raised by a young 4-H member. These exhibits offer a window into their makers' everyday lives—their families, farms, and communities—as well as into complex issues of American identity and culture.

The contributors to this book guide us through fairground venues to show how fairs connect people through craft. Sara Morris leads us to the most obvious locations: the creative arts and the fine arts displays. Elana Hain describes the importance of youth displays that showcase craft-based life skills like sewing, canning, and raising animals.

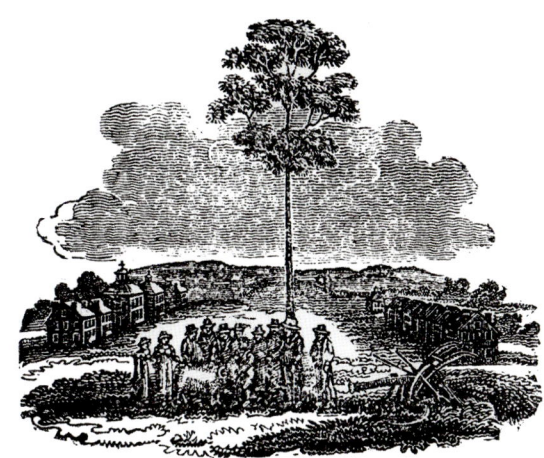

Elkanah Watson's sheep show of 1808.

Jon Kay invites us to a Pioneer Village where artists demonstrate traditional crafts refined over a lifetime. Amber-Dawn Bear Robe considers how Native American communities have created fairs and markets to showcase Indigenous art on their own terms. I mosey through the rest of the fairground to find places where craft might be hiding: tractor and machine halls, the horticulture and

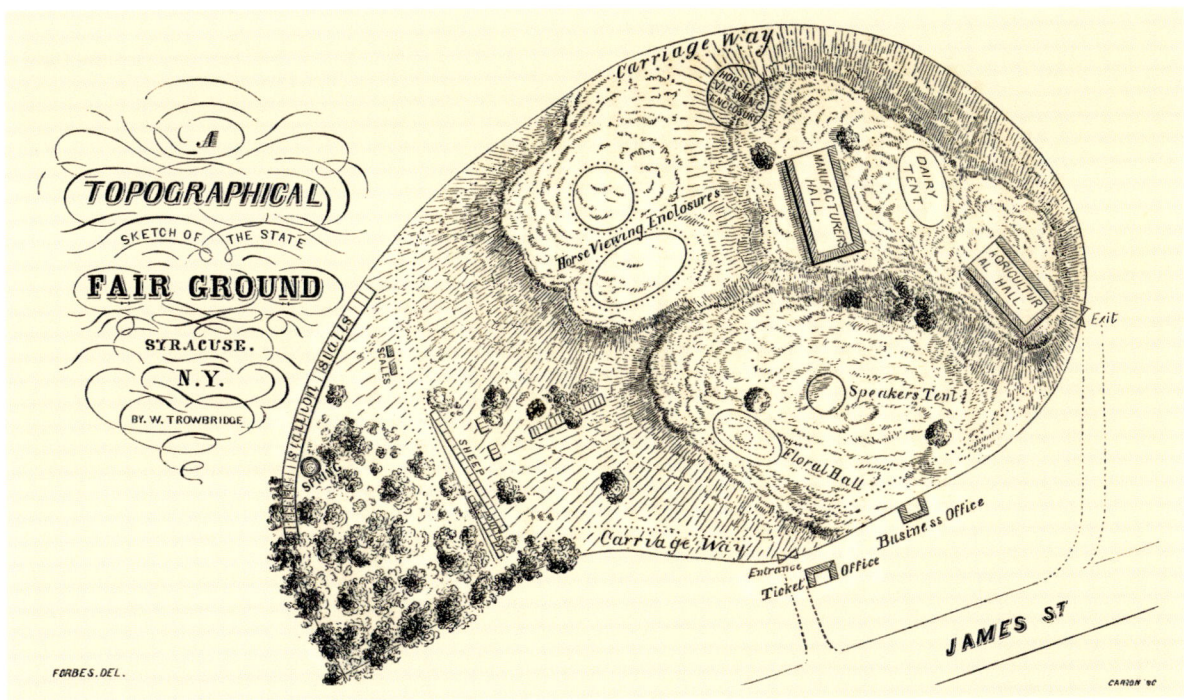

A map of the 1849 fair in Syracuse, New York, with some structures labeled, such as the Agricultural Hall, the Manufacturer's Hall, and the Dairy Tent.

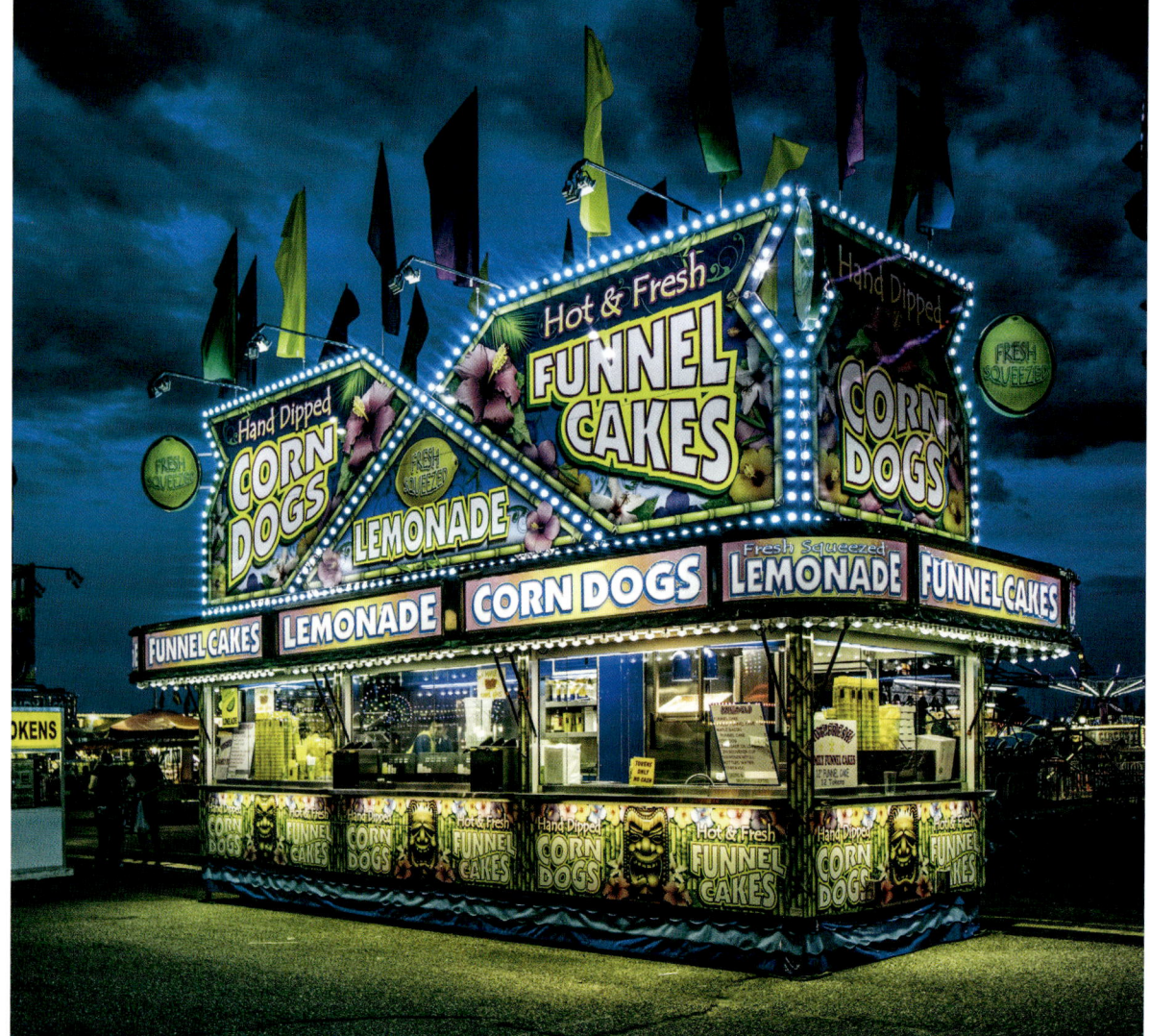

Concession stand purveying all sorts of fried foods and treats at the Colorado State Fair in Pueblo, Colorado, on September 2, 2015.

dairy displays, and the rodeos and horse races. Artists, engineers, cowboys, and butter queens all have their chance to shine at the fair.

The idea of an agricultural fair took root long before the first butter queen was crowned. Carnivals, medieval markets, cattle shows, harvest and barn-raising festivals, religious celebrations, and sheep-shearing feasts have all informed this tradition. State fairs have also been shaped by the American Revolution, world wars, and federal policies on international trade, domestic industry, and land management. They have been bolstered by expanding transportation infrastructure, including canals and railroads, along with interstate telecommunications infrastructure.

Every state fair has a different origin story. South Carolina held its first fair in 1853, when enslaved labor drove the plantation-based agricultural economy.[1] Nebraska organized its first "state" fair in 1859, when it was still a US territory.[2] The Mississippi Band of Choctaw Indians formalized their annual tribal fair in 1949 after a long history of Green Corn Festivals celebrating the ripening of corn.[3]

Like the fairgrounds themselves, media coverage of state fairs has tended to favor excess, recounting the attention-grabbing features like visits by presidents and celebrities, new amusements, daredevil performances, and bizarre (albeit delicious) fried foods. Many media outlets faithfully cover the annual rubber-chicken-throwing contest at the Iowa State Fair. But alongside the "hen-sational" stories about fair follies are stories about women and men winning prizes at the state fair for their pickled eggs, painted china, and livestock.

Back in 1808, citing the success of his sheep show, Elkanah Watson claimed credit for "inoculating this County [Berkshire County] with the Sheep Mania" and shared his vision of introducing his sheep to Massachusetts and beyond.[4] In reality, Watson, a retired land speculator and businessman, was following the lead of gentlemen farmers, lawyers, and merchants in Berkshire County who sought to protect their financial holdings against the changing tides of international trade.[5] The Embargo Act of 1807 restricted the export of American crops to Great Britain and the import of fine cloth from Great Britain. The gentlemen farmers saw an opportunity to improve and diversify their livestock herds by introducing new breeds (like Merino sheep), and the merchants saw an opportunity to expand the local textile industry. First, though, they had to convince working farmers, laborers, and craftspeople to raise more sheep and turn their fleece into wares.

In October 1810 several of the men organized a livestock show to educate working farmers about improved and imported breeds of cattle and sheep.[6] To enliven the event, some of the exhibitors paraded their animals around the public square, concluding with a chorus of cheers, led by Watson:

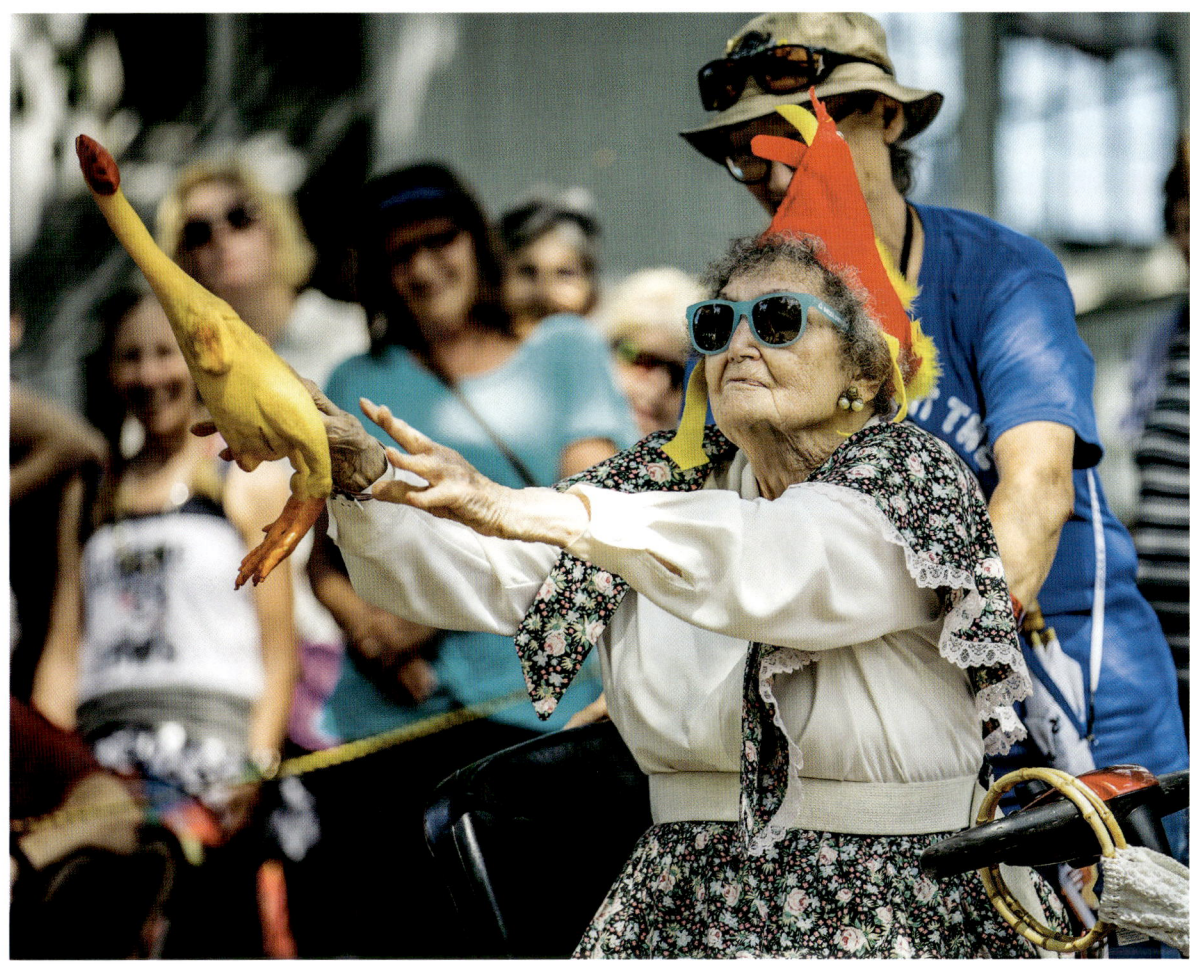

Bonnie Swalwell Eilert of Newton tosses in the "51 and over" category of the Ladies' Rubber Chicken Throwing Contest at the Iowa State Fair on Wednesday, August 15, 2018, in Des Moines.

"I was placed at the head of a procession of farmers, marching round the square … and to separate with some *éclat*, I stepped in front, gave three cheers, in which they all united—we then parted, well pleased with the day and with each other."[7]

Although Watson was not an especially capable farmer—he was once an object of ridicule after falling for a joke about a new breed of potato-picking chickens—he did identify, and take ownership of, a defining element of the American agricultural fair: *éclat*, meaning a sensational, dazzling display. According to Watson's biographer, Mark A. Mastromarino, "The march around the square probably did not result from an individual's decision but a crowd action. Watson was perspicacious enough to seize upon the notion that people needed to be attracted before they could be educated."[8] Following the success of the show, the organizers officially incorporated the Berkshire Agricultural Society.

At the 1811 fair, the society layered more éclat into the program. The day began with livestock competitions in Pittsfield's public square, for which the society offered $70 worth of prizes for the winners of the cattle and sheep competitions. At noon the sheriff conducted a parade from the square to the town meetinghouse. Highlights included sixty oxen drawing a plow guided by the county's two oldest men; members of the Berkshire Agricultural Society bearing signs; a musical band; a stagecoach displaying American-made wares; and another stagecoach carrying a weaving loom and a spinning jenny operated by English artisans.[9] Ever the showman, Watson bundled ears of wheat into ornaments for members and officers of the society to wear in their hats during the procession. At the end of the route, Watson gave a public address and announced the awards. He later summarized the event as "splendid, novel, and imposing, beyond any thing of the kind ever exhibited in America."[10]

The 1812 fair increased the prizes for the livestock competitions to $150 and introduced a new competitive category of superfine woolen broadcloth. Watson himself won a hefty prize of $50 for broadcloth woven by local women from the wool of his Merinos.[11] The 1813 fair increased its prizes to $400, including fifteen prizes for "domestic manufactures, exclusively for females."[12] Indeed, in the US Northeast at the time, cloth was mostly woven by women in their own homes. According to the historian Laurel Thatcher Ulrich, of the 19,276,043

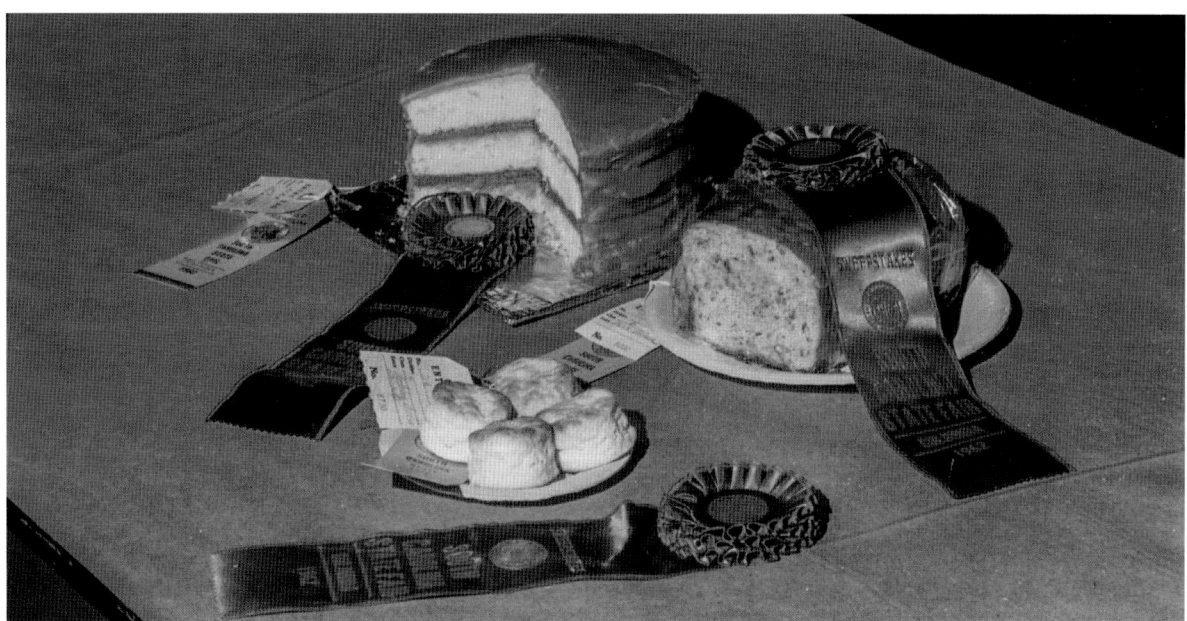

Prize winning baked goods at the South Carolina State Fair, 1962.

yards of cloth made in New England in 1810, only 4 percent was produced in woolen "manufactories." Most of it was woven "in families."[13] The fair provided a rare public platform for women to share their achievements.[14] The 1813 fair concluded with a ball, designed to attract younger townspeople, especially women. Watson observed that the ball further "promoted domestic manufactures, by exciting emulation, and inducing females to feel a pride in appearing decorated in the works of their own hands, on a public occasion."[15]

The Berkshire Agricultural Society established a new paradigm for displaying and celebrating agricultural advancement. In the following years, similar fairs, boasting events from sheep competitions to chic celebrations, spread to the US Midwest and South. These county-level events sowed the seeds for state fairs, the first of which was held in New York.

Art Follows the Plow

In 1832, the New York State Agricultural Society, the first of its kind, was established in Albany to promote and invest in agricultural growth in the state.[16] After several failed attempts throughout the 1830s, the society held the first New York State Fair in 1841. The state government allocated $8,000 for the "promotion of agriculture and household manufactures in the State."[17] Held in the farming town of Syracuse on September 29–30, the fair included an exhibition of three yoke (harnessed pairs) of oxen and a plowing contest. The fair became an annual event with ever-increasing attendance that traveled to numerous cities. Horse races and parades were added to drum up interest. The 1849 New York State Fair introduced a fifty-foot tall revolving wheel, a predecessor to the Ferris wheel, that rewarded its brave riders with views of the fairground.

Emulating New York, other states took advantage of the nation's ever-expanding network of railroads, canals, and roads to hold their own fairs. South Carolina held fairs in the early 1840s, and Vermont and Georgia held their first fairs in 1846.

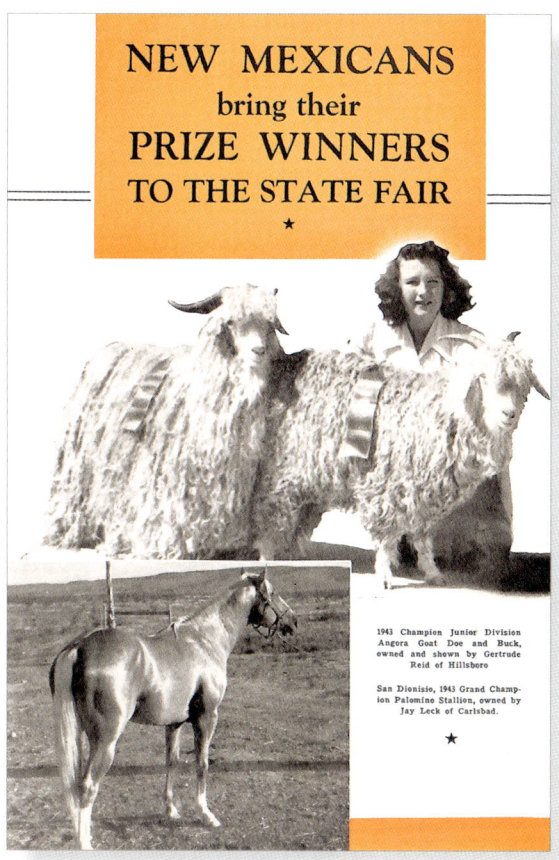

Both men and women participated in and won prizes contests at state fairs. Gertrude Reid was pictured with her prize-winning goats on the cover of a 1943 list of winners at the New Mexico State Fair.

In the emerging states of the Midwest, their populations swelling with white settlers and European immigrants, state fairs became sites of profound cultural influence. Michigan held its first state fair in 1849, followed by Ohio in 1850, Wisconsin in 1851, Indiana in 1852, Illinois in 1853, Iowa in 1854, and Minnesota in 1859. They were often the largest gatherings ever held in these states. Chris Rasmussen, a historian of the Iowa State Fair, describes the scene of the first fair: "In October 1854, thousands of Iowans hitched up their wagons and journeyed to Fairfield to attend the first Iowa State Fair … On the six-acre fairgrounds, hastily constructed buildings shielded the fair's exhibitions of crops, machines, cooking, crafts, and paintings from the sun and rain, if not the dust."[18]

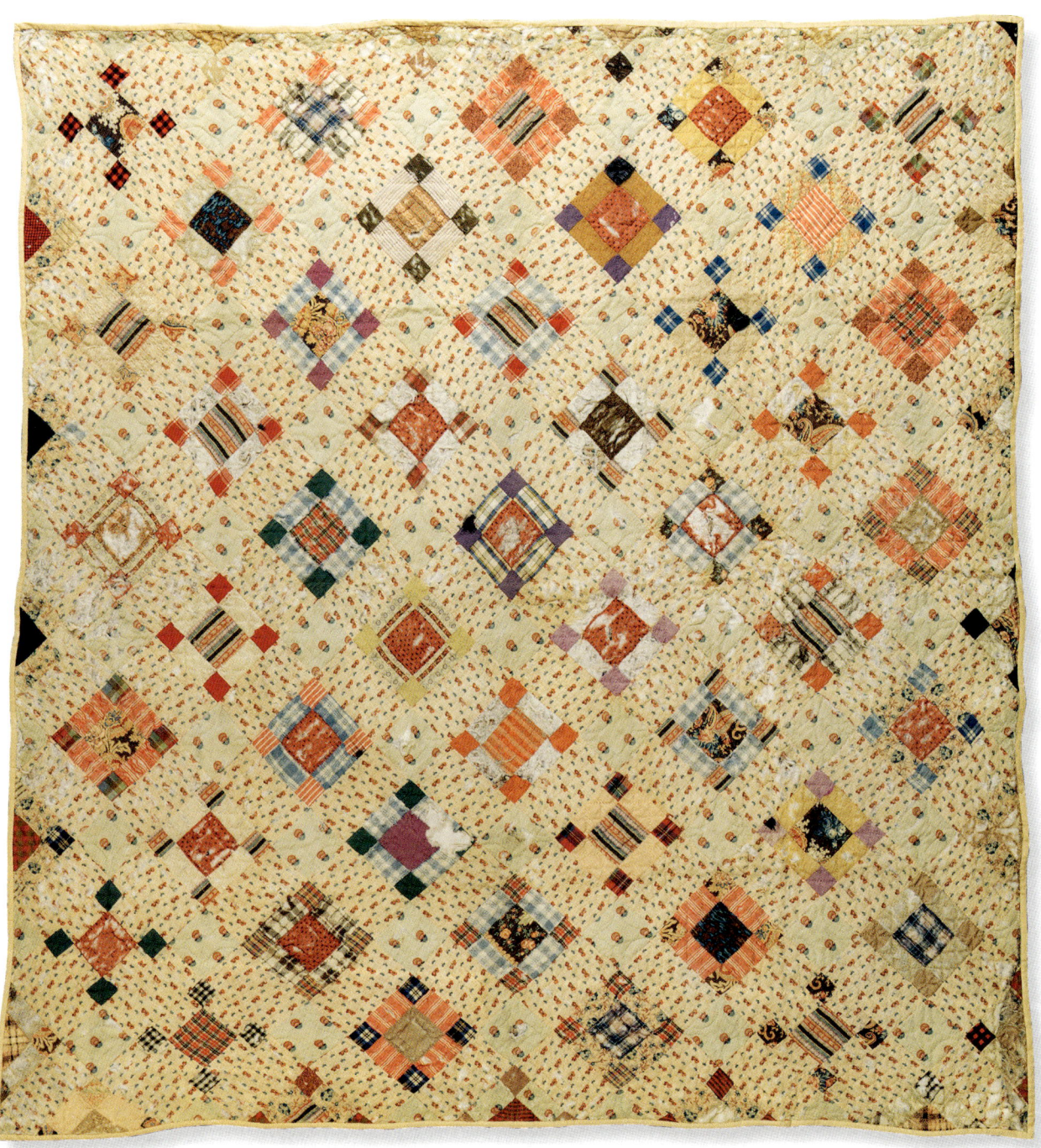

Marie Farrell, nine-patch cotton quilt, 1859, cotton, 78 × 83 in.

This list of exhibit categories exemplifies how state fair organizers continued to follow the Berkshire paradigm: the integration of agriculture with displays of commercial and domestic products, aligning the interests of farmers, craftspeople, and manufacturers. To recognize women's contributions to farm and community life, the inaugural exhibition of farm work at the Iowa State Fair offered two classes of "Domestic Manufactures."[19] One category offered awards for functional flannels, mittens, rag carpets, and fine white hose. The other category offered awards for less functional fancywork and ornamental needlework.[20] The Iowa State Agricultural Society described the women's work as "the most brilliant feature of the exhibition. This display spoke in volumes to the honor of the mothers, wives, and daughters of our state."[21]

The inclusion of art and craft competitions at state fairs reflects the relationship of *culture* to agriculture. In the 1840s, Massachusetts Senator Daniel Webster famously proclaimed, "When tillage begins, the other arts follow. The farmers, therefore, are the founders of civilization."[22] Such a sentiment energized art competitions at fairs, convincing rural participants that they were crafting a distinct "native" culture. Rasmussen argues that as "fairgoers gazed at exhibitions of livestock, handicrafts, or art, they were implicitly taking the measure of their state's economy, society, and culture."[23]

Fairs have developed categories for entries and a hierarchy of prizes. Along with prize ribbons, judges often award monetary "premiums" to winning entries. The first-place winners of a particular class—wheel-thrown pottery, for example—may be judged against the winners of other classes in related categories. The winners of those tiers of competition then compete for the "Best in Show" award (also known as the sweepstakes award), the top prize of the competition. Fairs and local art museums also make "Purchase Prize" awards, acquiring the selected artworks for their collections, and some fairs offer a "People's Choice" award, with the winner selected by fairgoers.

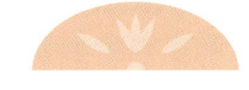

"When tillage begins, the other arts follow."

SENATOR DANIEL WEBSTER

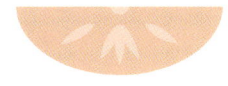

Competitions in traditionally feminine arts showcased a region's cultural values.[24] At the first Minnesota State Fair in 1859, Marie Farrell won first prize for her hand-stitched cotton quilt in the popular nine-patch design. A historian of the Minnesota State Fair, Karal Ann Marling, observes that "just as the judging of animals established a community standard for the breeder, so did inspections of intricate stitches and the flake of piecrust help to define the accomplishments expected of the superior housewife."[25] Rural women would continue to define and refine notions of culture through craft competitions.

A 1959 quilt by Dora Frink narrates the idealized story of how the American frontier was tilled to produce (white) American culture. To commemorate the one-hundredth anniversary of Oregon's statehood, Frink embroidered vignettes of the state's history on thirty-two squares that she pieced into a quilt. Frink's version of the story begins with a stereotypical depiction of

"Indians": A man aims his bow toward an elk, and a woman and child sit in front of a tipi. In the 1850s, numerous Indigenous peoples in Oregon were forcibly relocated to reservations, where most suffered poverty and illness. This part of the history is not told in the quilt. The arrival of covered wagons, shown in several squares, anticipates the end of the Indigenous story. The pioneers assume control over the land, chopping trees and building log homes. Then, as one square indicates, the land is "settled": a farmer tends to livestock, with a barn and a church in the background. From here, culture begins. Frink depicts government institutions like the State Highway Commission (whose establishment officially closed the chapter on the rugged Oregon Trail), the State Library, and the Public Service Building. In a final scene, Frink presents a vision of "Home in 1859," with a woman ironing in a room equipped with a lamp, a stove, a spinning wheel, and a rocking chair—symbols of home-spun American culture. This quilt won a blue ribbon at the 1959 Oregon State Fair.

The widely held assumption that a so-called native culture could sprout from previously untilled land willfully erases the presence of Indigenous nations that had known and cultivated that same land for generations. The success of farmers relied on the disenfranchisement and mass killing of Indigenous peoples across the United States. Following the American Revolution, the State of New York sought to attract settlers from New England to purchase and cultivate farmland. New York Governor George Clinton coerced the Haudenosaunee (Iroquois) to sell their land to the state and then made that land available for sale to incoming farmers and laborers.[26] In 1830, President Andrew Jackson signed into law the Indian Removal Act, forcing Indigenous nations to cede their ancestral lands in the Southeast and move to territory west of the Mississippi. The Indian Removal Act and subsequent treaties enabled the federal government to grant Indigenous land to settlers, primarily enterprising farmers.

County and state fairs also gained momentum from policies and tensions around slavery. Before the Civil War, President Abraham Lincoln's government invested in state agriculture programs to provide viable alternatives to plantation agriculture in the South, creating land-grant universities in the new Midwestern territories.[27] The Midwest began to stake out its claim as the nation's food basket. The historian Pamela H. Simpson notes that "King Corn was the midwestern challenge to the South's King Cotton, and the Civil War exacerbated that competition."[28] Following the Civil War, agriculture became more specialized.[29] Farmers formed new horticultural societies and unions to represent their interests to governments and businesses alike, and state fairs became social grounds for these organizations. Newly formed government programs and agencies and agricultural colleges catered to the needs of emerging agricultural sectors.

> ## Competitions in traditionally feminine arts showcased a region's cultural values.

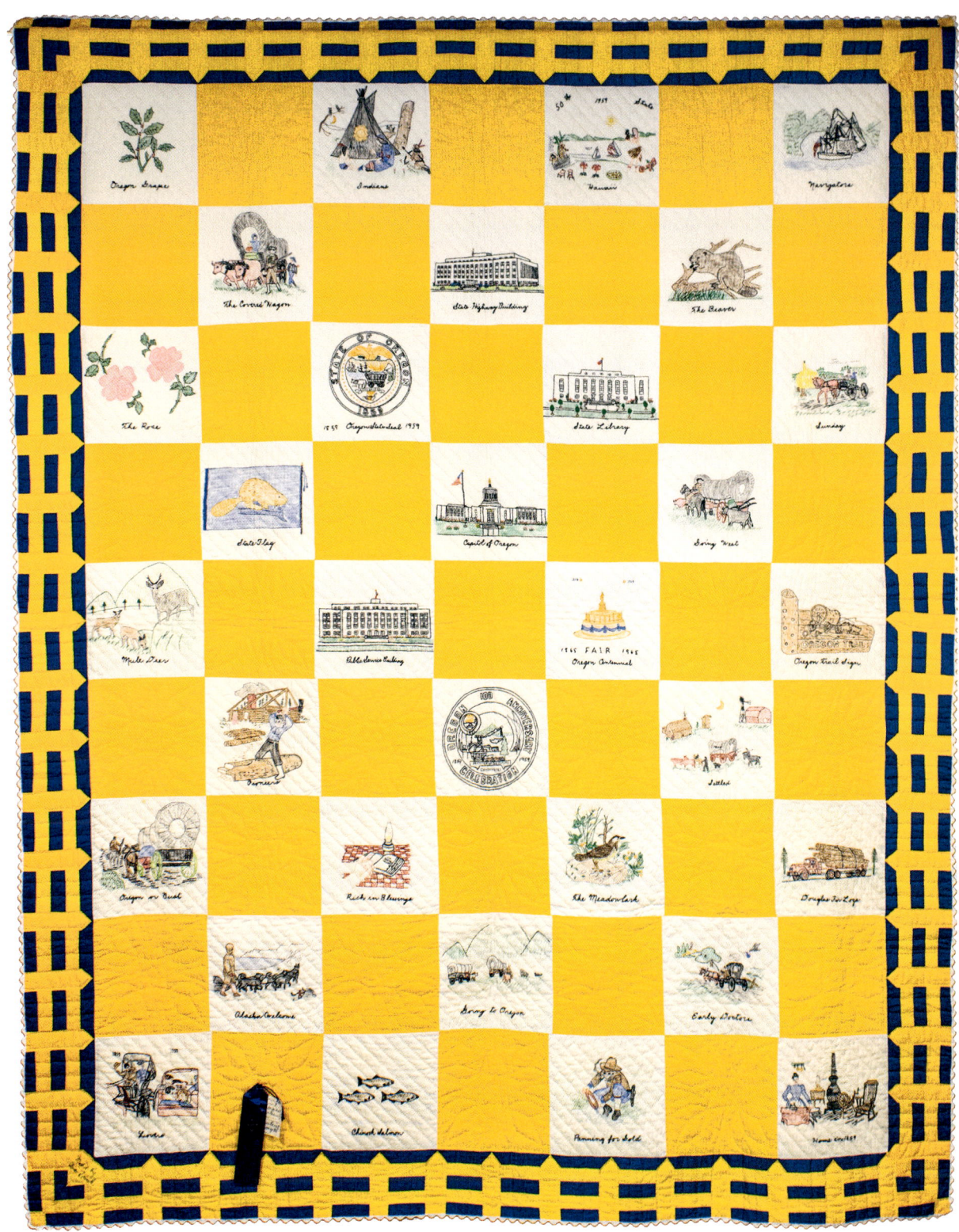

Dora Boles Frink, Pioneer Quilt, *1959, embroidery thread and crayon on cotton, 94 × 77 in.*

From Revolution to Retrospection

As state fairs grew, their management evolved into professional enterprises that invested in permanent locations and buildings: livestock barns, arenas, machinery halls, agricultural halls, women's and children's buildings, and more. The fairs hired professional staff and installed electricity, running water, and bathrooms on the grounds.[30] The improved facilities attracted better competitors and larger crowds, including urbanites. In the first quarter of the twentieth century, state fairs were recognized as key cultural institutions, growing bigger and flashier each year. Fairs conveyed images of optimism, even fantasy.

Meanwhile, industrial agriculture was beginning to eclipse the family farm. More families moved to cities as farmers found themselves economically vulnerable.[31] Handcrafted goods were being supplanted in the market by cheaper, mass-produced factory items. In consequence, the once-lively quilt competitions at the Minnesota State Fair became dominated by older participants, or as Marling describes them, "matriarchs of seventy-three, eighty-five, ninety, and ninety-eight years, who had moved into town from the farm and spent their retirement years recreating the beloved quilt patterns of girlhood."[32] As needlework declined in popularity in a "faster age" in which women could purchase an electric sewing machine or a ready-made bedcover, young city women took up the more elegant pursuits of china painting and lace making.[33]

In the Blue Ridge Mountains of western North Carolina, the educator Lucy Morgan saw the decline of home handicrafts as an economic opportunity for women. In 1923, Morgan established Penland Weavers, a craft school for local women. Morgan's goal was, first, to "revive and perpetuate the native arts and crafts of a mountain community, and secondly … to provide for the people of this mountain community an opportunity of supplementing the productions of their small farms with a little cash income."[34] Morgan sold the women's work at county fairs, churches, and resorts. In 1924, Morgan and weaving instructor Amy Burt drove to Raleigh to showcase Penland Weavers products at the North Carolina State Fair. Morgan recalled, "This was 1924; and most of the persons who stopped at our booth actually had never seen hand-weaving done, unless they were old enough to have seen their grandmothers engaged in such a task."[35] While at the state fair, Morgan and Burt met George Coggin, state supervisor of trade and industrial education, who helped Penland Weavers obtain state aid. The weavers developed a strong market that sustained many families through the Great Depression. The school is still in operation as the Penland School of Craft.

The agricultural collapse accompanying the Great Depression compelled a restructuring of state fairs. With vast numbers of American workers unemployed, President Franklin D. Roosevelt established the New Deal, a series of public programs and public works projects meant to provide employment and financial assistance in hard times. Projects to construct new buildings on fairgrounds created work for architects and laborers, and scientists, writers, and artists were engaged to create educational displays about issues like soil and food conservation. The photographer Russell Lee was hired as part of a photography initiative under the Farm Security Administration to document poor (mostly white) American life from 1935 to 1944. At the 1938 Louisiana State Fair, Russell provided illustrations for a poster display about the virtue and practicalities of conservation. In 1940, he photographed a farmer from Casa Grande Valley Farms displaying her prize-winning canned goods at the Arizona State Fair. During World War II, the government encouraged the planting of victory gardens and the canning of home-grown food to supplement food rations.

During these years the ambiance of craft displays at fairs became increasingly retrospective. Like fertile topsoil or a summer crop of beans, craft was worth preserving. In the 1930s, for

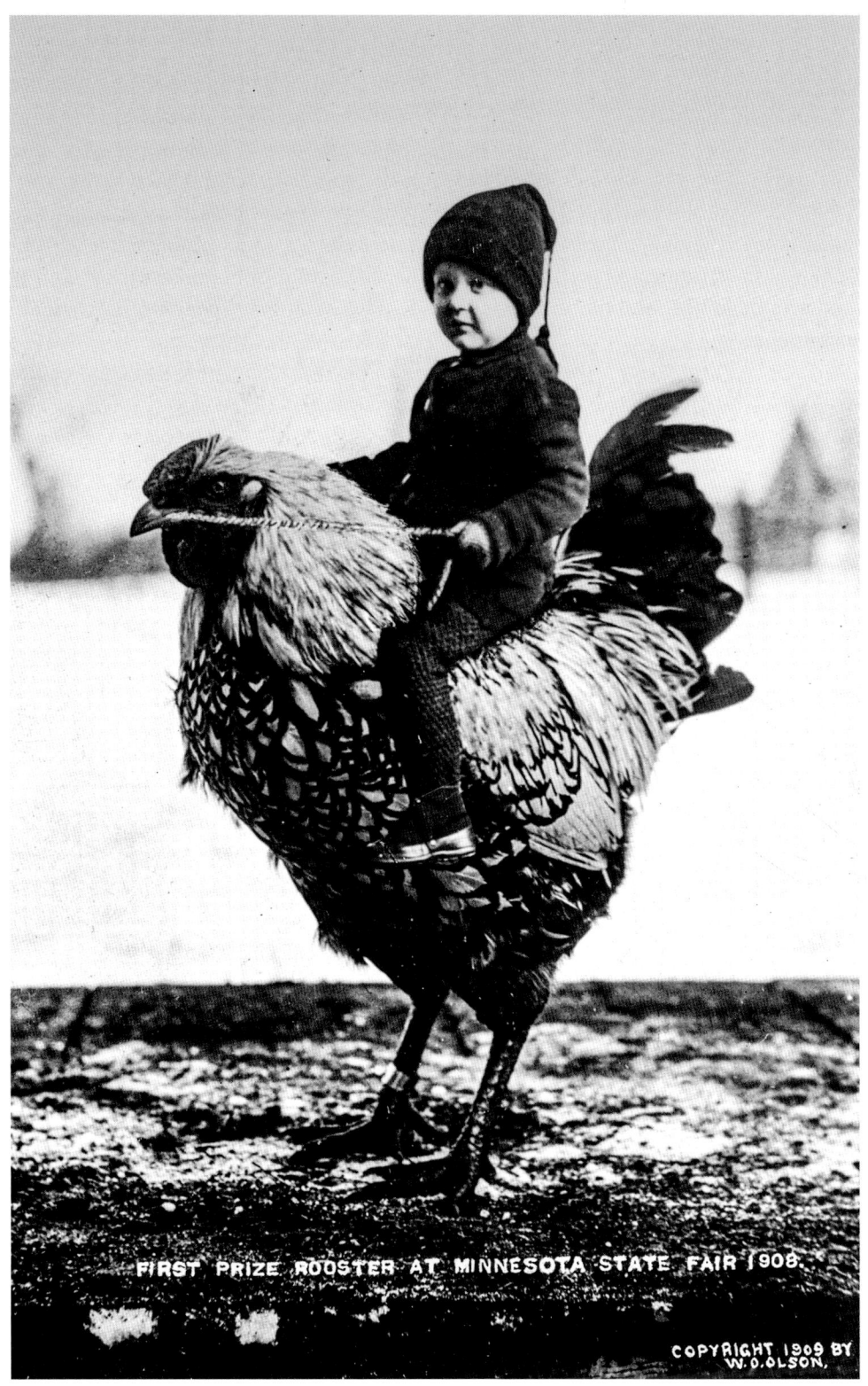

FIRST PRIZE ROOSTER AT MINNESOTA STATE FAIR 1908.

COPYRIGHT 1909 BY
W.O.OLSON.

A 1908 postcard from the Minnesota State Fair features a manipulated photograph of a "first prize rooster" so massive that a young child could ride it like a horse.

example, the Minnesota State Fair added a folk painting category to its woman's activities division (now known as creative activities) to reflect the state's significant population of Scandinavian Americans.[36] Many competitors painted in the tradition of rosemåling, a decorative freehand painting style, incorporating floral motifs, introduced to the United States by Norwegian immigrants in the nineteenth century. In the 1980s, in the wake of the nation's Bicentennial, rosemåling experienced another wave of revival. Third- and fourth-generation Scandinavian immigrants in Minnesota took up rosemåling to establish or deepen connections to their heritage.[37] Rosemåling became an official competition category at the fair in 2006.

In the 1950s, James Schwalbach, professor of rural sociology at the University of Wisconsin and the superintendent of the arts and crafts division of the Wisconsin State Fair, organized a novel color broadcast of a weaving demonstration on NBC's daytime television program *Home*. The cameras picked up the "rainbow range of colors" of threads on Josephine Le Mieux's loom and then "roved about the studio to pick up the brilliance of the setting and the fine workmanship of jewelry fashioned from silver and bowls made of ceramic with fine lines of design."[38] The color camera brought new focus to the state's craft programs.

State fairs began to introduce displays and demonstrations of "native" folk and rural traditions, in dedicated spaces called heritage or pioneer villages. The movement gained momentum with the nation's Bicentennial celebration in 1976. In 1979, for example, the Florida State Fair opened a rural living history museum, Cracker Country, to re-create the everyday lives of white settlers in the nineteenth-century Florida.

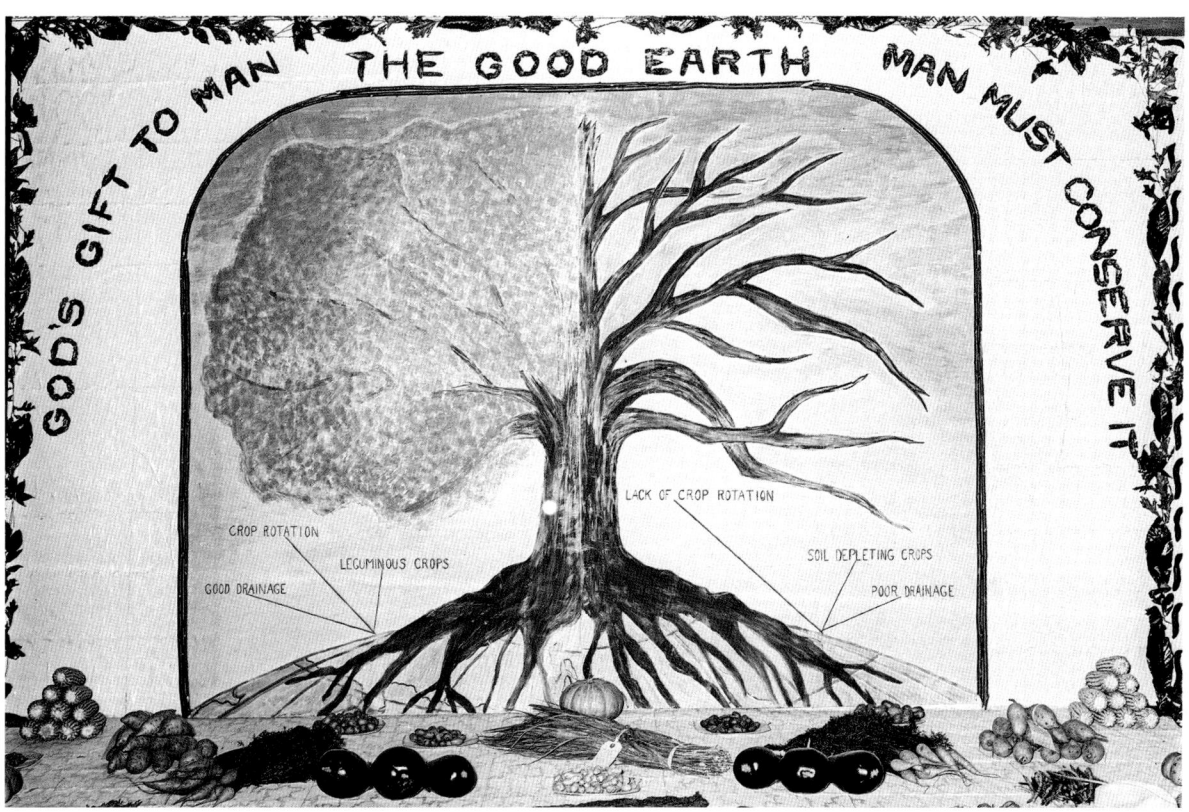

Above: *As part of the Farm Security Administration's photography initiative, Russell Lee captured images of the 1938 Louisiana State Fair, such as this display of corn, eggplants, and other produce.* **Right:** *At the 1940 Arizona State Fair, Lee photographed a proud woman displaying her prize-winning canned goods.*

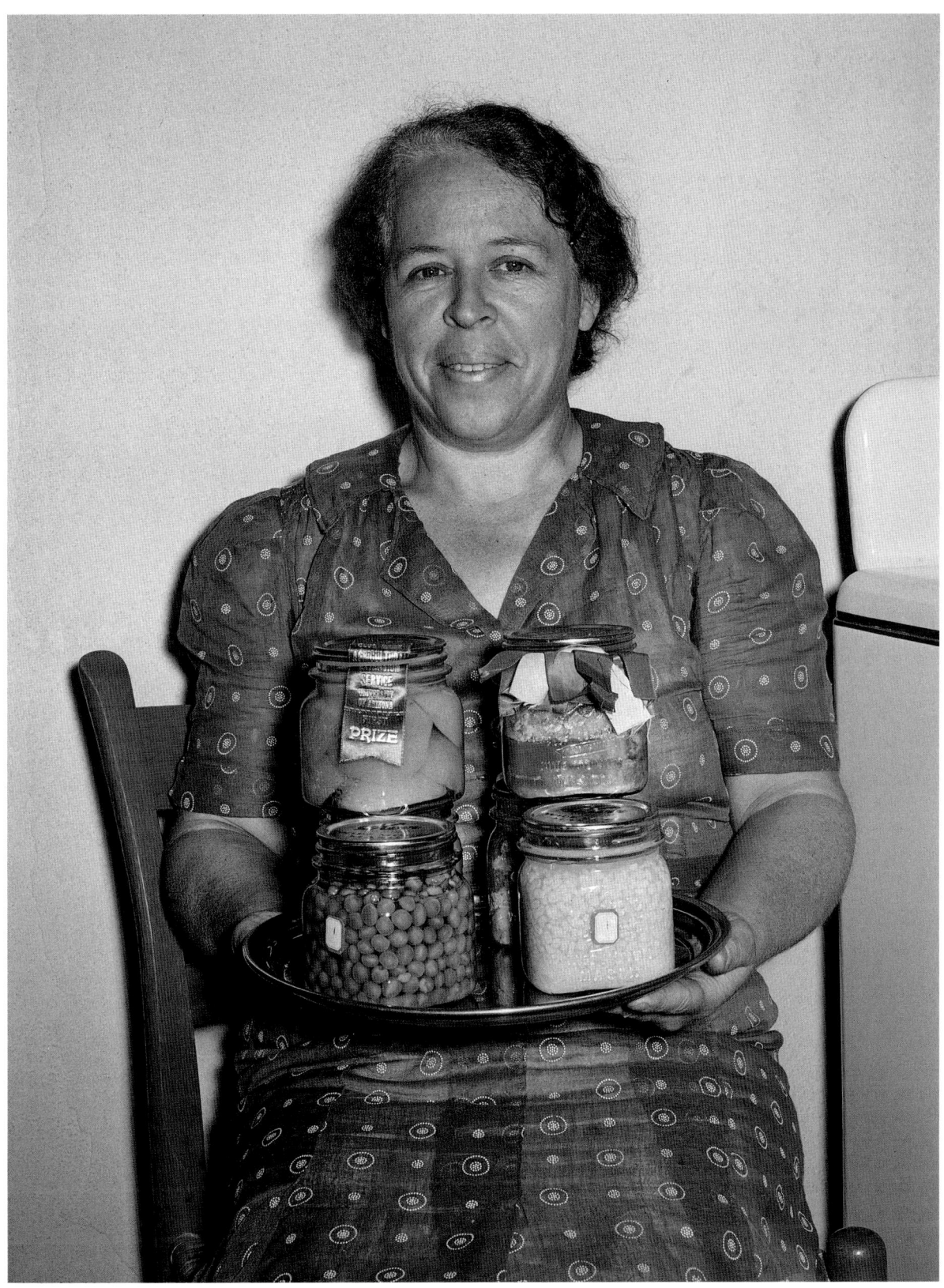

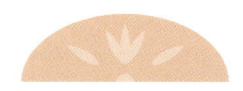

Like fertile topsoil or a summer crop of beans, craft was worth preserving.

During the twentieth century, fairgrounds became increasingly complex cultural sites, resisting easy generalizations about their overall purpose and influence. Simply put, state fairs do not follow the image of progress they often try to convey. At varying points, they have boosted suffragism, birth control, and gay rights while simultaneously staging eugenics displays and racist sideshows, and many fairs enforced segregation through the period of the civil rights movement. They continued (and continue) to revolve around farming even as farms grew more industrialized and less familiar to many Americans.

As a result of these shifts, the crafts aspect of fairs became less tightly bound to the agricultural economy. Craft made its own way on the fairgrounds, propelled by the will of artists. Crafters continued to consider their relationship to agriculture and land, but they did so through more critical takes on progress and with more diverse and personal stories.

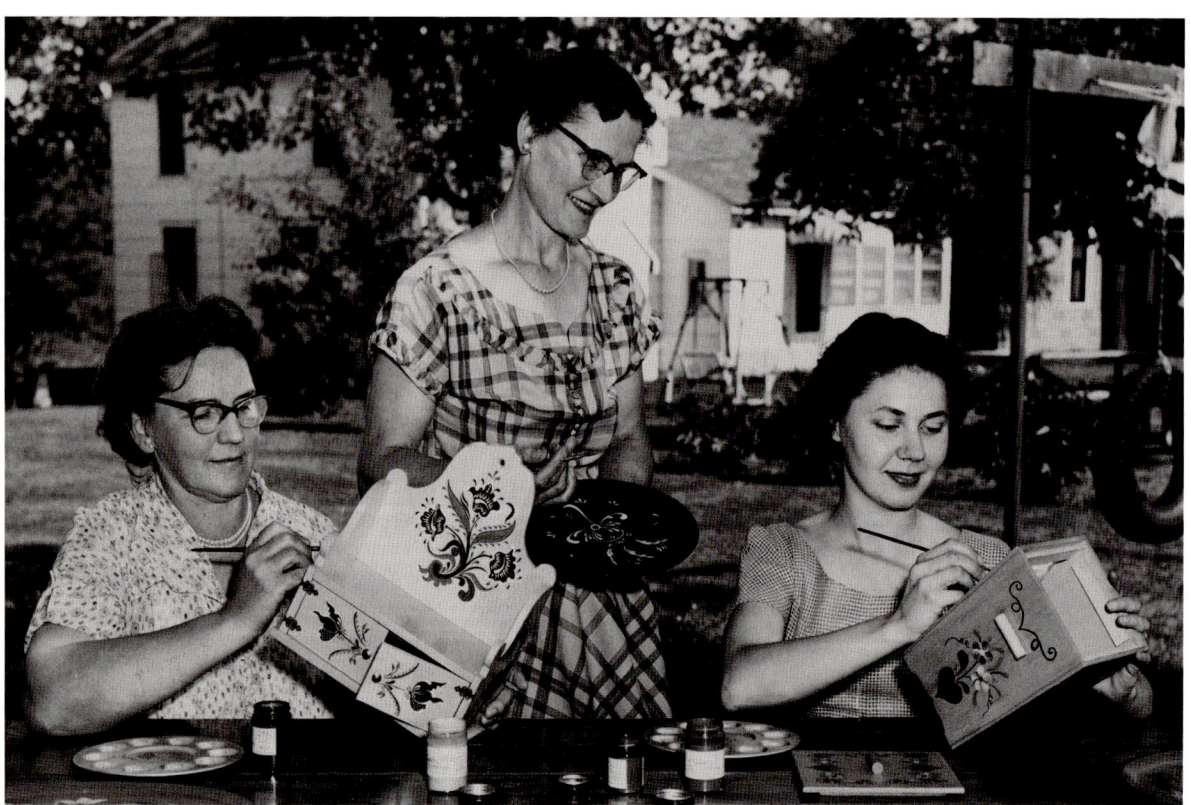

Mrs. Walter Wolf (center) *teaching rosemåling to her pupils, Mrs. Raymond Kern and Mrs. Ronayne Lee.*

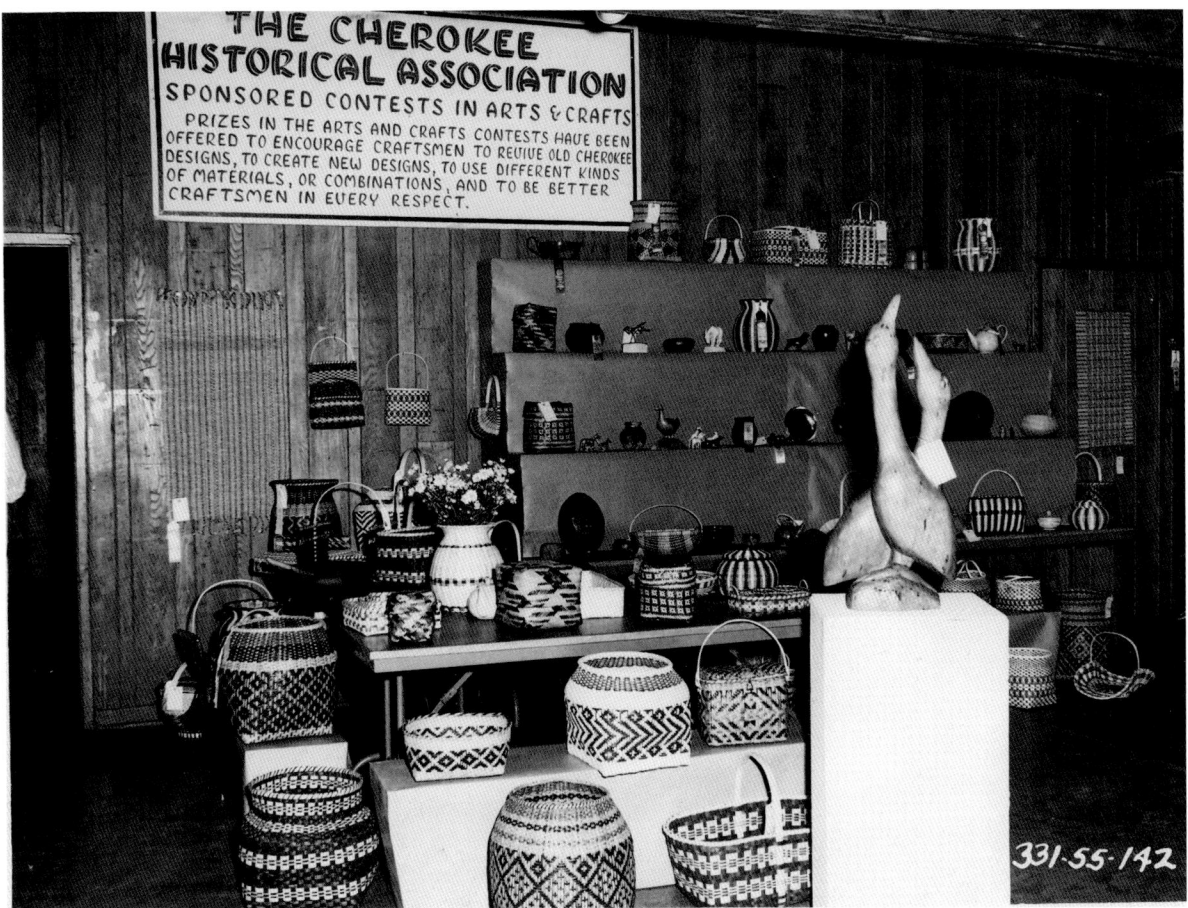

THE CHEROKEE
HISTORICAL ASSOCIATION
SPONSORED CONTESTS IN ARTS & CRAFTS
PRIZES IN THE ARTS AND CRAFTS CONTESTS HAVE BEEN
OFFERED TO ENCOURAGE CRAFTSMEN TO REVIVE OLD CHEROKEE
DESIGNS, TO CREATE NEW DESIGNS, TO USE DIFFERENT KINDS
OF MATERIALS, OR COMBINATIONS, AND TO BE BETTER
CRAFTSMEN IN EVERY RESPECT.

331·55·142

An exhibit at the Cherokee Indian Fair, held by the Eastern Band of Cherokee Indians.

In 1914, the Eastern Band of Cherokee Indians (EBCI) established the Cherokee Indian Fair, an annual fair modeled on state fairs, which continues to thrive today.[39] The tribal council sought to reunite Cherokee citizens dispersed by the Indian Removal Act and to attract tourists to its ancestral lands in western North Carolina. The fair program highlighted Cherokee cultural practices. For example, Cherokee could participate in Green Corn dances, a tradition that celebrated the yearly corn harvest. The 1935 program shored up affinities between agriculture and art. The program noted, "The agricultural and home making exhibits will be of exceptional quality and number and will demonstrate recent Indian advancement in these fields."[40] Craft exhibits and competitions have historically featured Cherokee

basketry, pottery, masks, blowguns and darts, and wood carving.

The potter Amanda Sequoyah Swimmer grew up in a farming family on the Qualla Boundary, a territory of ancestral land in western North Carolina purchased by the EBCI, who collectively allowed the US federal government to hold the land in trust. The family grew corn, cane, and tobacco, but she became interested in the raw clay near her home. When she married, she started experimenting with pottery, using wood-firing techniques and incised designs on her pots. She began earning a reputation for her work in the 1950s.[41] "After I got married, I decided to hunt that clay right above where I lived. I made some small bowls and told my husband, I said, 'Let me try to burn them. Just make a hole right there in

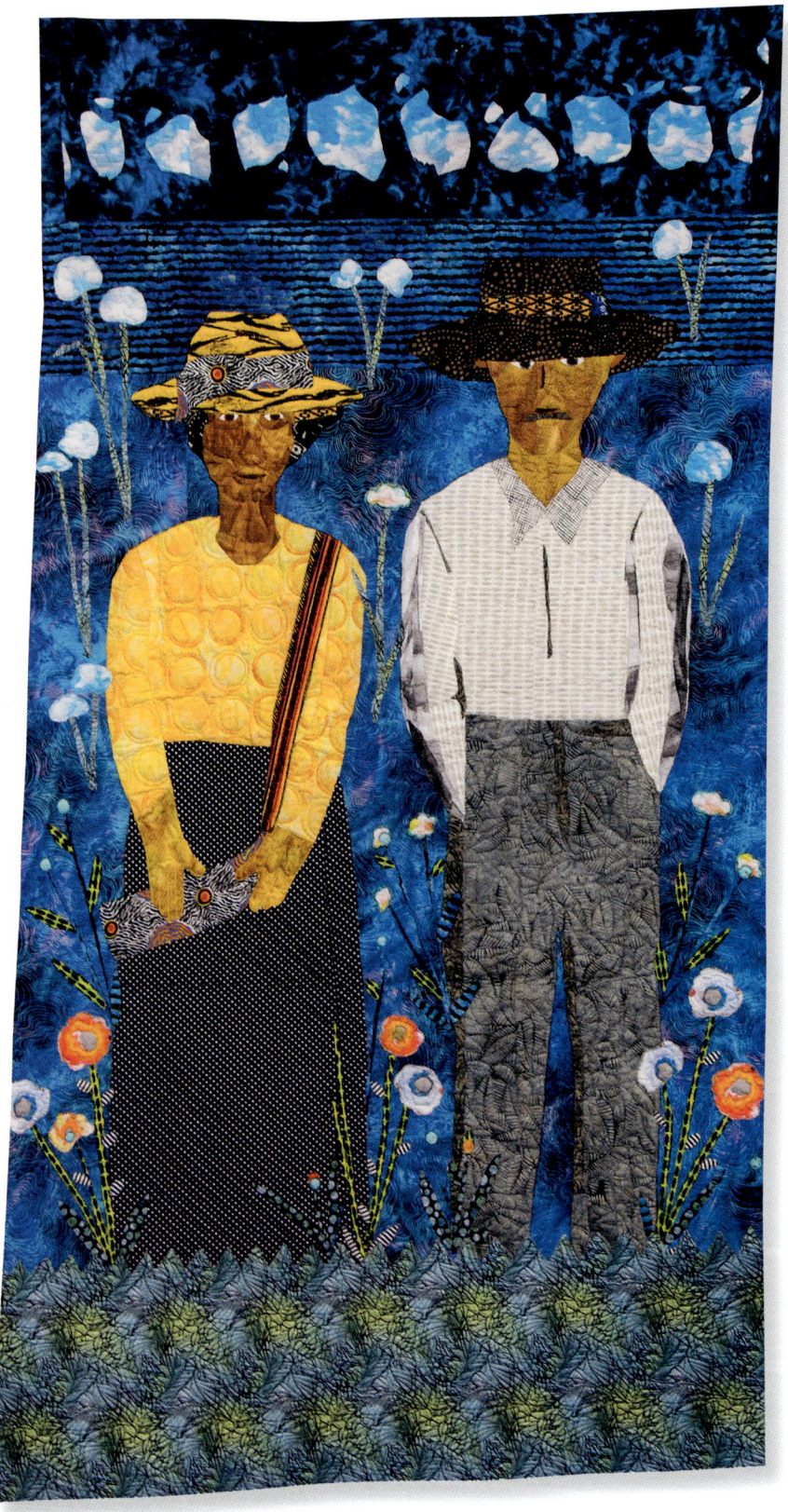

the yard.' We just piled wood in there and burned my pottery. And that came out pretty good. I just kept on playing with that wood, off and on."[42] Swimmer researched the history of Cherokee pottery, rediscovering techniques lost during the forced relocation and assimilation of the Cherokee. She demonstrated pottery to generations of young Cherokee children for more than fifty years. For much of her career she competed at the Cherokee Indian Fair as well as other shows and festivals, reviving interest in Native American pottery and intergenerational knowledge of the land.

Peggie Hartwell's quilts also tell the story of her family and land. Hartwell was born into a large extended family of farmers and quilters living on her grandfather's land in South Carolina. Hartwell recalls: "This was a very good childhood because all the women did some type of needlework or some type of craft. Most of the men were storytellers, so that my life was rich with oral history; it was rich with sewing and churchgoing and day-to-day existence on a farm."[43] For years Hartwell taught fairgoers how to make a nine-patch quilt at the South Carolina State Fair. In 2022 her quilts were shown in an exhibition organized by the McKissick Museum of Art of the University of South Carolina, Columbia.

As a child, Hartwell moved with her parents to New York as part of the Great Migration, which saw approximately six million Black people leave the South and settle in other parts of the United States during the early and middle years of the twentieth century. One quilt pays homage to her grandparents, William and Annie Tyler, as she remembers them in the 1940s. Annie wears a cow horn on her shoulder strap to call the family in for dinner. Together they stand in a field surrounded by the cotton they picked as sharecroppers, with flowers blossoming at their feet.

Another artist, Corey Alston, demonstrated Gullah basketry for several years at the South Carolina State Fair. Gullah people have been making sweetgrass baskets in the Low Country of South

Left: *Peggie L. Hartwell, Ode to William and Annie Tyler, 2022, thread, cotton fabric, and batting, 90 × 55 in.*

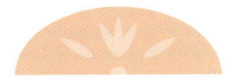

"My life was rich with oral history; it was rich with sewing and churchgoing and day-to-day existence on a farm."

PEGGIE HARTWELL

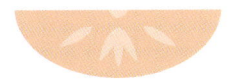

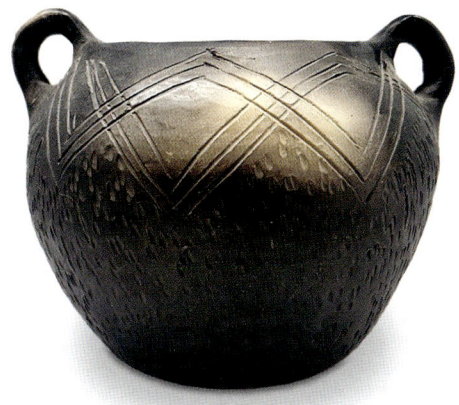

Amanda Sequoyah Swimmer, Pottery vessel with two handles, ceramic. Measurements are 8½ × 5½ × 6½ in.

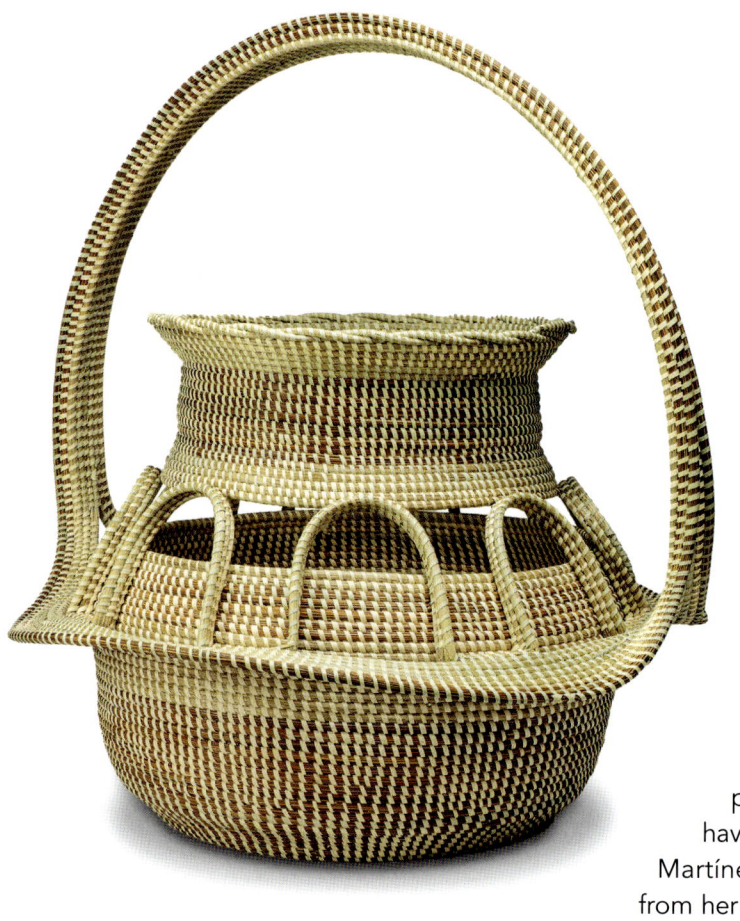

Carolina since the seventeenth century, when enslaved Africans made baskets for use in the cultivation of rice on plantations. Alston, a fifth-generation maker, educated fairgoers on the process of making baskets, from harvesting the grass to passing on knowledge to the next generation. Hartwell's and Alston's participation at fairs speaks not only to intergenerational agricultural connections but also to the history of agriculture in the South—a history built on the exploited labor and knowledge of their ancestors.

State fairs in other parts of the country also celebrated local craft traditions. When fairs were established in the Southwest, the region already had a long history of agriculture and ranching. Navajo-Churro sheep had been introduced to the region by Spanish colonizers in the 1500s. Settlers and Native Americans began raising these sheep for food and fleece, and they became central to the lives and cultural practices of Diné (Navajo) and

Hispanic families. Thick, strong wool is spun by hand from Navajo-Churro fleece, dyed with natural pigments, and woven into rugs. Displays and competitions at the New Mexico State Fair have helped sustain these traditions. Agueda Martínez wove history, ideals, and materials from her farm into acc laimed rugs in the Chimayo style. Martínez and her husband, also a weaver, supported their family of ten children by working as subsistence farmers during the day and weaving at night. They gathered plants for dye and spun yarn recovered from worn clothing to make rugs. At first they sold their work through blanket dealers, and later, as they became well-known, from their home. By the 1970s, Doña Agueda Martínez was nationally renowned. In 1975 she won her first blue ribbon at the New Mexico State Fair.

While for most artists the fair is a backdrop for their work, for Linda Nez it is the subject. Nez grew up in the Navajo Nation tending to her family's sheep and goats. She learned how to weave pictorial textiles from her aunt, Susie Black, even though such images were less popular with rug collectors and tourists than geometric designs. In one of her pieces she depicts the Northern Navajo Nation Fair, the oldest fair in the Navajo Nation. Nez shows a festive midway: a Ferris

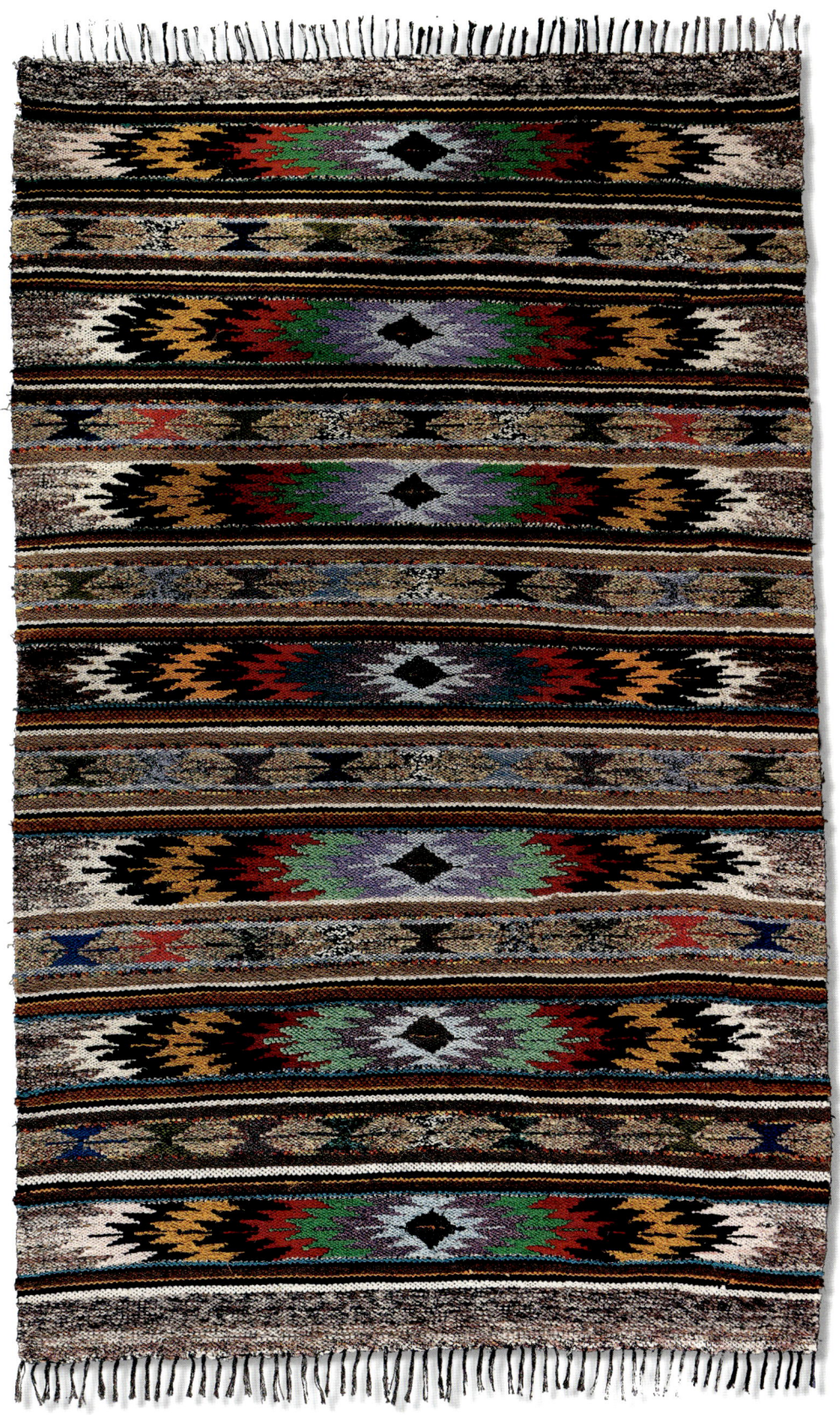

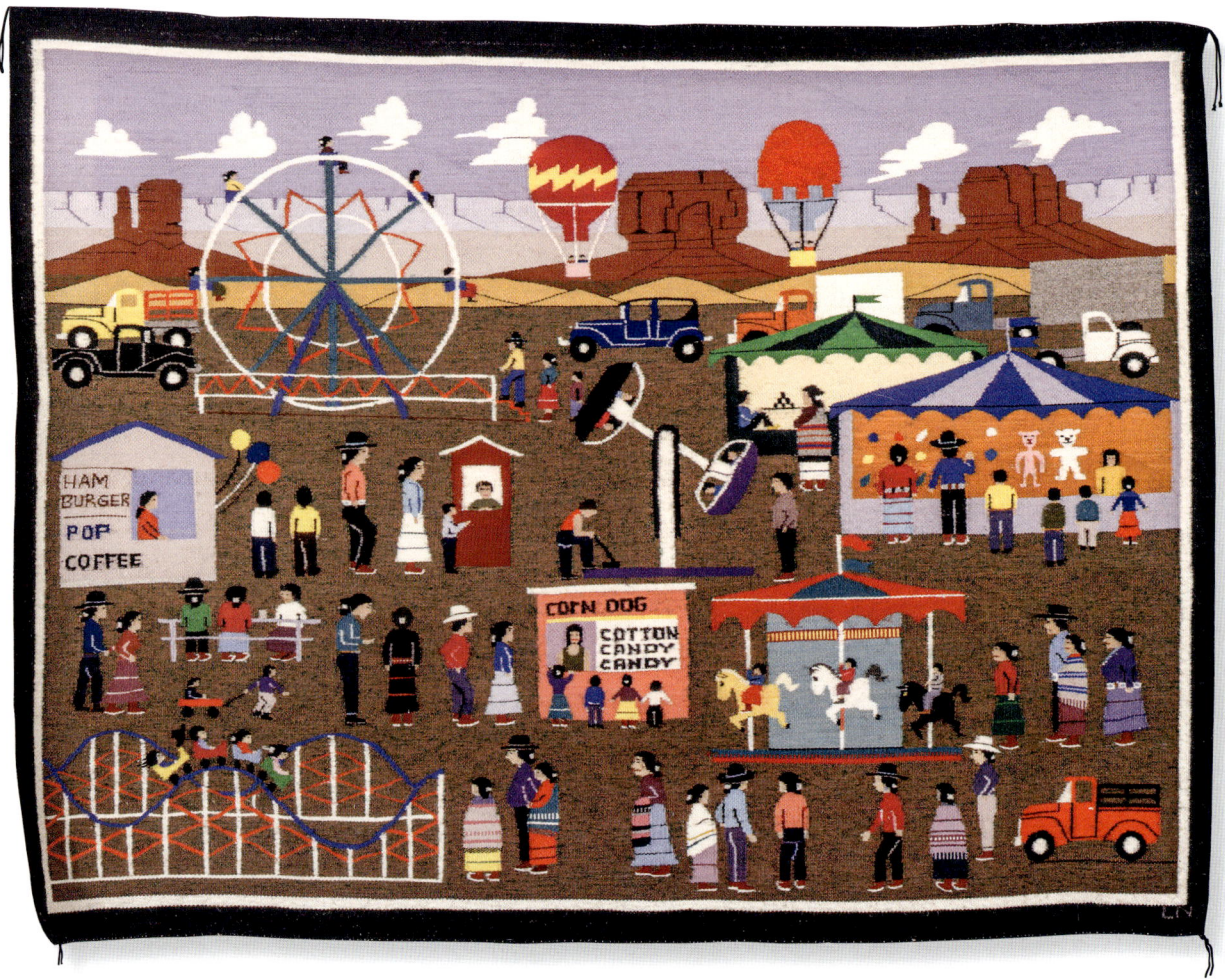

Linda Nez, Carnival, 1992, woven tapestry with commercial yarn, 43 × 57½ in.

wheel, a hot-air balloon, carnival games, and the classic concession stands offering hamburgers, corn dogs, and cotton candy. The fairgrounds are set against the even dreamier landscape of the Monument Valley, which spans the Utah-Arizona border. The fairgoers are identified as Navajo, not tourists, in their velvet blouses and skirts, cowboy hats, and deer-hide moccasins.[44]

These examples of narratives told through craft illustrate the profound relationship between agriculture and creative work. The "Blue Ribbon Gallery" in this book shows how craft displays at fairgrounds continue to reflect state demographics, aesthetics, and technologies—although often in disproportionate and sometimes unfair ways.

State fairgrounds have served as dynamic sites of social and cultural discourse. And while key elements of fairs remain the same—the sheep, the quilts, the Ferris wheels—the educational purpose of fairs has shifted. Fair programs once celebrated farmers as central to a state's diversified economy. Today farming is largely out of sight and marginalized: most fairgoers—and even many agricultural workers—have never milked a cow, let alone sat at a loom. Less than 2 percent of the US population lives on farms, and only 1 percent claims farming as an occupation.[45] One 2016 study of fairs notes that because so much of the population lives in urban and suburban areas, "people's ability to obtain firsthand knowledge of agriculture may be limited to annual local, county or state fairs."[46] Fairs help connect contemporary consumers to agricultural practices.

For the past fifty years, the Las Arañas Spinners and Weavers Guild and the New Mexico Wool Growers have run a "sheep to shawl" demonstration at the New Mexico State Fair. Just outside the Livestock Building, fairgoers can watch a sheep being sheared and then follow the sheep's fleece inside as it is prepared for spinning. Bundles of fleece are spun into yarn while the team of demonstrators engages the public in conversation. Finally, the wool is woven into cloth on a loom. Such activities were common in most homes in the Northeast in 1808, when Watson exhibited his two Merino sheep. Now they are arguably more novel than virtual reality, turned into spectacles at state fairs and wool festivals throughout the nation.

State fairs hold the past, present, and future in tension: they continue to encourage and showcase innovations that might change how we make and consume things. And while the media gives prime-time coverage to the soapbox speeches of visiting politicians at fairs during big election years, the fairs continue to give artists their own platform through competitions and demonstrations. Artists share powerful personal stories to invite collective reflection and inquiry. Through their subject matter, materials, and processes, artworks reveal intimate stories of families and communities that may span generations. The diversity of artworks and competition categories reflects changing aesthetic trends and invites viewers to consider developments in agriculture, industry, and home life. Fairs are places to be seen, heard, and recognized. The many makers whose work appears in this book and exhibition proudly display their intertwined creative and practical skills. Likewise, the diverse and democratic approach of fairground displays often represents the best of local and cultural traditions. Together, fair artworks and objects, like the fairgrounds themselves, offer a vibrant portrait of American life.

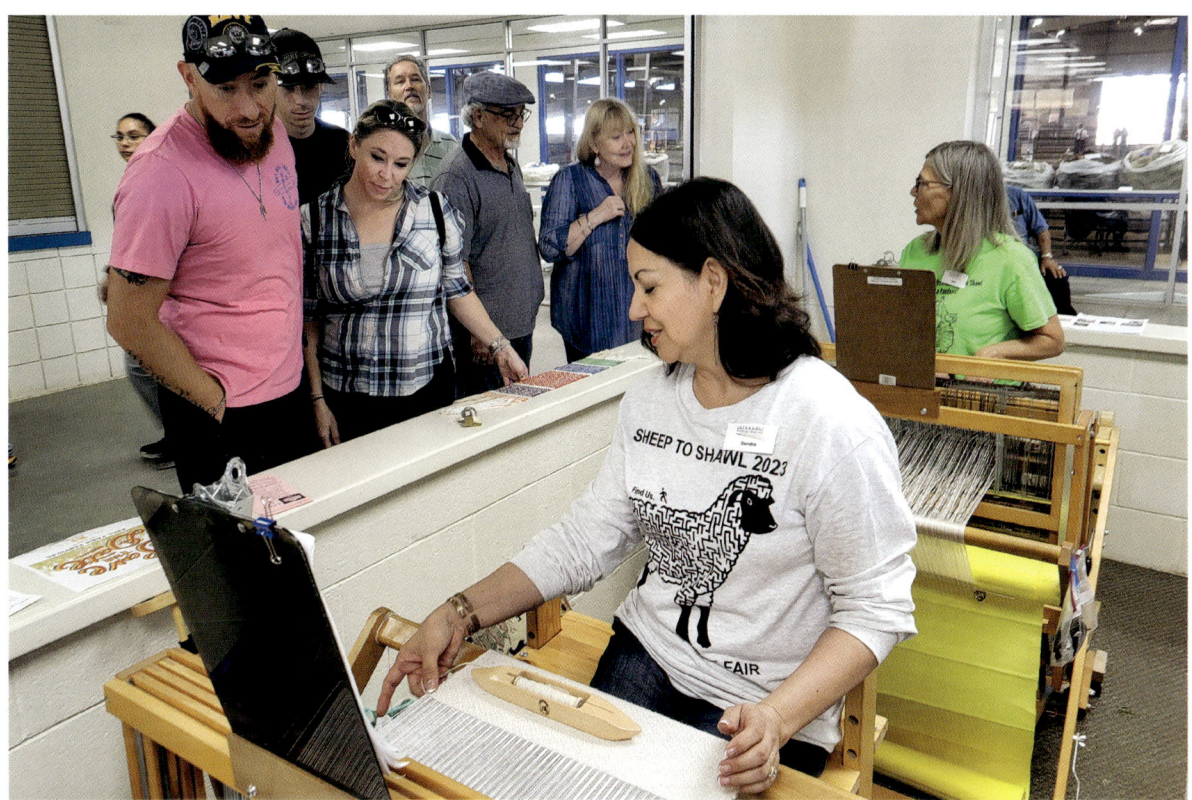

"Sheep to Shawl" volunteers Sandra Baldonado and Beth Dykstra demonstrate weaving techniques in front of fairgoers.

Creative Arts Competitions and Women's Collectivity

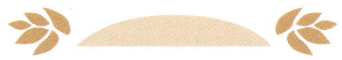

SARA MORRIS

Step inside a Creative Arts Building or Women's Building at a state fairground anywhere in the United States and behold sumptuous displays of quilts, doilies, flower arrangements, cakes, jams, and more. During the mid-nineteenth century, fairs sought to boost attendance and women's participation by featuring displays of domestic work, such as sewing, knitting, weaving, baking, and canning, in addition to agricultural and farm work. Competitions celebrating these homespun activities, rooted in necessity, acknowledged women's contributions to farm labor, and it wasn't long before women began participating in horticultural and dairy competitions as well.[1] The continuity and popularity of these exhibits exemplifies how handwork, historically known as "women's work" and "the domestic arts," has become closely identified with the state fair. These often elaborate displays showcase a year's worth of labor and highlight the cultural heritage and aesthetics of local communities.

In today's fairs, participants submit their artworks to be judged by a panel of experts on criteria such as execution, technique, and creativity. At especially competitive fairs like those of Iowa, Minnesota, and Nebraska, thousands of artworks must be documented, sorted, and displayed in short order, and with great care. None of this would be possible without fair volunteers—mostly women—who often work long shifts to arrange the eye-catching displays. When the display opens to the public, award-winning contributions are identified by ribbons, with the most coveted being "Best in Show."

Craft guilds and collectives are the driving force of creative arts displays. Members of the Nebraska State Quilt Guild (NSQG) offer their time and expertise to arrange the exhibition of quilts at the Nebraska State Fair. Guilds may

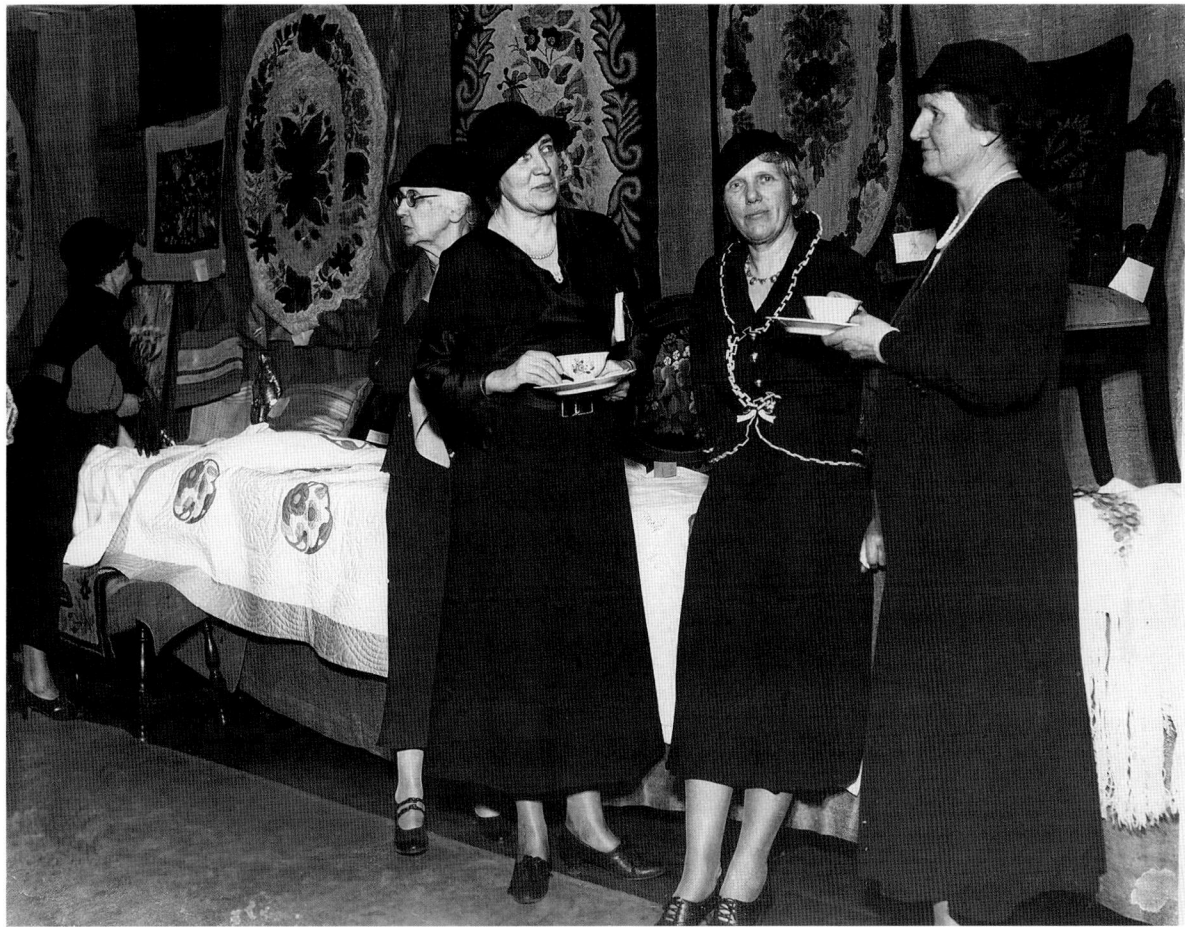

The interior of the Women's Activities Building at the Minnesota State Fair, around 1935.

also sponsor special awards at the fair, such as the NSQG's "Pride of Nebraska" prize, which is awarded to the best original or traditional quilt design conveying Nebraska's heritage or culture.

If the organization of fair displays testifies to women's collaborative efforts, so do many of the artworks on show. For example, pieced and appliquéd quilts surviving from the nineteenth and early twentieth centuries were created by quilting groups or family members. These were often passed down through generations, exemplifying women's art, labor, and collective endeavor.[2] The collections of historical societies and libraries across the country include ribbon quilts, assembled from collections of prize ribbons, which are a self-referential form of such art. Elizabeth Milward

of Madison, Wisconsin, pieced together a quilt containing hundreds of fair ribbons won by her husband, William Henry Milward, for his fruit, flowers, and poultry at the Wisconsin State Fair between 1908 and 1934 and at the 1933 Chicago World's Fair.[3] As with bountiful horticultural exhibits showing off the best of the harvest, the ribbon quilts and other examples of creative arts reinforce themes of prosperity and abundance. The exhibition halls themselves communicate narratives of nostalgia and patriotism.

Although creative arts competitions engaged white women, fairs often practiced overt or tacit exclusion or segregation of African Americans and the creation of separate competitions. From 1890 to 1969, the Palmetto State Fair (formerly

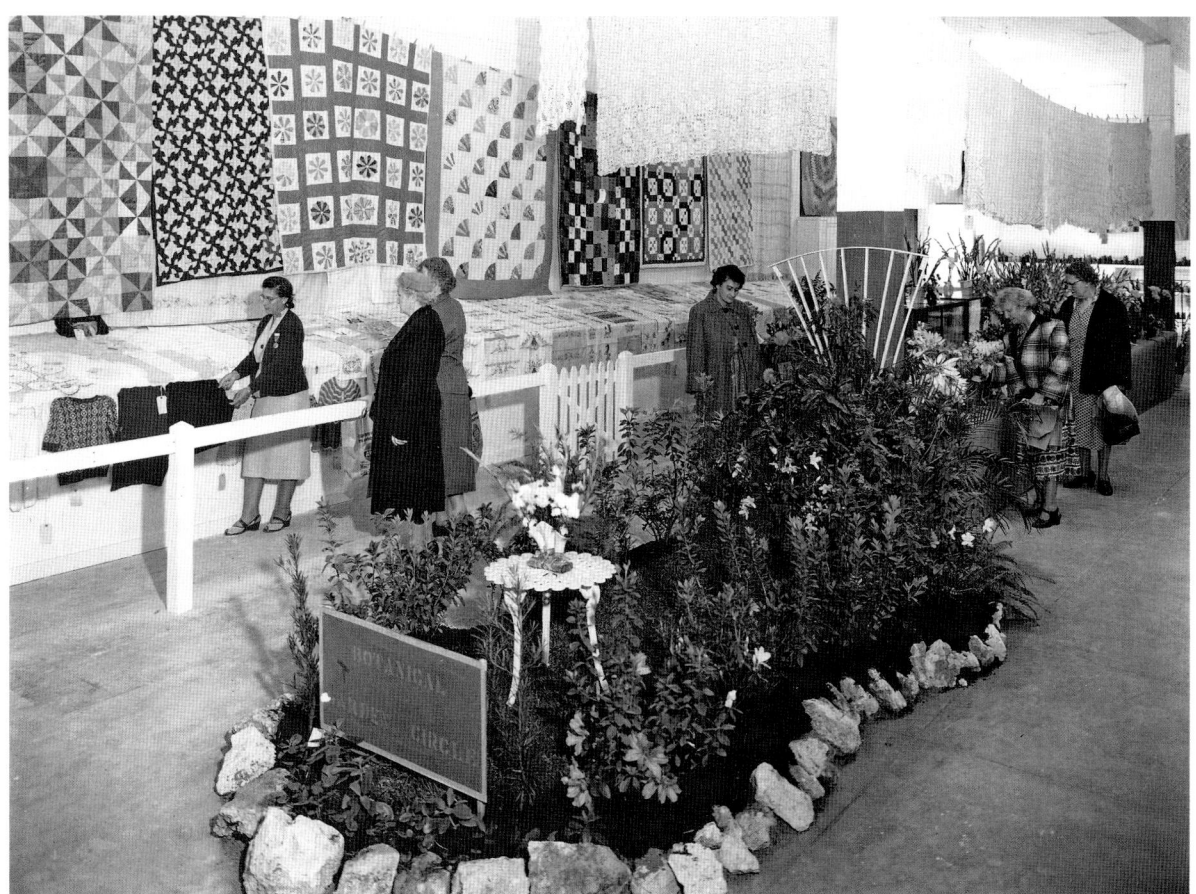

Women looking at handmade sweaters, quilts, and flowers at the Florida State Fair in 1953.

the Colored State Fair) in Columbia, South Carolina, was a separate fair organized by African Americans and held the week following the South Carolina State Fair.[4] During the 1950s in Dallas, Texas, the civil rights advocate and politician Juanita J. Craft, along with members of the NAACP Youth Council, protested at the State Fair of Texas, where African Americans were permitted to participate in the fair's activities only on "Negro Achievement Day."[5] Both state fairs integrated their events following the Civil Rights Act of 1964.

The Harriet Tubman Quilt, created by the Negro History Quilt Club of Marin City and Sausalito, represents an effort to break down such barriers. The quilt must have been a spectacular sight at the 1952 California State Fair, where it took second place. Designed by the architect Ben

Irvin, its subject was chosen and the quilt sewn by the group, which is said to have brought together Black women from Marin City and white women from nearby Sausalito. In its center, the quilt depicts Tubman, a looming figure in a striped skirt and blue coat, standing with a rifle under cover of night. Three figures in the background represent the enslaved people she led north to freedom. An owl perched in a tree stands guard, another embodiment of Tubman herself. When asked about making the quilt, which took nearly two years to complete, one quilter commented, "When we're quilting, I like to let my thoughts run back over the years to other quilting bees I've known. We talk about Harriet Tubman and Frederick Douglass, too, and that's the way you really get to know about our history."[6]

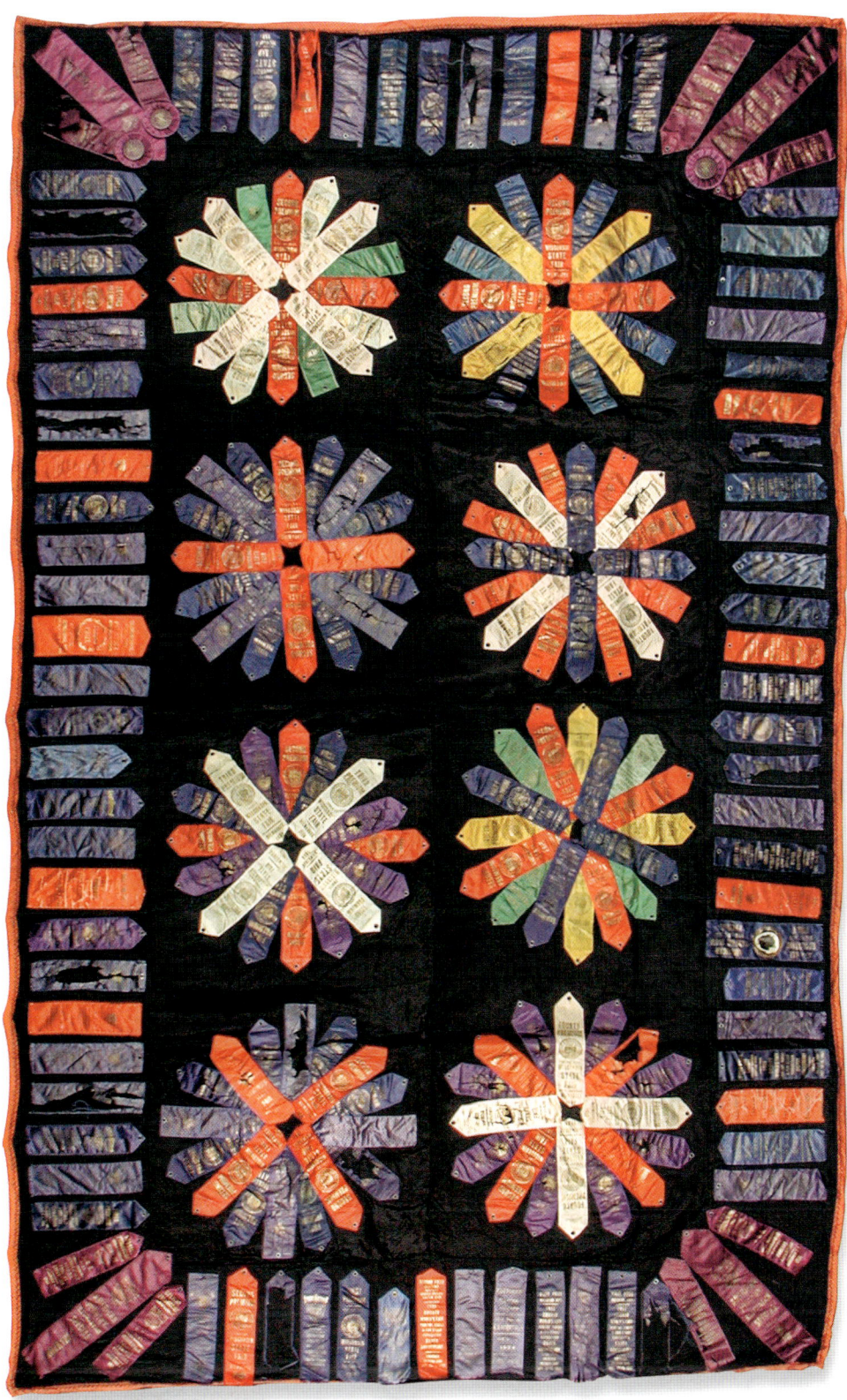

Elizabeth (Meibohn) Milward, Fair Ribbon Quilt, 1934–35, prize ribbons appliquéd on black rayon, 87 × 53½ in.

Stitching the personal with the collective, quilts representing community and group endeavors inspire action and in some cases effect political change. In 1995, the members of the Battered Offenders Self-Help (BOSH) group at the Kentucky Correctional Institution for Women displayed a quilt at the Kentucky State Fair that depicted their stories of domestic abuse. Incarcerated women inscribed their personal stories with magic markers on patches of cloth. The quilt's large central panel features a red heart overlaid by a weeping eye, seen through jail bars. Below the heart, the names and prison sentences of the quilters are listed. Together, the fifty-two squares tell a harrowing tale. While on display at the fair, the quilt deeply moved Kentucky Governor Brereton Jones, leading him to work toward commuting the women's sentences. "This was a very basic way to communicate, but a very personal and articulate way," explained Jones. "Had that quilt not been made, I am quite confident that I, in the midst of all the other responsibilities of the job, would not have looked into this issue in the in-depth way that I did."[7]

These quilts signal an ongoing shift in attitudes about the creative arts. After World War II, many state fairs witnessed waning interest and skill in the creative arts competitions, followed by a revival of enthusiasm. The quilt historians Kari Ronning and Barbara Brackman suggest that the feminist movement encouraged women to see textile arts in a new light—as a valued and serious mode of self-expression by, and often for, women. They also argue that the counterculture movement of the 1960s and 1970s revived interest in so-called hobby crafts as a political stance against consumerism.[8]

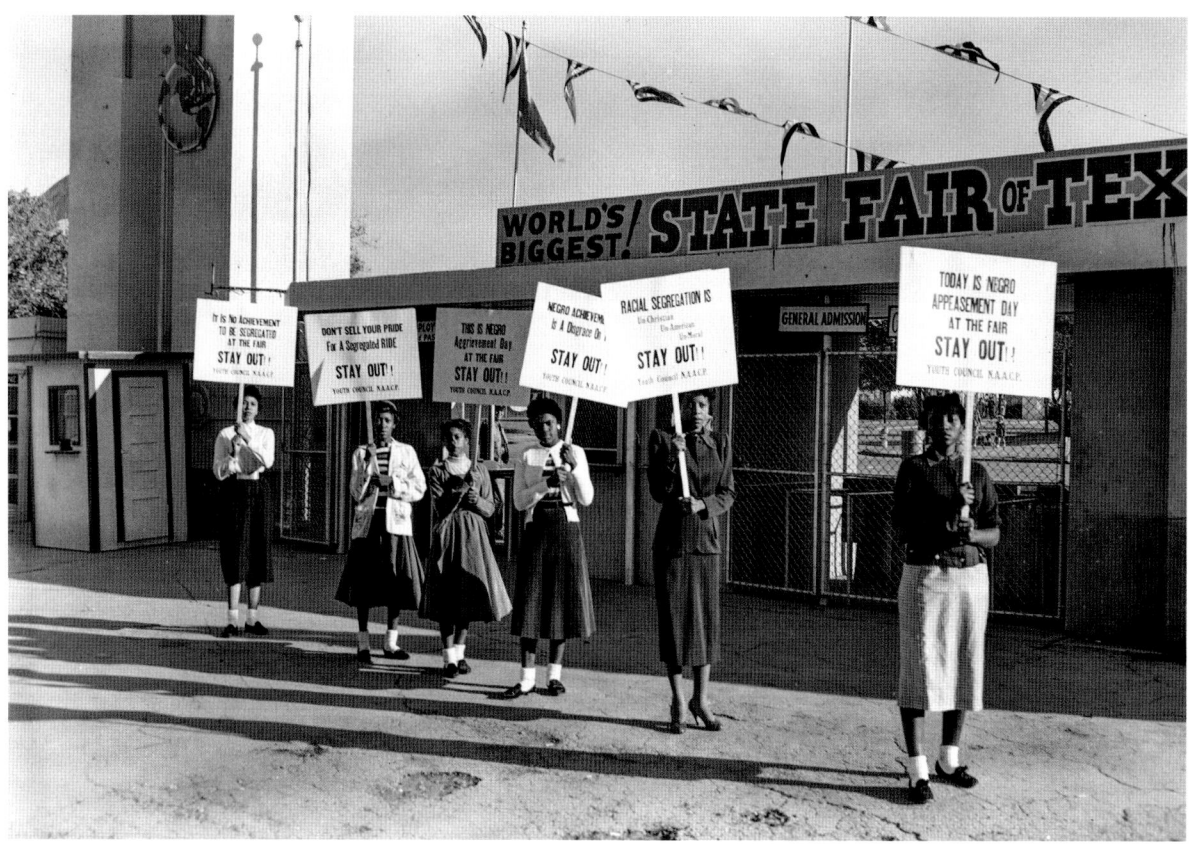

Above: *Members of the NAACP Youth Council protest segregation at the State Fair of Texas in October 1955. While their protest was not immediately successful, it drew attention to discrimination against Black fairgoers, and the fair fully integrated in the 1960s.* **Right:** *Negro History Club of Marin City and Sausalito,* Harriet Tubman Quilt, *1951, cotton, 120 × 96 in.*

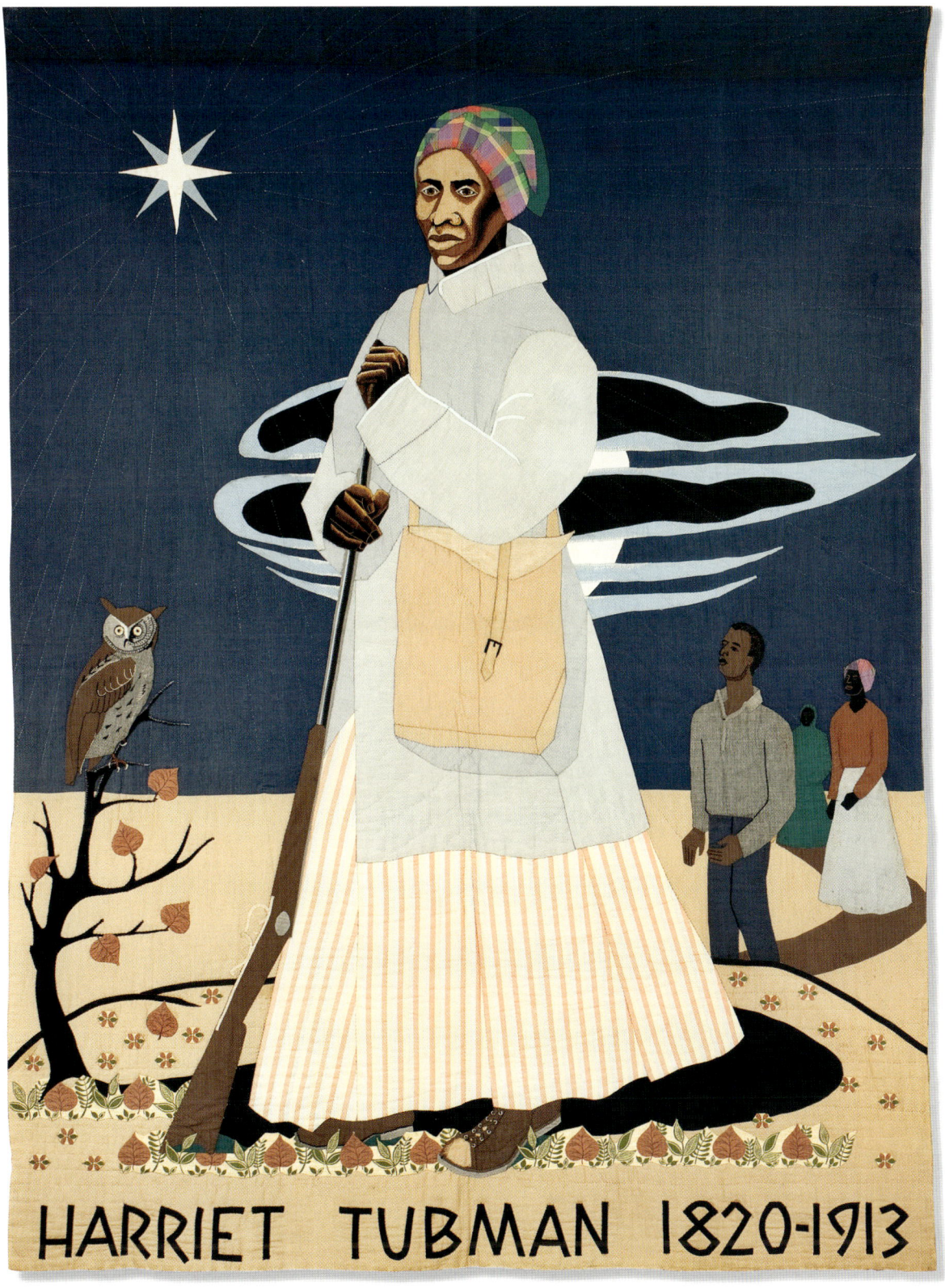

HARRIET TUBMAN 1820-1913

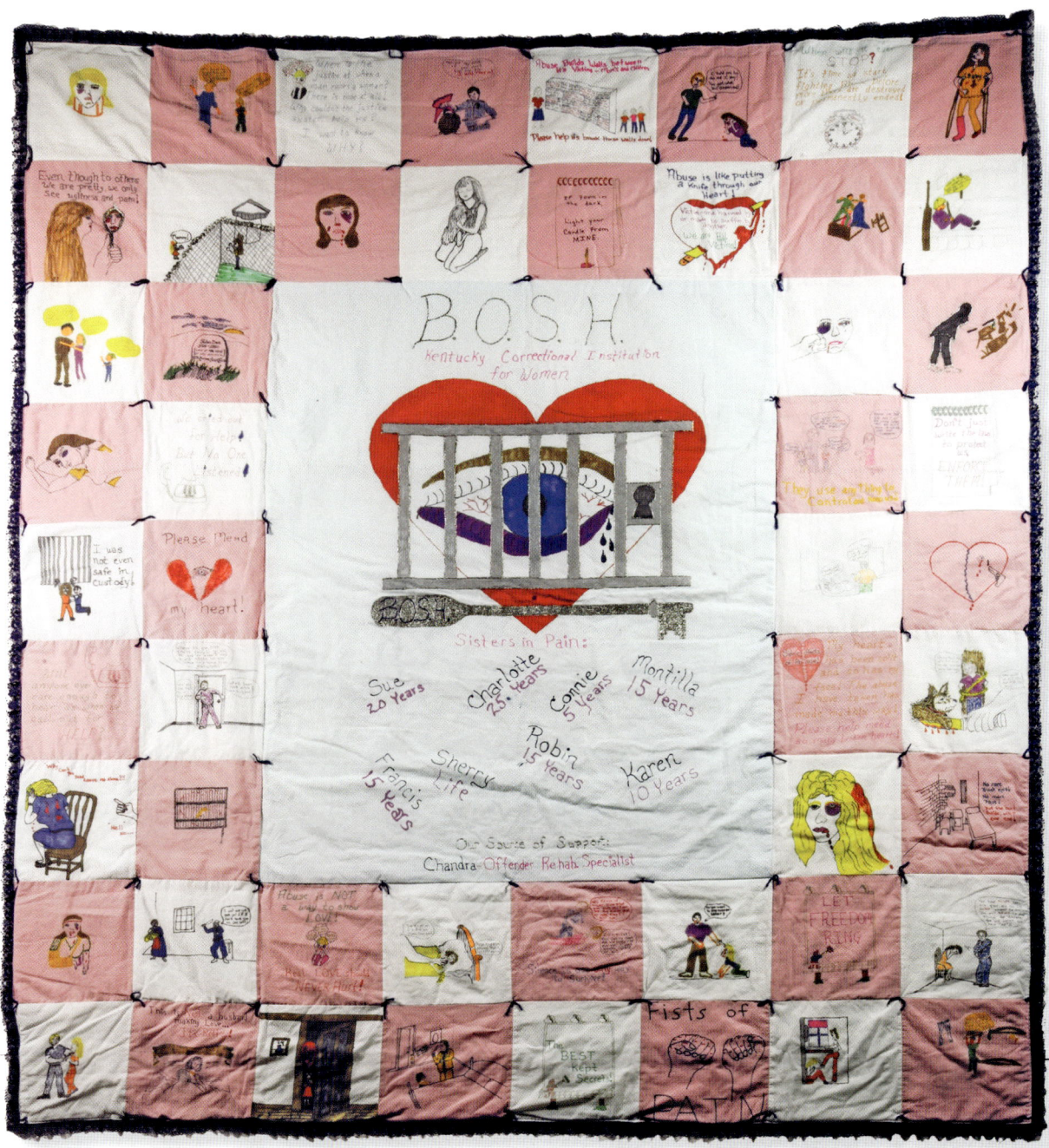

Battered Offenders Self-Help (BOSH) Group, Quilt, 1995, cotton, paint, ink, 102¾ × 88½ in. The names and prison sentences of the quilters are listed: Sue, twenty years; Charlotte, twenty-five years; Connie, five years; Montilla, fifteen years; Francis, fifteen years; Sherry, life; Robin, fifteen years; Karen, ten years.

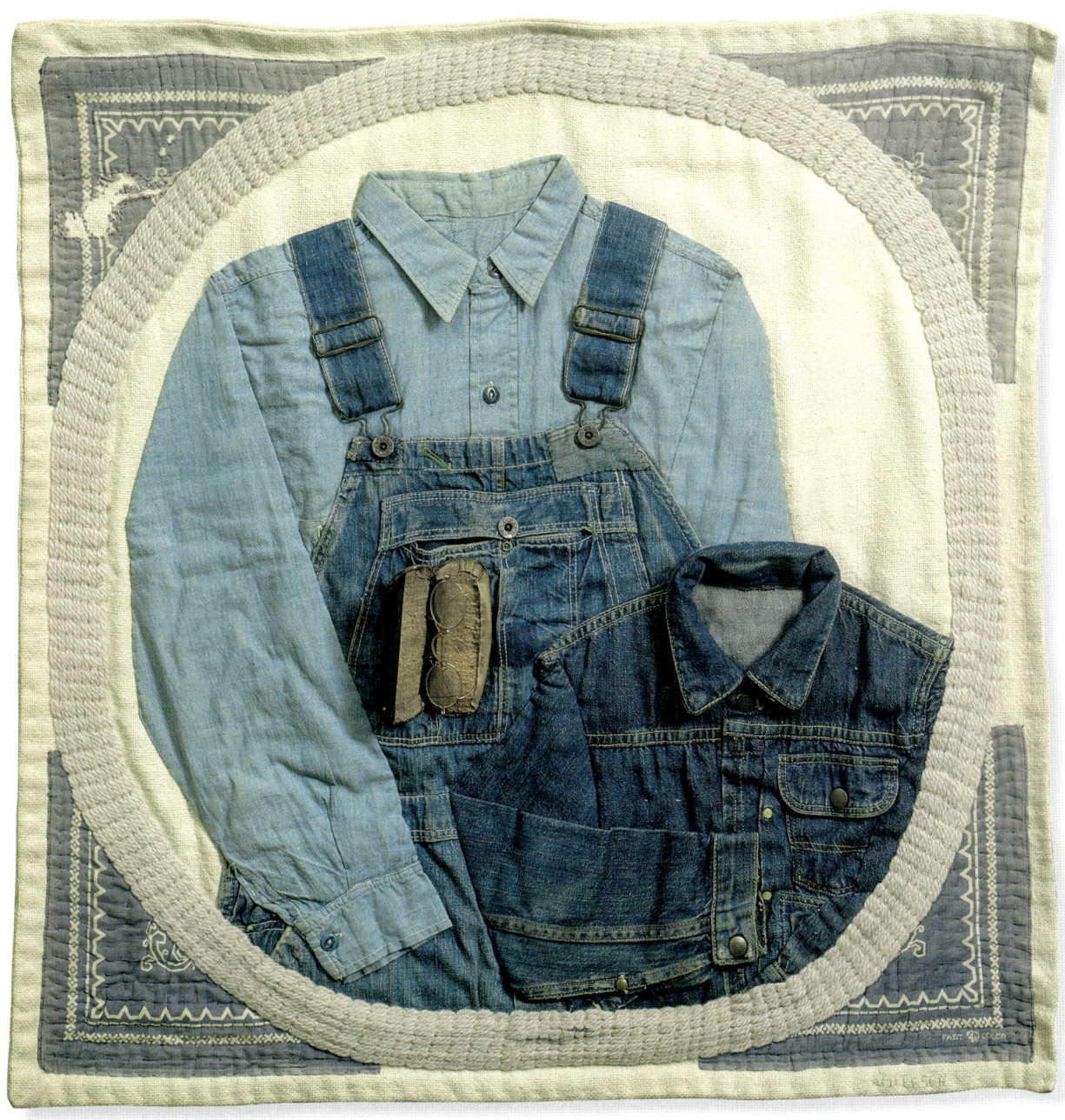

Alma Wallace Lesch, Like Father, Like Son, *1967, cotton denim, vintage clothing, wool yarn, thread, eyeglasses, 32½ × 32½ in.*

Creative arts competitions at fairs have often welcomed more original, varied, and sometimes subversive entries than traditional art and crafts genres have done. Even intricate forms of fancywork (decorative needlework) have historically been dismissed as sentimental and unworthy of attention from art museums or the fine arts categories in fair competitions, but they have been accepted into creative arts competitions, along with embroidery, crochet, and even Victorian hair wreaths. In the 1960s, Alma Wallace Lesch, a fiber artist and instructor, took top prizes in the Women's Department at the Kentucky State Fair with works in embroidery, weaving, ceramics, and collage. Lesch soon became nationally known for her collaged fabric portraits, such as *Like Father, Like Son,* made from personal clothing and everyday objects with gendered associations. These works contributed to the feminist reevaluation of women's work in the 1970s. In the twentieth century, Women's Buildings and creative arts displays made room for exhibits and demonstrations by 4-H clubs and home economics departments that covered politically charged topics such as food security, sustainability, labor conditions, and public health—a departure from the traditional categories of domestic and agricultural work.

Showcasing the collective creative efforts of women has long been the principal objective of creative arts competitions at fairs. Although the categories listed in premium books, which serve as exhibitors' guides to fair competitions, offer insight into how these events evolved in tandem with shifting cultural values and social dynamics, they tell us little about the visual impact of the entries and displays or the stories of the people who created them. Other evidence, including archival images, newspaper clippings, and oral histories, reminds us that women's collectivity has been central to organizing creative arts competitions and displays, underscoring the fair's role in shaping communal belonging.

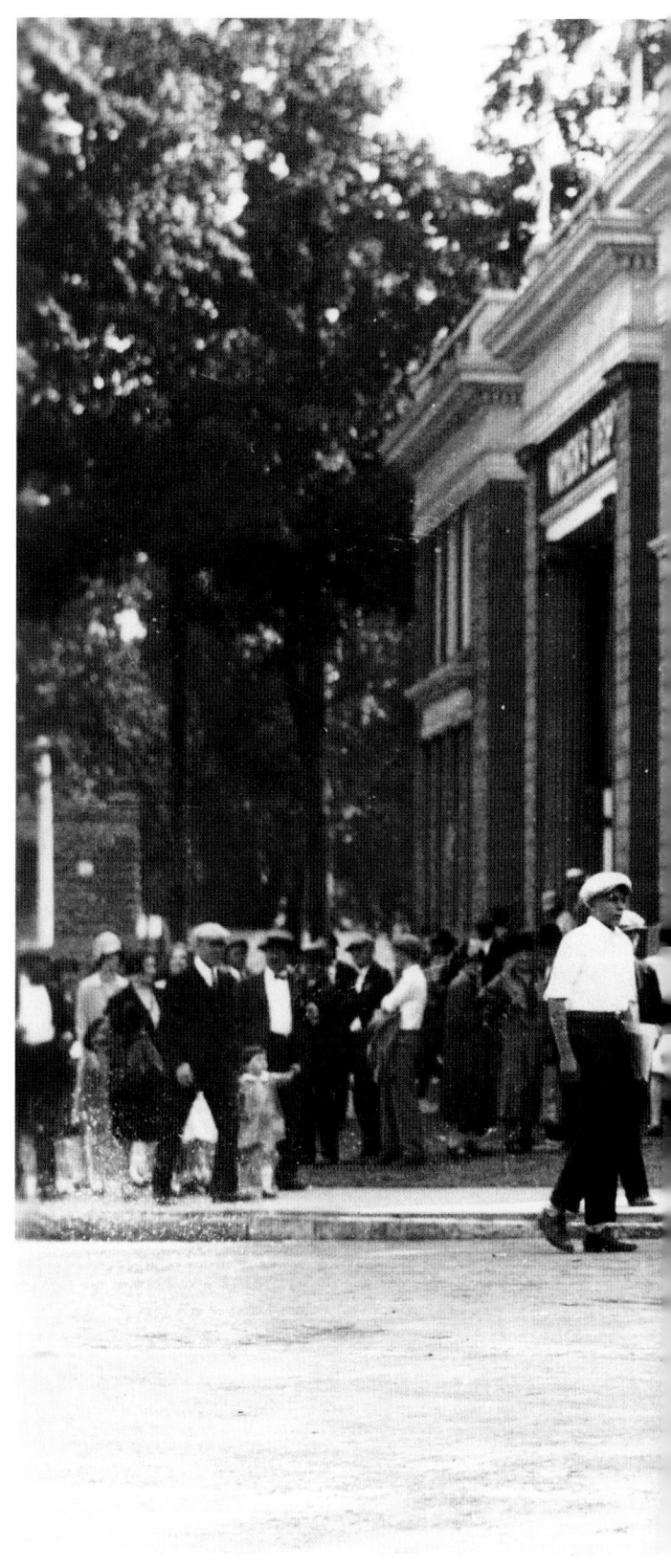

The Women's Building at the Wisconsin State Fair, around 1920. Fairs used Women's Buildings to display craft typically created by or associated with women, such as flower arrangements and cake decorating.

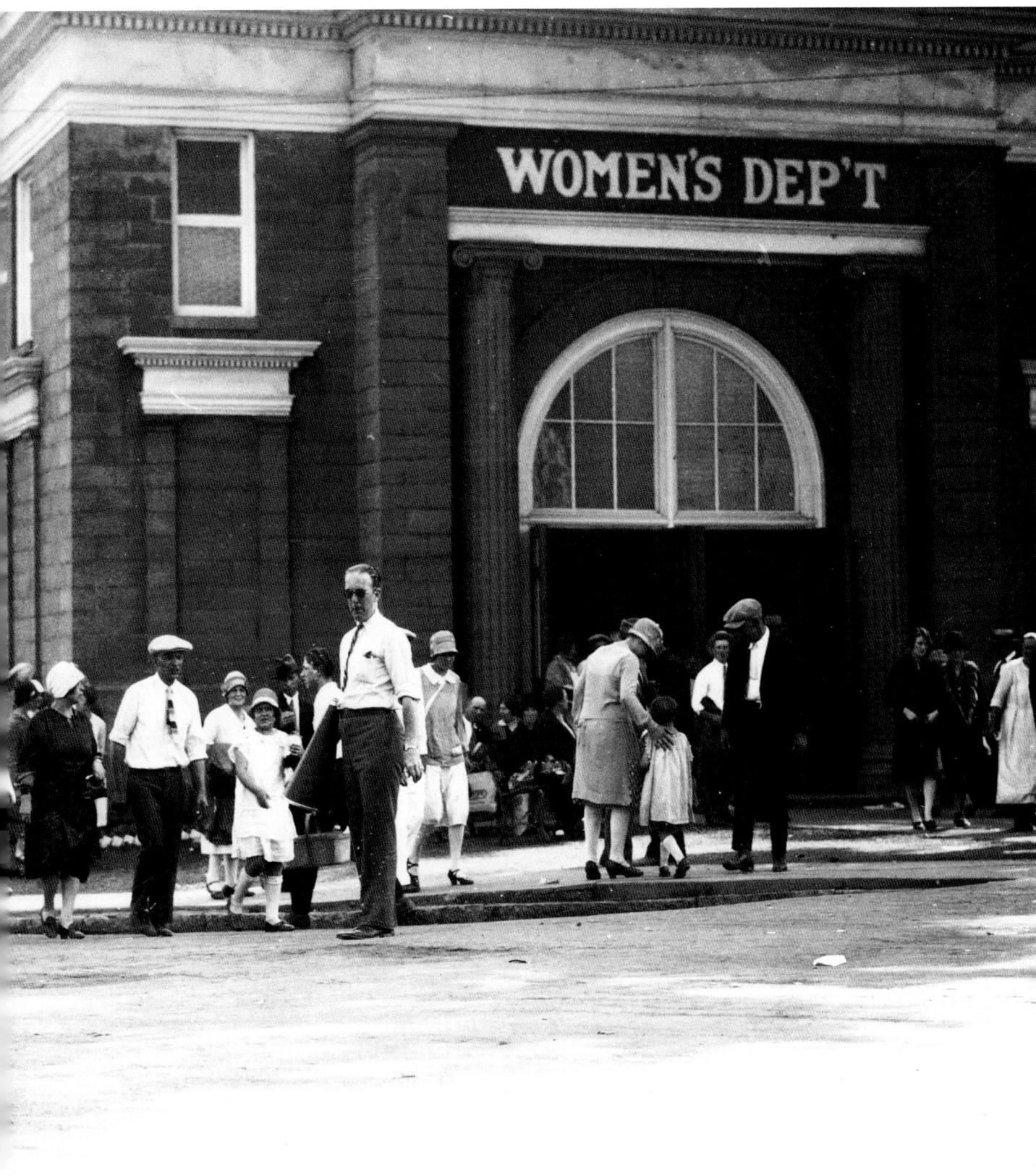

Studio Craft Competitions and Workshops

SARA MORRIS

I n the United States, the histories of studio craft and state fairs have always been inter-twined. Indeed, the popularity of state fairs after World War II—a period of economic prosperity that saw fairground expansions and record-breaking attendance—offered a public stage for the work of professional craftspeople. Fine arts competitions (whose entries were previously limited to painting and sculpture) began to include categories for ceramics, fiber arts, glass, metals, and jewelry. Though exhibiting in the Fine Arts Buildings of state fairgrounds did not carry the same prestige as displays in art museums, fairs provided artists with unprecedented exposure, especially women and emerging artists operating outside mainstream gallery systems. For many exhibitors, a bigger reward than the ribbons and prize money was recognition in exhibition catalogs, newspapers, and craft magazines.

The well-regarded fine arts competition at the California State Fair helped bring into focus artists who were largely excluded from postwar art histories, and it expanded audiences for studio craft on the West Coast. The fair's exhibition catalogs from the 1940s show the increase in categories of artwork recognized as "fine art." By the mid-1950s, the fair's fine arts competitions had earned national recognition through publications like Craft Horizons. In a 1956 issue, Richard Petterson, director of arts and crafts at the Los Angeles County Fair, praised the state fair as a showcase for young artists.[1] A visitor to the fair in 1950 would have encountered the prize-winning ceramics and enamels by Katherine Po-Yu Choy, who entered them in the fair competitions while still a graduate student at Mills College in Oakland. Amid stiff competition that year, she won the first-prize purchase award for her Ceramic Group over ceramics entered by such contemporaries as

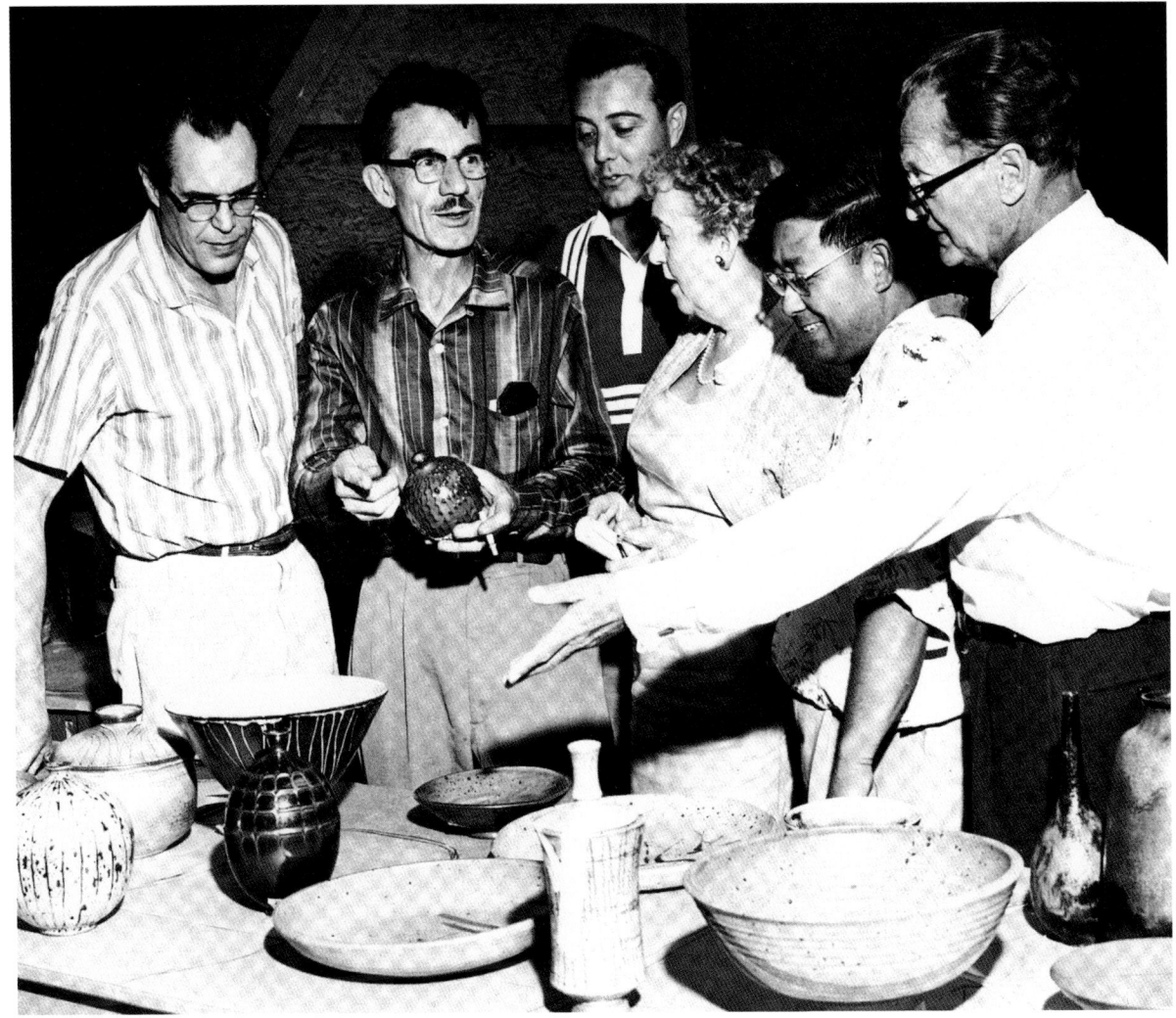

Crafts jury making selection for the 1957 California State Fair Art Show. **Left to right:** *Carlton Ball, Albert King, Russ Brown, Eleanor Forbes, Harry Osaki, Dr. Karl With.*

James Lovera, Harrison McIntosh, Edith Heath, and Ruth Rippon.[2]

With awards and recognition at stake, expert judges and juries were crucial to the success of the art competitions. Typically, juries were composed of experienced artists and professionals in the field. For example, the fiber artist Kay Sekimachi, who won second prize for her handweaving at the California State Fair in 1952 and third prize in 1954, served as a juror in 1959. Judges were sometimes also expected to weigh in on other class categories, a practice that stirred

controversy. At the first Annual Conference of American Craftsmen at Asilomar, California, in 1957, Karl With, a curator and art historian, questioned whether members of a jury should be specialists: "If it is your consideration that only the weaver can judge the weaving, only the potter can judge the ceramic, that sounds to me very clannish … For what do you judge? For the general public? For the market that you want to build up? … Do you make your pots for other potters?" He gave his own answer: "No. In order to enjoy the omelet you don't have to be the hen who lays the egg."[3] At this time, however, many of the jurors were indeed hens.

Even if visitors came to the California State Fair mostly to watch a 4-H sheep competition or taste a funnel cake, they would have also had the opportunity to view and participate in live art demonstrations. Adjacent to the Fine Arts Building, the Art in Action area hosted hands-on workshops on enameling, ceramics, and metalwork led by professional artists. Art in Action highlighted correlations between making and learning, principles fundamental to studio-craft pedagogies that were, in large part, community focused.

For some, demonstrating was truly a family affair. As a young man, the Sacramento artist Fred Uhl Ball dazzled crowds with his skilled enameling demonstrations. He was continuing the tradition established by his parents, Kathryn Uhl Ball and F. Carlton Ball, who were fair participants, judges, and demonstrators. Antonio Prieto and Eunice Prieto, a married couple, demonstrated throwing pottery as well as exhibiting their work. Antonio Prieto's bulbous *Engobe Bottle* features a semiabstract figure that echoes the form of the vessel, glazed using a watered-down clay slurry known as engobe. After Antonio Prieto's death, the 1967 fair catalog paid tribute to him for his longstanding involvement, making special mention of his showmanship on the pottery wheel and thoughtful explanations for visitors.

Robert Arneson experienced a breakthrough moment at the Art in Action program. On a September afternoon in 1961, Arneson gave

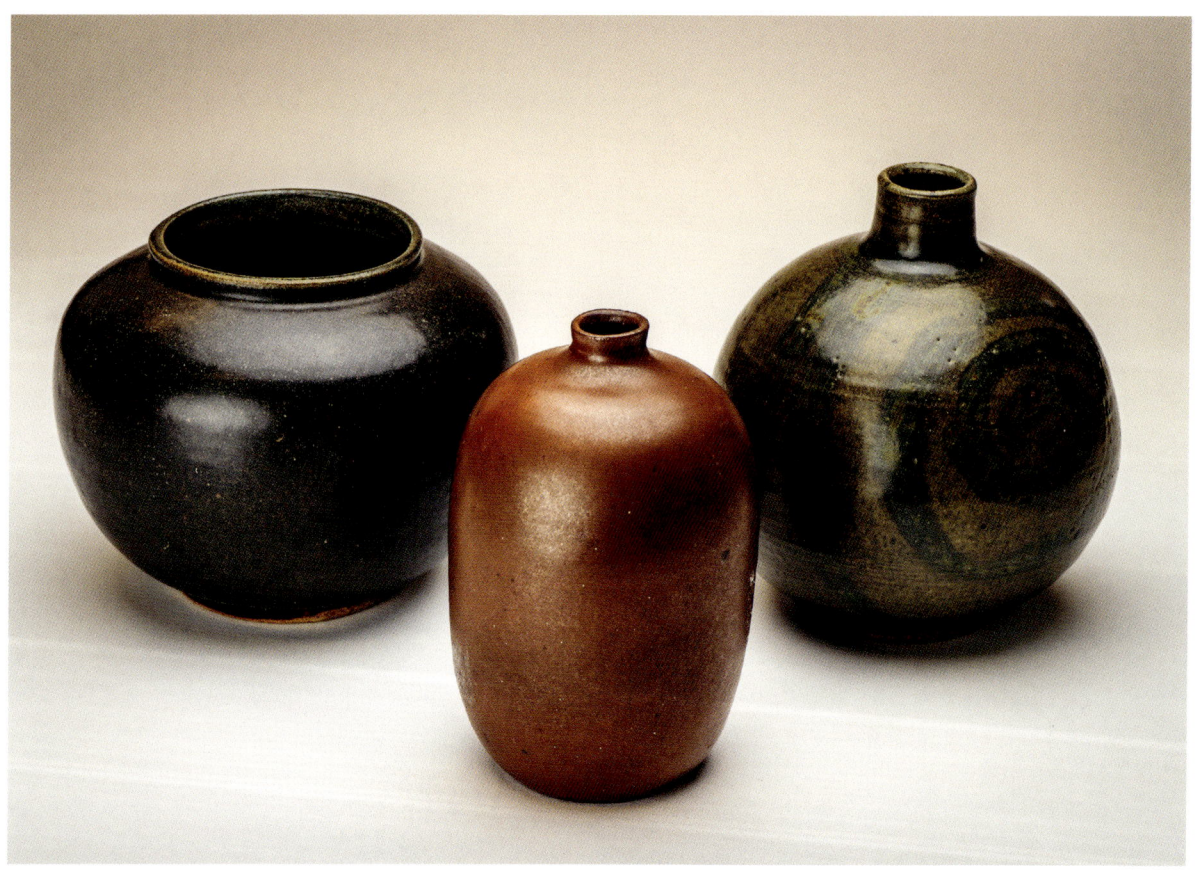

Above: *Katherine Po-Yu Choy, Group of Pots, 1950, glazed stoneware; center: 6 × 4 in. diameter; left: 6½ × 6 in. diameter; right: 5¼ × 6½ in. diameter.* **Right:** *Kay Sekimachi, Wall hanging, 1959, cotton, rayon, wool, jute, wood, 62 × 21½ in.*

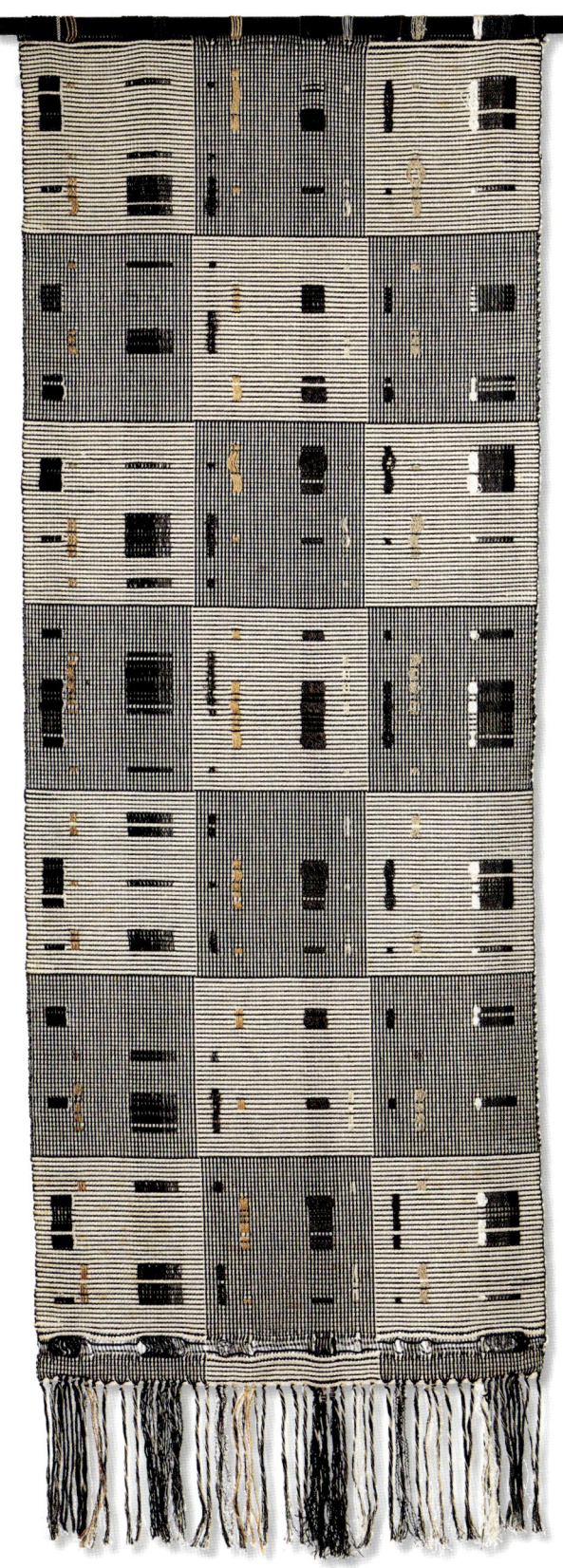

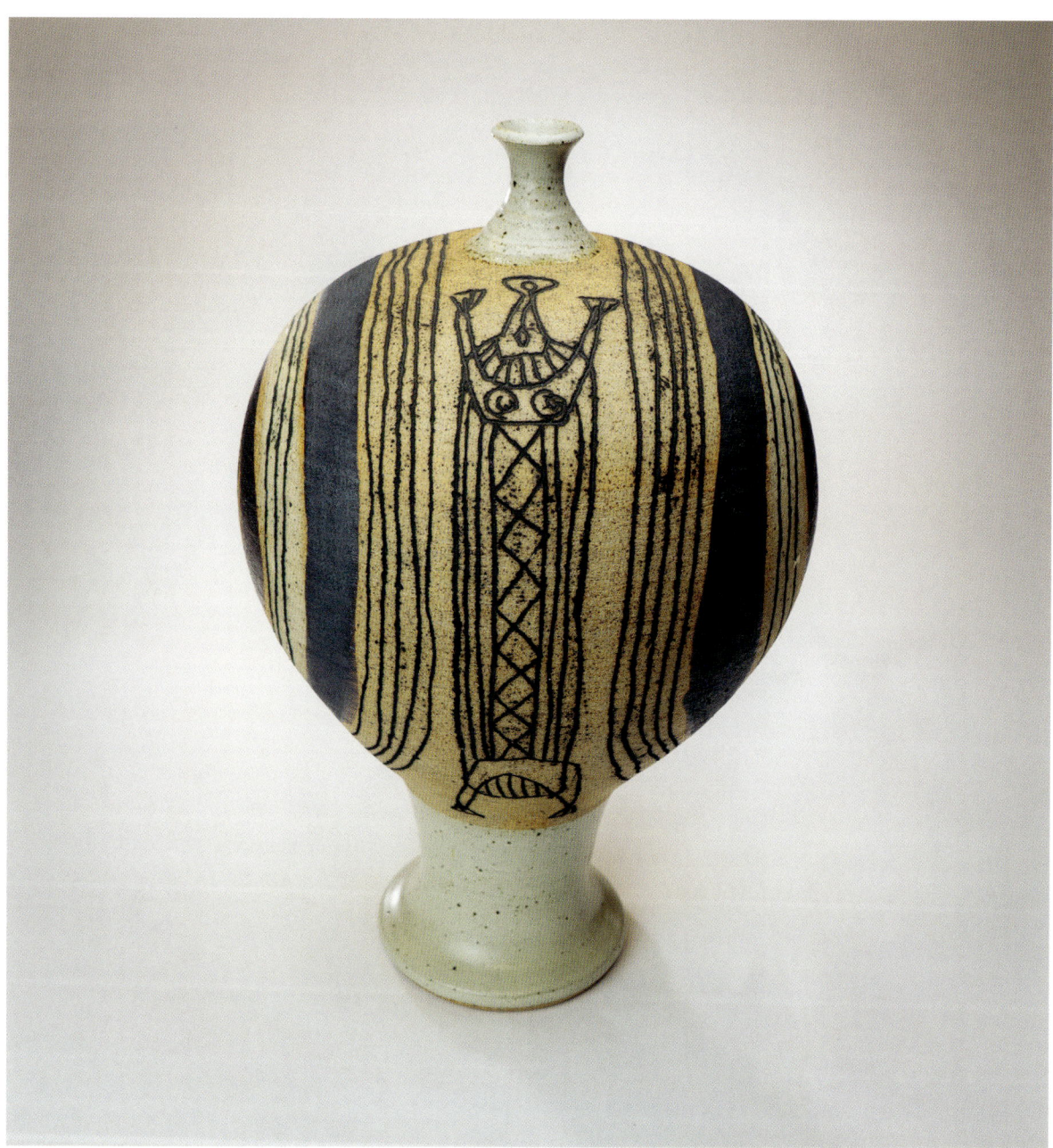

a demonstration, throwing what he described in a letter to museum director Paul Smith as "a handsome, sturdy bottle about quart size."[4] The artwork in question is *No Deposit, No Return,* a ceramic bottle marked with an X and the words "NO DEPOSIT." By sealing the bottle closed—rendering it useless in a traditional sense—Arneson signaled his rejection of functionality in ceramics.

Countless other artists have found opportunities for expression at fairs across the country. In 1974, Arturo Alonzo Sandoval submitted *Moth III* to the Illinois State Fair's fine arts competition. According to Sandoval, the moth is a symbol of transformation—a fitting theme, given that the artist had recently graduated from the Cran-brook Academy of Art, where he studied fiber art,

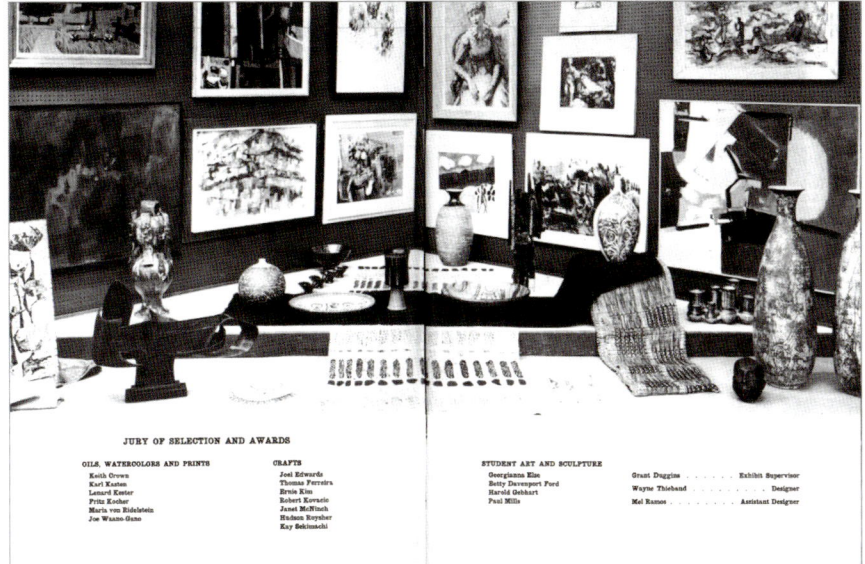

JURY OF SELECTION AND AWARDS

OILS, WATERCOLORS AND PRINTS

Keith Crown
Karl Kasten
Lenard Kester
Fritz Kocher
Maria von Bidelstein
Joe Wessn-Gano

CRAFTS

Joel Edwards
Thomas Ferreira
Ernie Kim
Robert Kovacic
Janet McNinch
Hudson Roysher
Kay Sekimachi

STUDENT ART AND SCULPTURE

Georgianna Rim
Betty Davenport Ford
Harold Gebhart
Paul Mills

Grant Duggins . . . . . . Exhibit Supervisor
Wayne Thiebaud . . . . Designer
Mel Ramos . . . . Assistant Designer

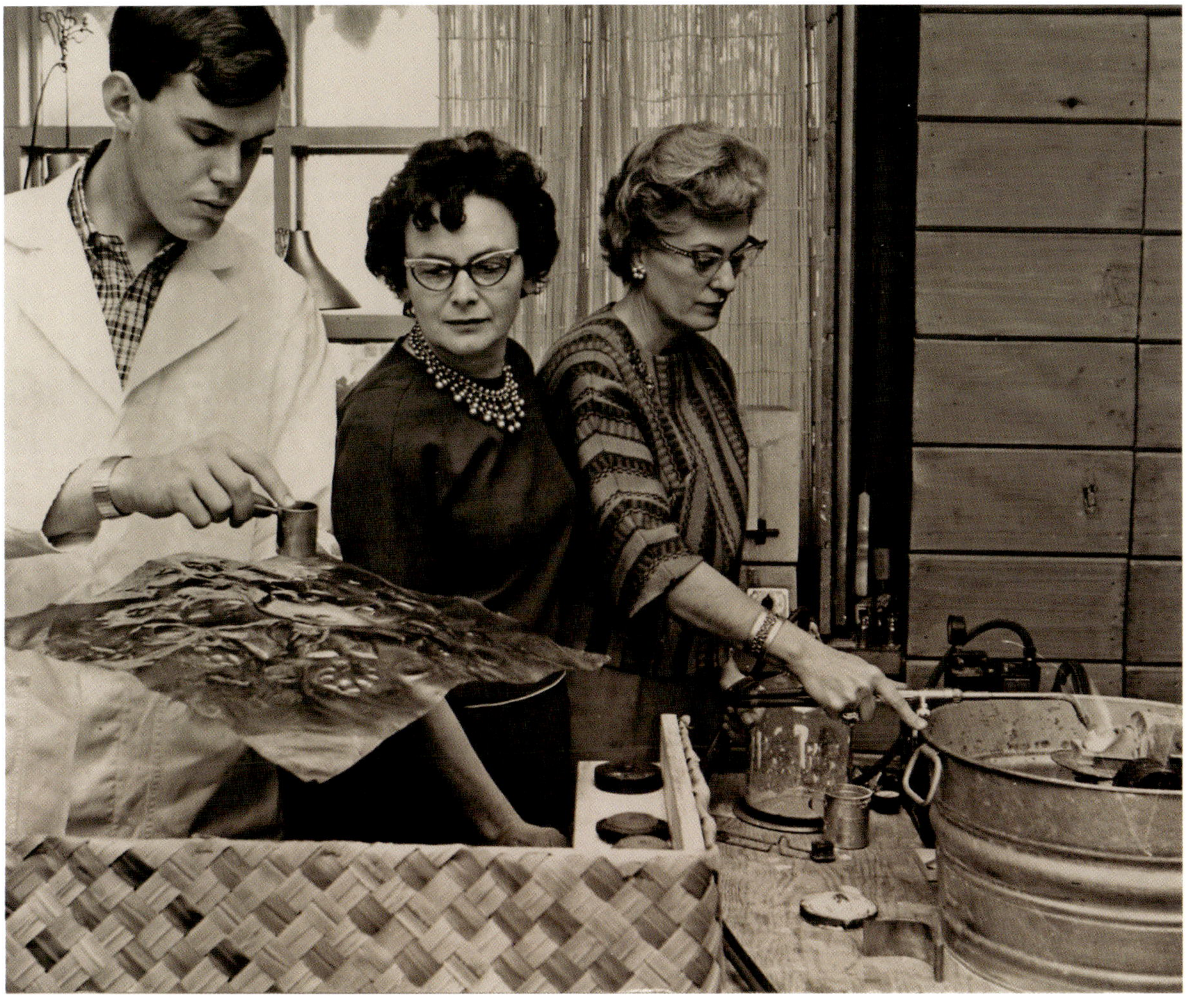

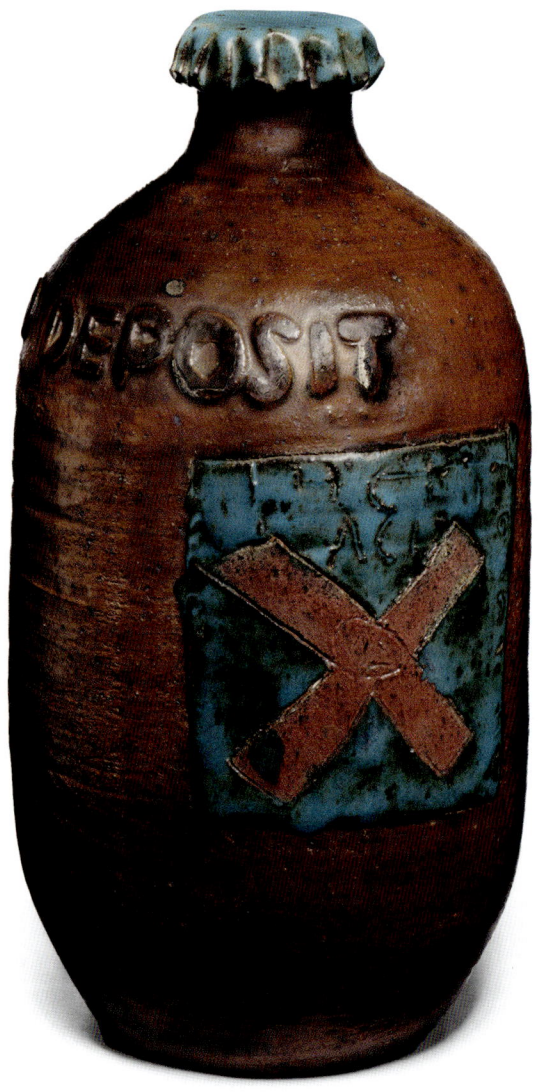

Robert Arneson, No Deposit, No Return, *1961, earthenware, 5 × 10¾ in.*

and become an instructor on the art and design faculty at Southern Illinois University (SIU). At SIU, his colleagues encouraged him to submit his weaving to the fair to bulk up his resumé. *Moth III* earned first place and was purchased directly from the fair's exhibition by the influential collector and conductor George Macaulay Irwin.

Fine arts competitions at state fairs have provided artists, especially newcomers and mid-career

artists, with opportunities to show their work to large audiences. The role of the fair as an arena and testing ground for studio art runs counter to its traditional associations with provincial styles and homespun tastes. Yet the fairground has shaped the trajectory of studio craft and modern art more broadly, making it an integral yet often overlooked part of the nation's artistic legacy.

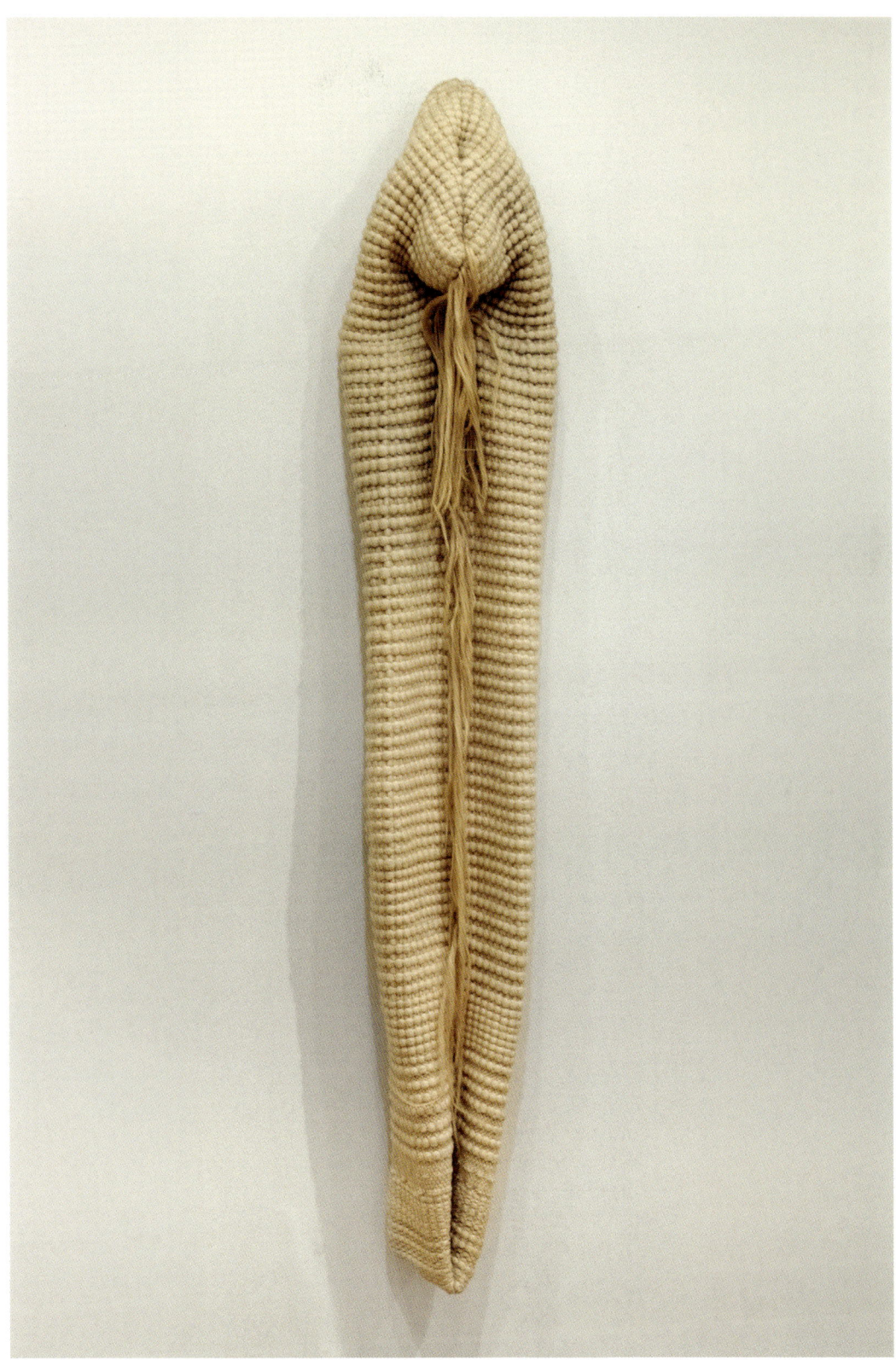

Arturo Alonzo Sandoval, Moth III, 1971, wool, Lurex, and flax, 86 in.

4-H and Youth Participation

ELANA HAIN

From midway games and carnival rides to livestock birthing barns and contests for activities such as joke-telling and mom-calling, fairgrounds have long offered young people a variety of activities to enjoy. Children's participation in fairs dates back to the late nineteenth century, when agricultural organizations began to offer educational programs for rural youth. In 1888, the National Grange of Order of the Patrons of Husbandry, a progressive farming advocacy group, established the Junior Grange as its leadership development program for children. In 1898 the president of the Farm Institute, Will B. Otwell, organized corn-growing contests for boys in Macoupin County, Illinois, and in 1902 A. B. Graham initiated an agricultural program for rural youth in Clark County, Ohio. Over the next few years, agricultural clubs for children sprouted across the nation, including the Tomato Club and the Pig Club. In recognition of their shared interests and goals, many of these local clubs assembled into the 4-H movement in 1912. Today 4-H, with over six million members aged five and up, describes itself as the largest youth development organization in the country.[1] Since 4-H and similar organizations first came into being, their engagement in state fairs has provided a range of opportunities for kids to learn and demonstrate artistic and agricultural skills, setting them up for a lifetime of engagement with craft-based pursuits.

The original mission of 4-H—whose name signifies the organization's four values of "head, heart, hands, and health"—was to disseminate improved farming and home economics methods by teaching them to the children of farmers. These included the use of hybrid corn seed, milk sanitation, and better home-canning procedures. Organizers hoped the students would relay this information to their (often apprehensive) parents as well as to the public.[2] In 1910 Oklahoma A&M College sponsored the

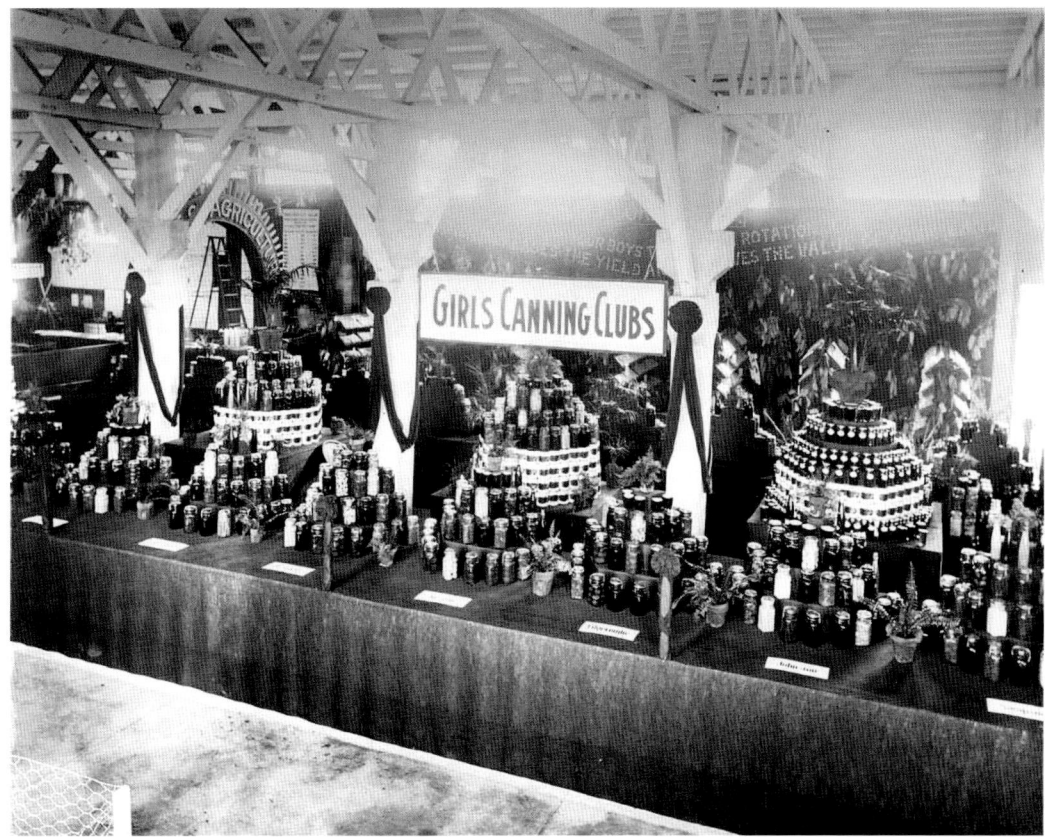

first booth for 4-H members at a state fair, featuring demonstrations of these new techniques and technologies by the children who had won the top prizes in their county competitions.[3]

As 4-H and other youth agricultural organizations gained traction, they built permanent structures on fairgrounds, such as dedicated youth buildings and dormitories for exhibitors. Here children and young adults from all over the state could come together and engage in many of the same undertakings as adult participants, such as arts, clothing, foods, horticulture, and livestock demonstrations. Buildings such as the Bruce Rastetter 4-H Exhibits Building at the Iowa State Fair and the 4-H Building at the Minnesota State Fair were constructed as part of New Deal employment programs and have been distinctive features of fairgrounds ever since.

In addition to promoting agricultural and home economics methods and bringing together isolated rural families, 4-H and state fair organizers

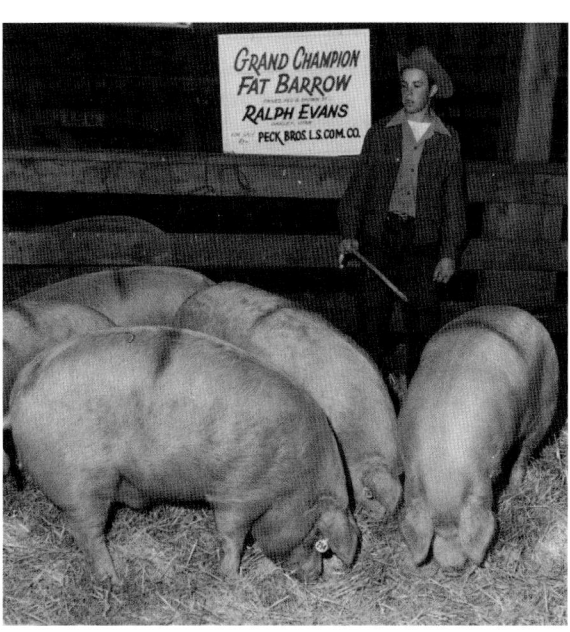

Top: *Products from various girls' canning clubs on display at the North Carolina State Fair in 1918.* **Above:** *Ralph Evans owned and showed pigs, including the grand champion fat barrow, at a fair in Utah in 1939.*

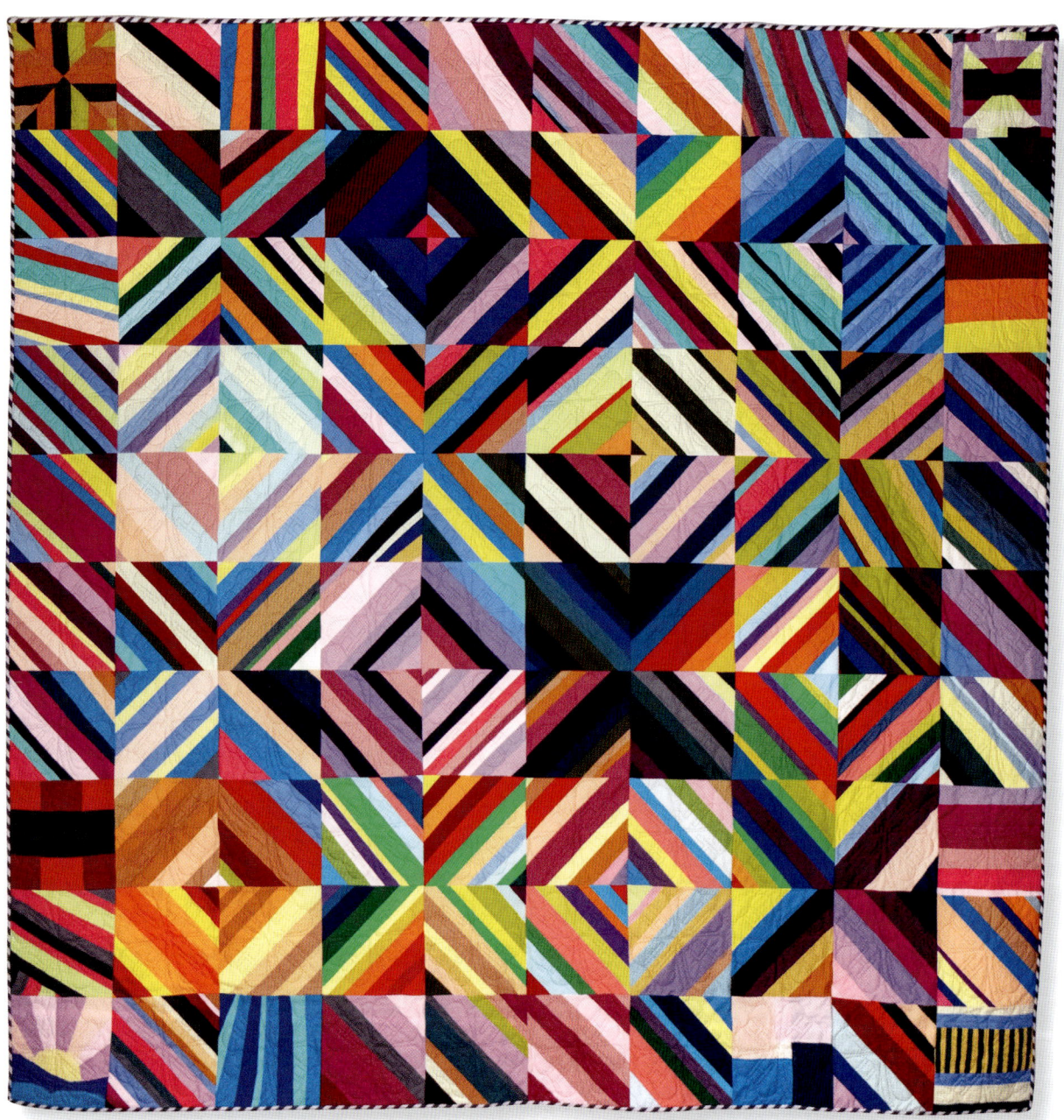

4-H Interaction of Color String Quilt, 2025, cotton fabric, batting, and thread, 110in × 110in. Organized and assembled by Susie Brandt, machine quilted by Stacey Bendure, and quilt blocks made by 4-H Clubs in Alaska, New Jersey, West Virginia, and Utah.

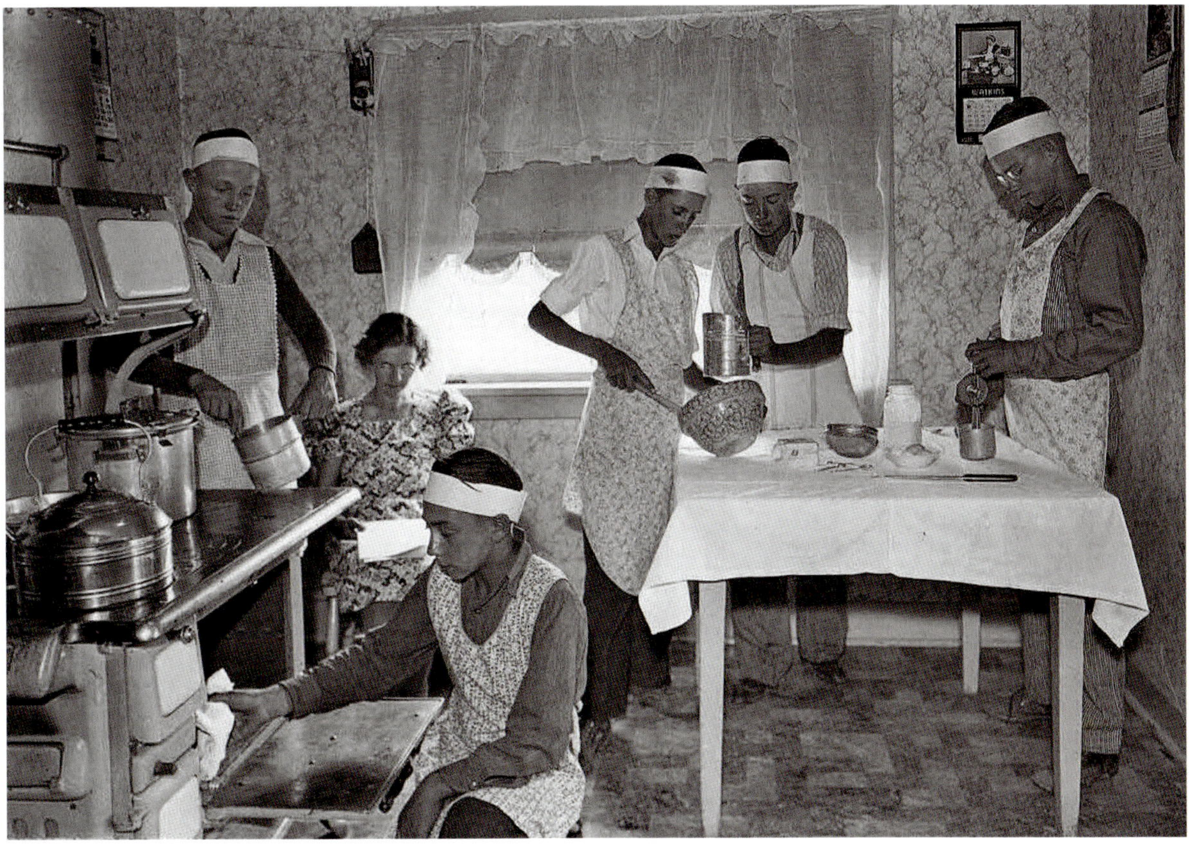

A 4-H food club for boys in Syracuse, Utah, in 1939.

encouraged participants to "learn by doing," which is still 4-H's slogan today. In 1902, a publicity campaign for the Minnesota State Fair argued that "children who attend can learn more of the state of Minnesota in a short time at the fair than in a year of the school room."[4] State fair competitions and demonstrations remain valuable learning opportunities for members of 4-H, Junior Grange, and the Future Farmers of America (FFA), another youth-focused agricultural association that was convened as a national organization in Kansas in 1928. A prominent example is the livestock show, in which children as young as five present small animals they have raised from birth, such as chickens and rabbits, while older kids show cattle, goats, horses, pigs, sheep, and other livestock. As in other state fair competitions, judges evaluate the aesthetic qualities of the exhibitor's "project" (in this case, traits like the animal's muscle mass,

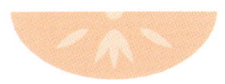

"Our hands are the antennas of our soul."

ELENA BERNABÉ

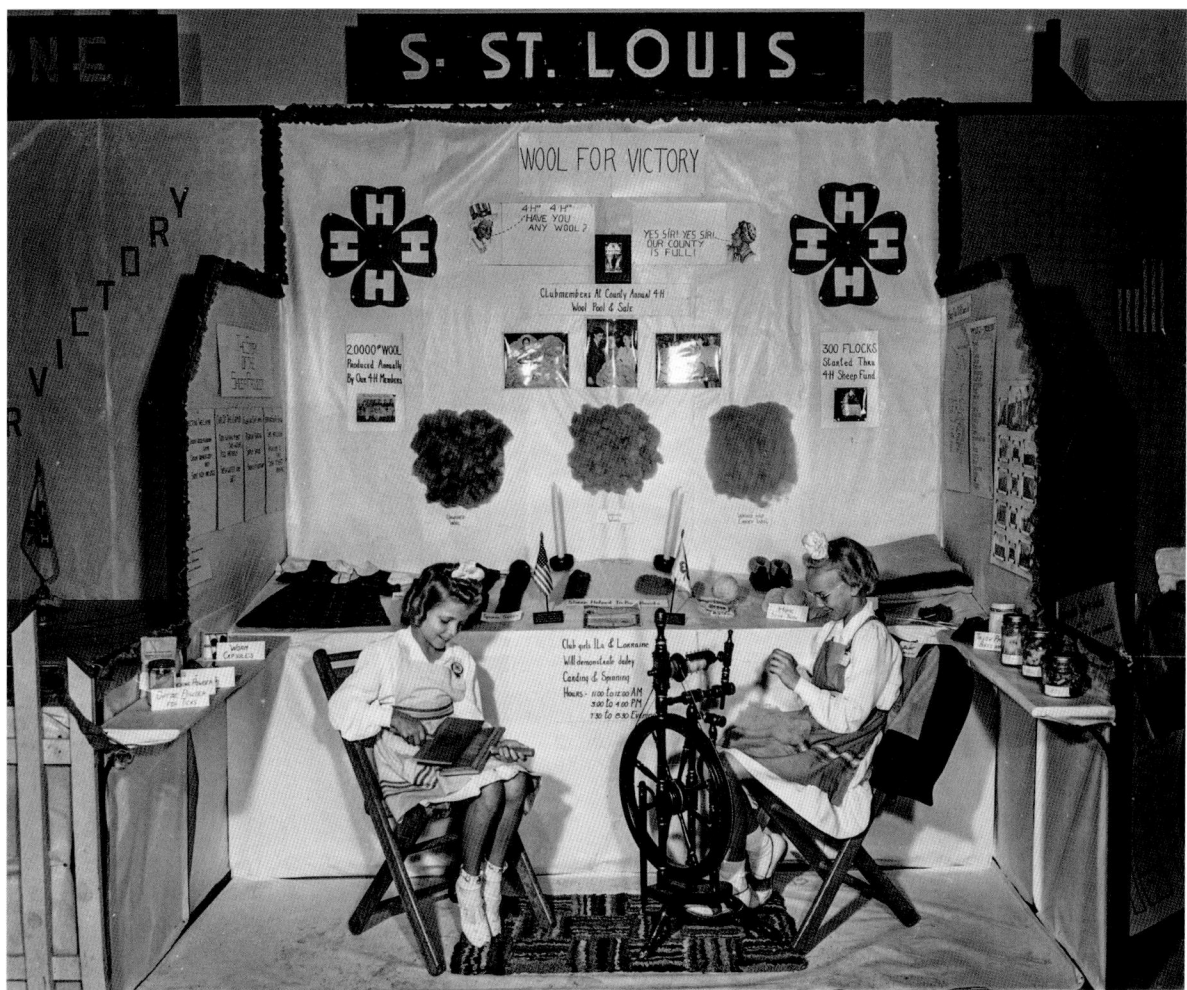

Above: *Hermantown 4-H Club members demonstrate carding and spinning wool at the Minnesota State Fair in 1942.*
Right: *4-H Club Dress Revue winners during the 1949 Indiana State Fair.*

movement, and overall appearance), as well as the exhibitor's showmanship skills and ability to answer questions about the animal and its care.

Many competitions at the fair were historically gendered in the same way as daily farm chores, though participation varied by organization. Until the 1960s, FFA was open only to boys, whereas the Junior Grange included activities for the whole family and created leadership positions for girls. At 4-H, boys were encouraged to raise animals and crops, though some local programs also taught boys cooking and canning skills in "food clubs." Girls were more likely to participate in canning, baking, and handicrafts such as quilting,

beadwork, and making clothing for the popular Dress Revue competitions. These "homemaking" activities have played a crucial role in farm life—especially during the Great Depression and world wars, when thrift and self-sufficiency were essential—and are often highly skilled and creative. For a 4-H display at the 1931 Wisconsin State Fair, thirteen-year-old Elda Strahm spent sixty-five hours cutting 1,152 fabric diamonds from flour and chicken-feed sacks and sewing them together to make her exquisite *Broken Star Quilt*.[5]

In addition to espousing gender bias, 4-H and FFA also perpetuated racial inequality. Until the Civil Rights Act of 1964, many states' agricultural programs were segregated. African American clubs received significantly less funding than white clubs, and Black members were excluded from national events.[6] Although both organizations have since striven to increase diversity—in part by expanding from rural farming communities to urban areas, suburban neighborhoods, and Native American reservations—around three-quarters of their members still identify as white, and participation often does not represent the significant Latinx agricultural workforce throughout the United States.[7]

Despite these significant absences, the commitment to learning by doing in these organizations and at fairs remains central to US agricultural education, and also develops participants' craft-based skills and insights. Whether they are raising animals and crops, sewing quilts, or learning baking skills, young people are gaining

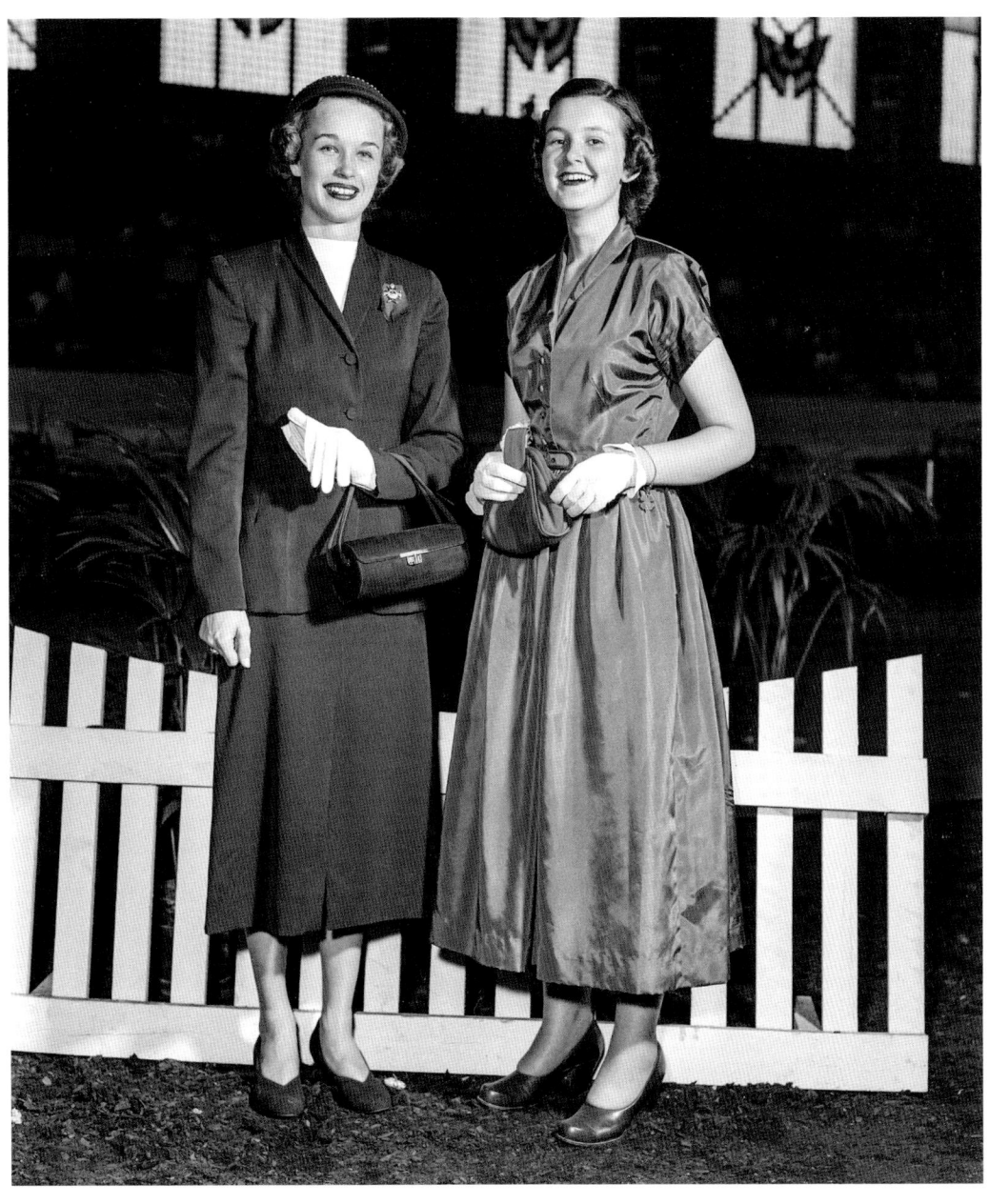

proficiency, learning through experience, and acquiring material knowledge. They can connect with the artistic and agricultural traditions of their own family or community as well as learn about the traditions of other groups they might not otherwise encounter. And all participants discover the possibilities of working with their hands. As the Italian author Elena Bernabé writes, "Our hands are the antennas of our soul. When you move them by sewing, cooking, painting, touching the earth, or sinking it into the earth, they send signals of caring to the deepest part of you and your soul calms down."[8] These experiences have inspired millions of kids to use their hands (as well as their heads and hearts) to become life-long practitioners of their skills and to advance 4-H's mission to "make the best better."

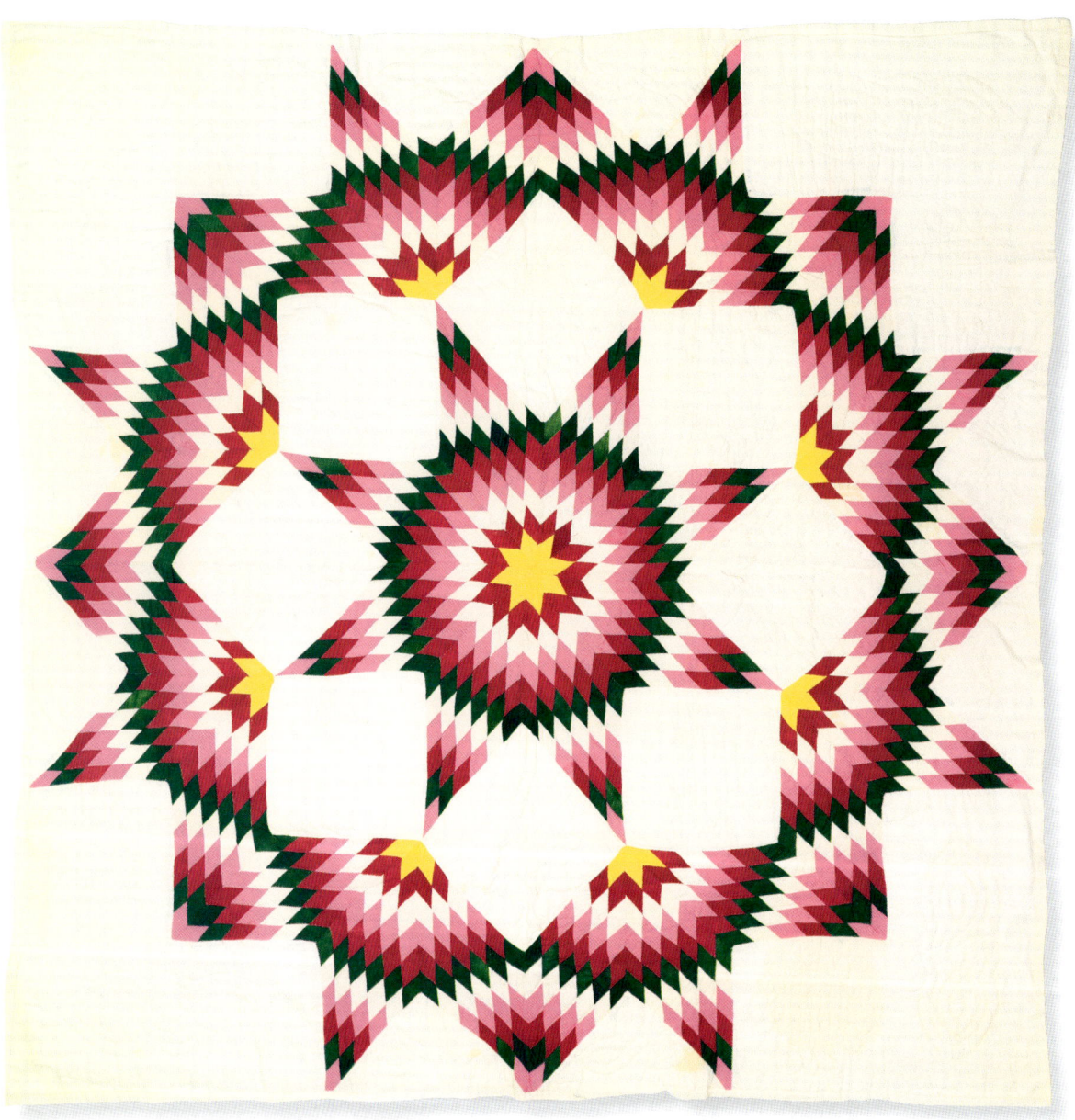

Elda Strahm, "Broken Star" quilt, 1931, dyed and pieced flour and feed sacks, 72½ × 72 in.

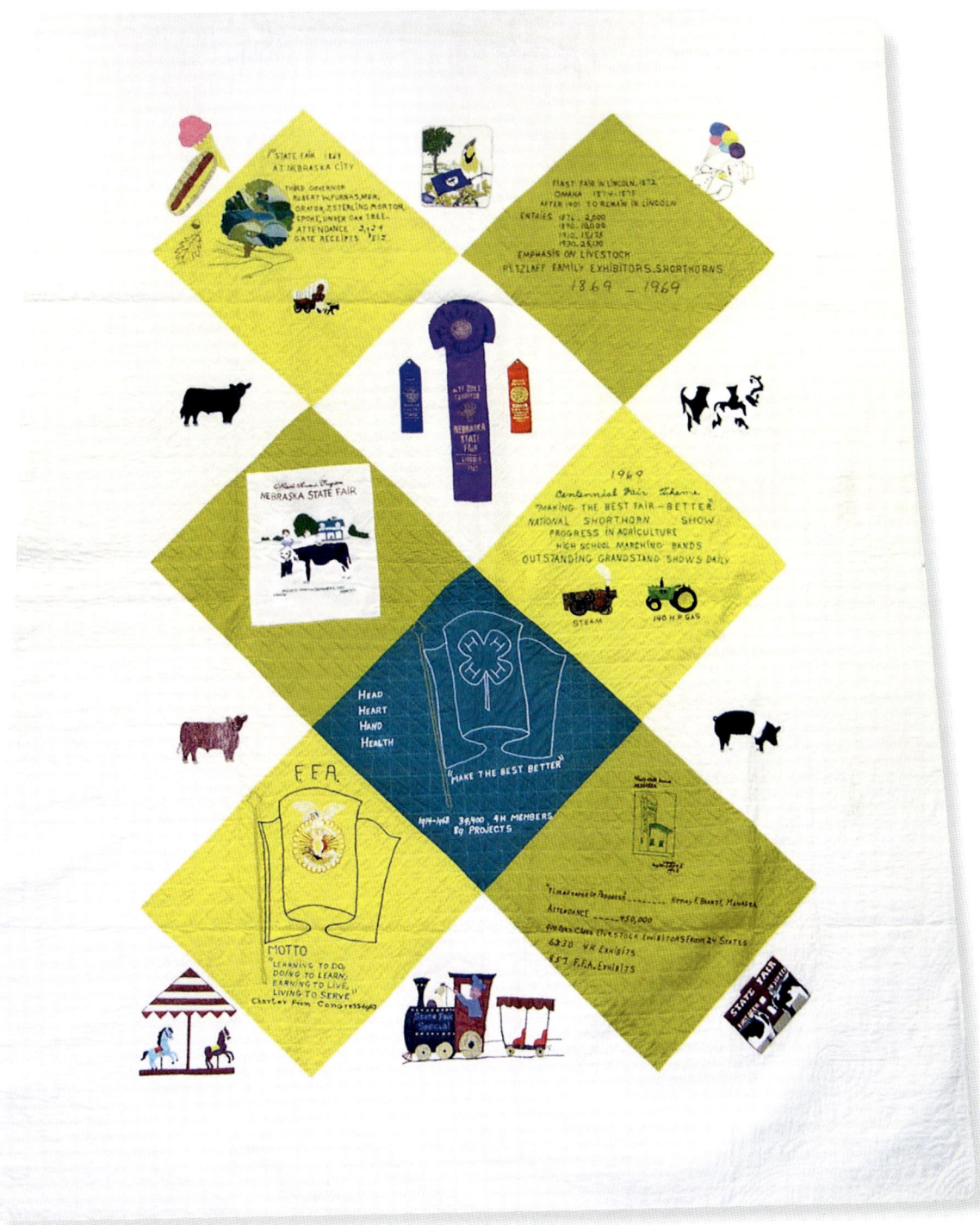

Hazel M. Meyers, Quilt commemorating the centennial of the Nebraska State Fair, 1969, fair ribbons, thread, paint, and ink on pieced cotton, 93 × 70 in. Meyers, who entered quilts in the fair from 1957 to 1969, appliquéd her prize ribbons onto this piece. The quilt represents the progress of each decade and includes scenes of Meyers's children participating in 4-H at the fair, as well as 4-H's motto and clover emblem.

The Indiana State Fair Pioneer Village and Folklife

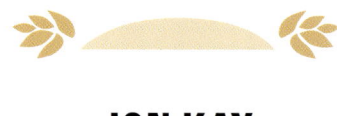

JON KAY

Folklife and living-history displays have become fixtures at state and county fairs across the United States. The Iowa State Fair's Pioneer Hall, for example, includes antique and craft displays, as well as traditional music performances. The State Fair of Virginia's Heritage Village exhibits vintage tractors, steam engines, and tools, as well as demonstrations of glassblowing, blacksmithing, and rope making.[1] Each year at the Indiana State Fair, volunteers, vendors, and employees convene to produce the Pioneer Village, a living display celebrating the traditions of the small family farms that were once common throughout the state. In addition to displays of antique tractors, wagons, and agricultural implements, the village offers fairgoers the opportunity to see demonstrators making quilts, splitting shingles, threshing wheat, and hewing wooden bowls. For many of the participants, Pioneer Village is a form of critical nostalgia, the presentation of the past as an effort to shape the future.[2]

The Pioneer Village began in 1961, when Mauri Williamson, the secretary of the Purdue Agricultural Alumni Association, brought a collection of antique farming tools and artifacts from Purdue University to display at the Indiana State Fair.[3] Before this, the fair had focused on the future of agriculture in the state, but Williamson's display offered a nostalgic glimpse into the past. In 1968 a dedicated barn was built on the fairgrounds to permanently house this collection. That year Williamson added threshing machine demonstrations, and the expanded vintage farm-equipment display became "the place to be" at the fair. Over the next fifty years, the village grew to include a blacksmith's forge, a wheelwright's shop, barns, and outbuildings to house both livestock and demonstrations.[4]

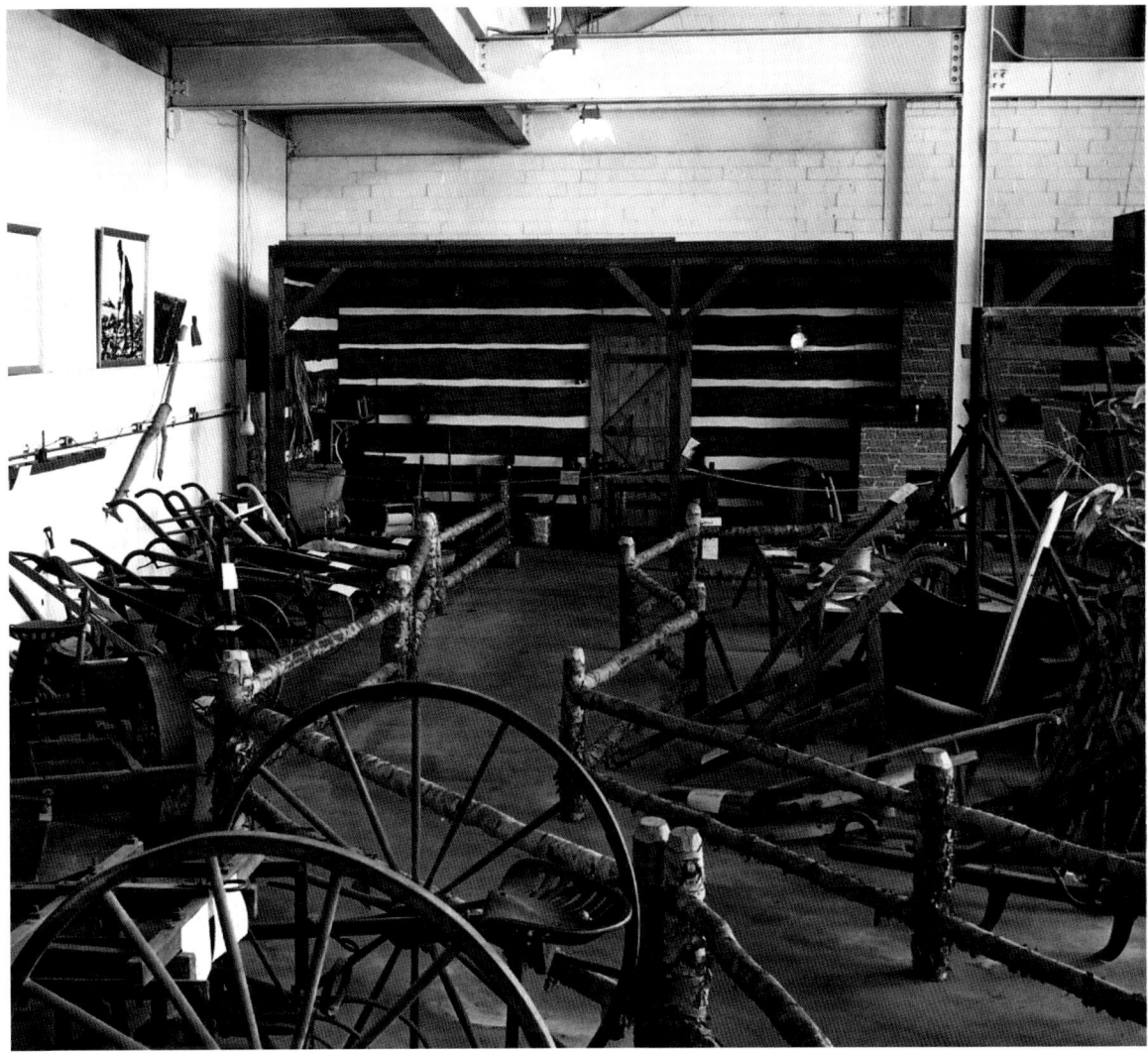

Pioneer Farm display at the 1965 Indiana State Fair, showing a variety of plows and other period farm implements.

To bring the village to life, the fair enlists the help of dozens of artisans, musicians, and demonstrators. Daily during the fair, the village demonstrates the use of antique threshing machines, sawmills, and other machinery once commonly found on Indiana farms, powered by historical steam engines. In 1996, Williamson, reflecting on the purpose of the village, wrote: "Our demonstrations, explanations of hundreds of agricultural antiques, and our interpreters who roam the showgrounds point all their actions toward the American consumer of food and fiber, who sadly knows little about it. The task is a formidable and rewarding one."[5]

While the village provides insights into the history of food and fiber production, it also stands in contrast to today's highly industrialized agricultural practices. Donya Lester, a former executive director of the Purdue Agricultural Alumni Association and a friend of Williamson, observed: "Farmers of all kinds were his heroes, and he was especially drawn to the stories of pioneer farmers who carved out a life for their families and built communities in wild, unsettled lands … Their ingenuity and resourcefulness were a continual inspiration to him, and he always looked for ways to share their stories so they could continue to inspire

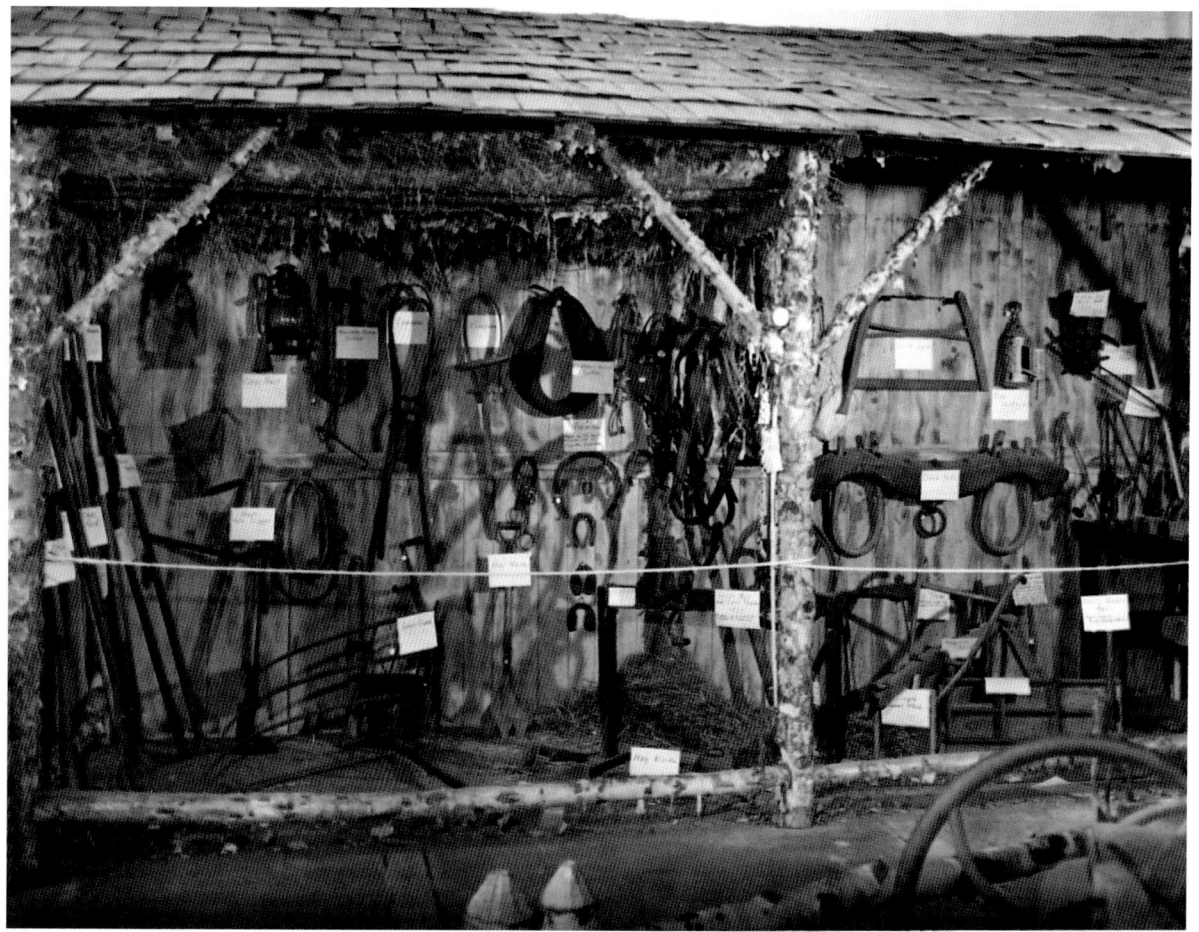

A variety of period tools, including a horse collar, buck saw, and ox yoke, on display as part of the 1969 Indiana State Fair's Pioneer Farm display.

others."[6] Williamson's vision for the village was a romantic re-creation of the farming communities of his youth.

In 1975, Williamson invited Ellsworth Christmas to demonstrate chair caning. Christmas has volunteered at the Pioneer Village ever since, teaching fairgoers about Indiana's traditional crafts and agricultural practices. He grew up on a farm in rural Warrick County, Indiana, at a time when plowing with a mule was slowly giving way to cultivation by tractor.[7] Christmas constructed a smokehouse for the village and built the pin-framed barn. In 1978 he worked with another volunteer, Keith Ruble, to build the Johnson Cabin, a replica of the 1822 log house that once

stood on the fairgrounds. A timberman and Vigo County Park superintendent, Ruble was experienced in hewing logs and working with his hands.

At the fair that year, Ruble met an old farmer who was chopping wooden bowls on a stump with a hand adze. Bill Day would become a life-long friend and mentor. Day's interest in hewing bowls began when his wife, Marion, brought home a hand-carved bowl from an antique store and he wondered how it was made. Day taught himself the nearly forgotten craft through trial and error. Using unseasoned or green wood, he hewed bowls in a range of shapes and sizes, each with a uniquely textured surface. Once the wood

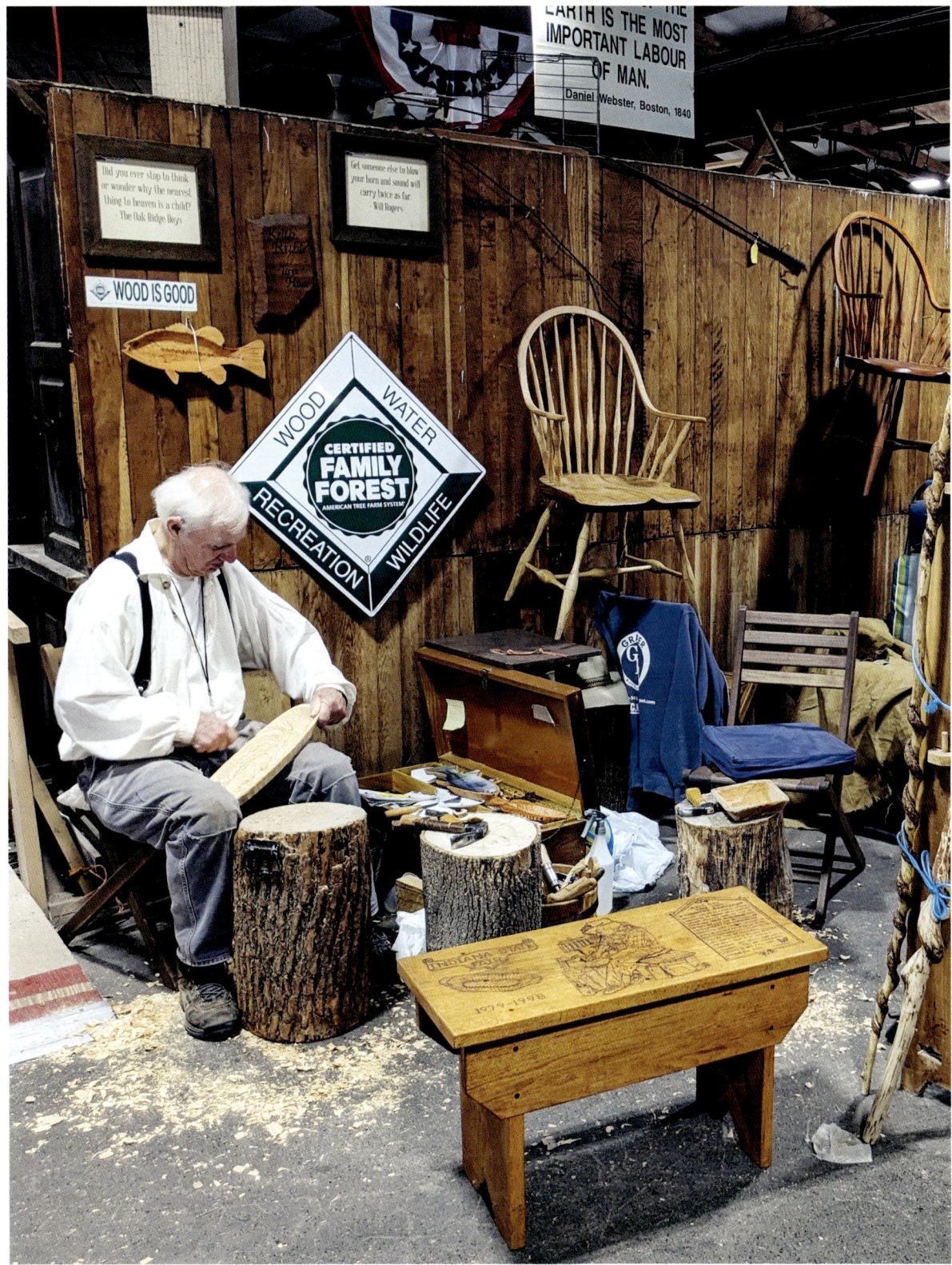

Pioneer Village volunteer Keith Ruble carving a bowl in his booth at the 2024 Indiana State Fair.

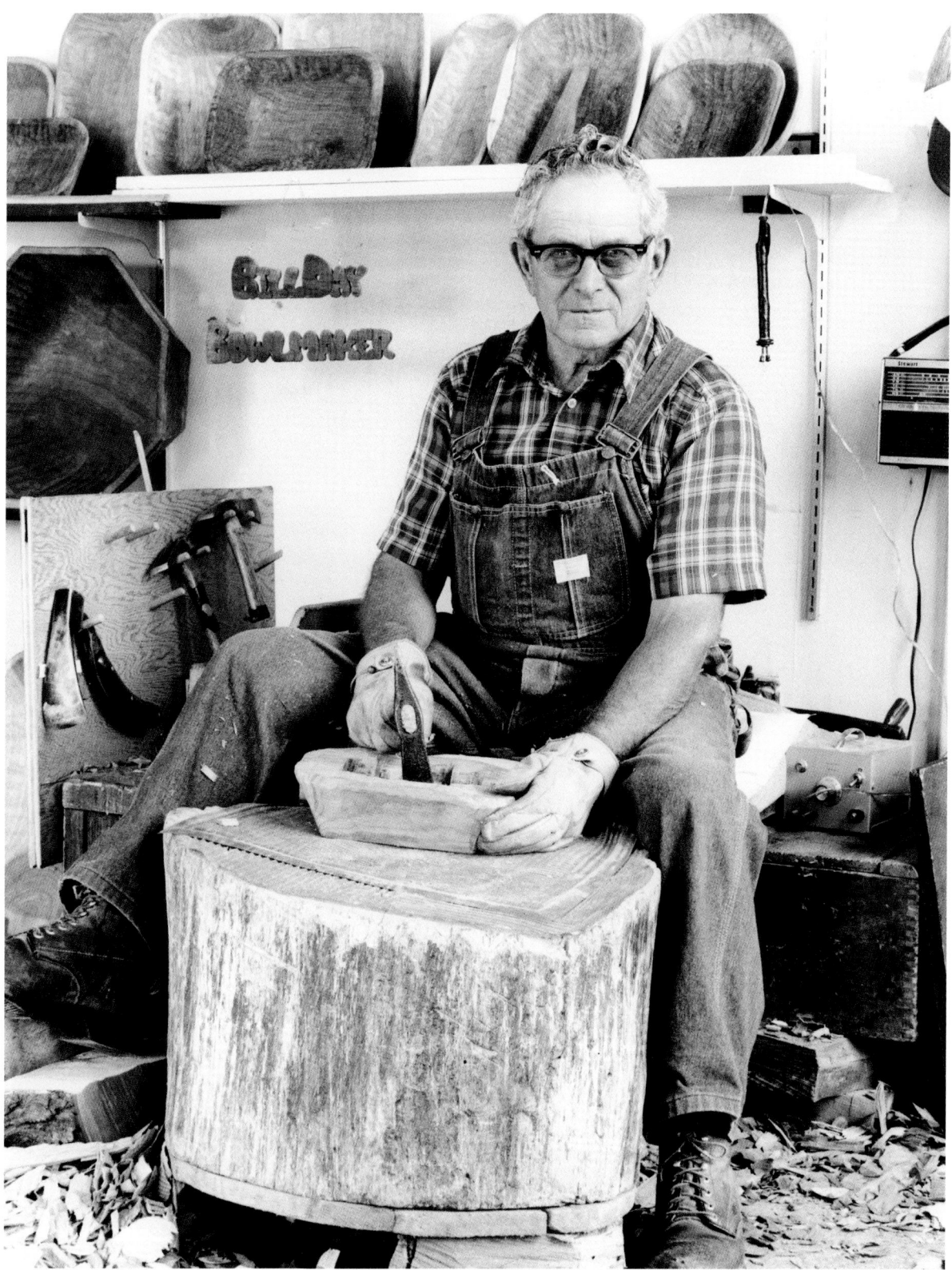

Bill Day at his Chop Shop in West Lebanon, Indiana, in 1983.

was dry, he oiled it and burned his name and the date onto the bottom of the bowl, along with the species of wood from which it was made. Making bowls became his retirement career. At his Chop Shop in West Lebanon, Indiana, he made bowls, chatted with customers, and sold his wares.

Day introduced millions of fairgoers to bowl hewing. He excelled at demonstrating: quick-witted and generous with his time, he was always ready to explain the process and share his talents with others. He even demonstrated his hewing skills at the Smithsonian Institution's Festival of American Folklife in 1991. He demonstrated bowl hewing with Ruble at the Pioneer Village each year until his death in 1999. Since then Ruble has maintained the tradition, teaching dozens of people to chop bowls (including the volunteers Blaine

Berry and Charlie Carson, who have demonstrated a range of other traditional woodworking and agricultural skills at the fair), and he continues to refine the craft he learned from Day.[8] Like many of the demonstrators in the village, Ruble works year-round to make enough bowls to sell at the fair each summer.

When Minnie Marchant visited the Pioneer Village in 1981, she noticed that it featured no quilters. She contacted Williamson and suggested that members of the Piecemakers group from the Salem United Methodist Church in Evansville could fill this void. For nearly three decades, Marchant, along with Jane Eberhart, Carol Kastner, Emmy Schmidt, Pat Shelton, and Roberta Smith, quilted at the fair. They also met on Mondays throughout the year to make a quilt to sell

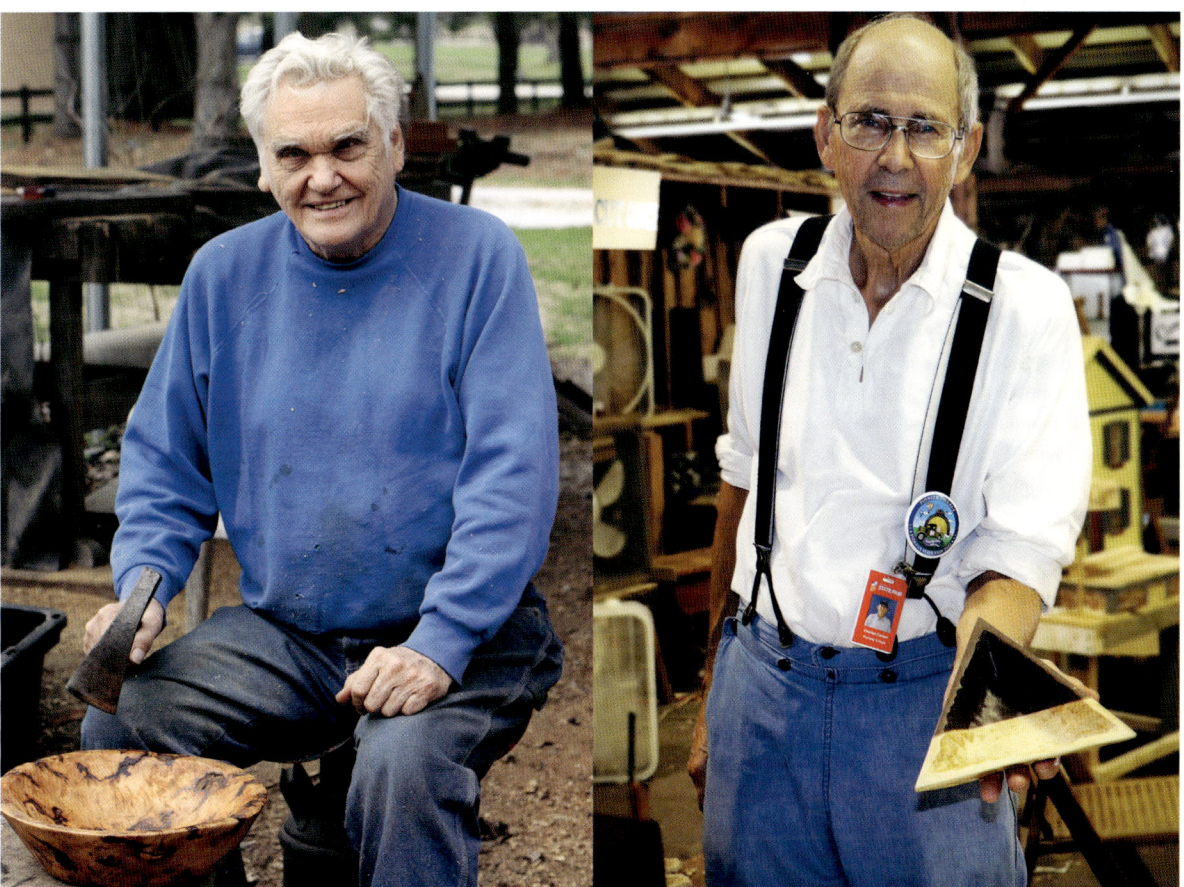

Left: *Blaine Berry with a maple-burl bowl that he made to sell at the 2022 Indiana State Fair.* **Right:** *Charlie Carson at the 2022 Indiana State Fair, showing his triangle-shaped walnut bowl made with both heartwood and lighter-colored sapwood.*

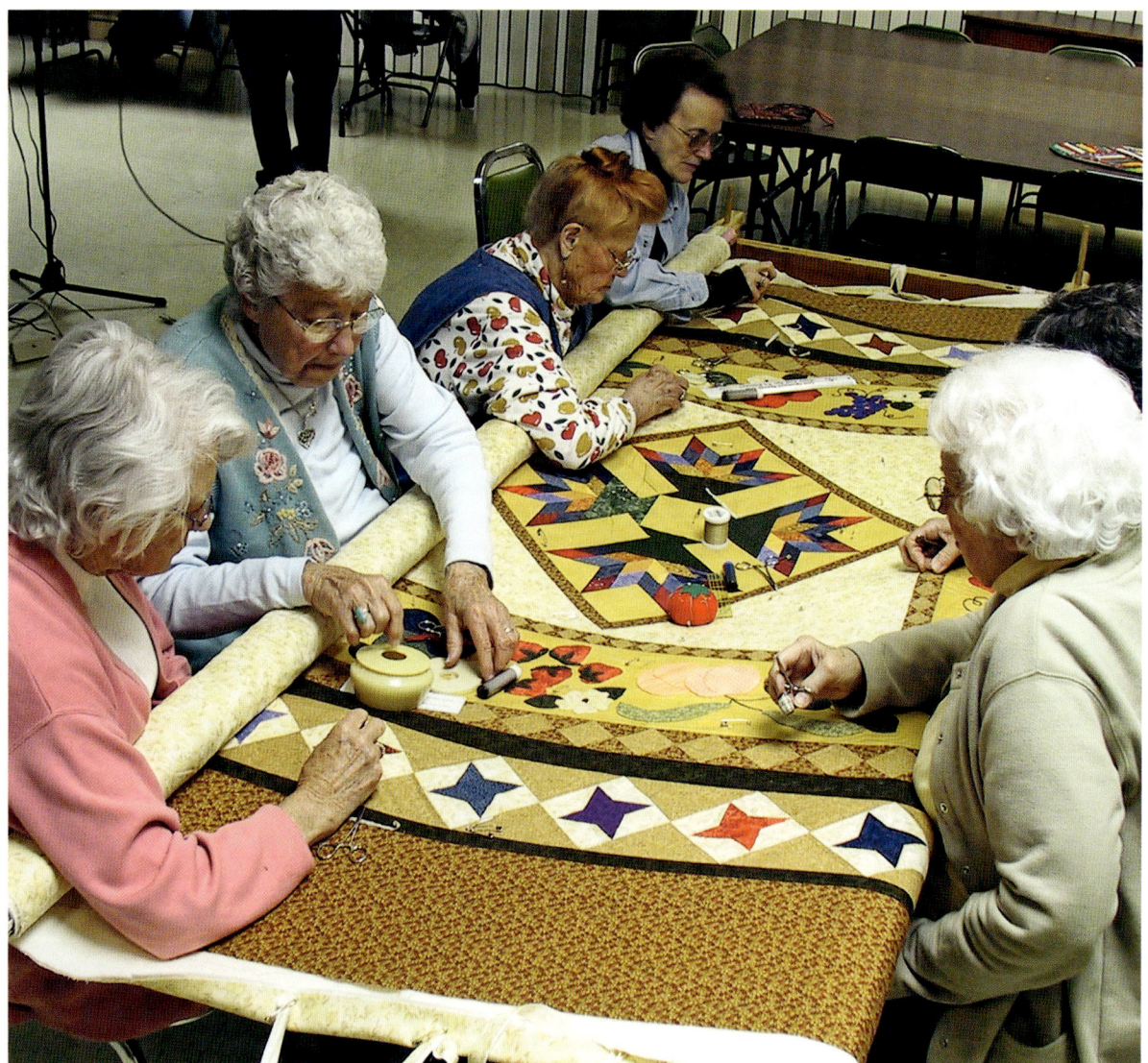

*The Piecemakers (**clockwise from left:** Minnie Marchant, Emmy Schmidt, Norma Jean Ice, Pat Shelton, Roberta Smith, Jane Eberhart) making a quilt for the Indiana State Fair in the basement of the Salem United Methodist Church in 2005.*

at the Pioneer Village auction, to raise money for the upkeep and development of the village.[9] For village participants like the Piecemakers and Keith Ruble, craft and heritage practices are meaningful beyond their aesthetic qualities and historical significance: they are practices that bring satisfaction and purpose to their lives.

Many of the older volunteers demonstrate practices they learned in their youth. Harold Stark demonstrated at the Pioneer Village for forty years. As a boy, watching his grandfather

work an eighty-acre farm in Rush County, Indiana, Stark learned about operating and maintaining steam engines for various purposes, from plowing fields to powering buzz saws. Stark worked in quality control at the Allison Corporation, a large transmission and engine manufacturing company in Indiana. Shortly before he retired, he built a half-scale replica of the 1909 Gaar-Scott steam engine that his grandfather had used years before, and displayed it in the village from 1980 to 2020. Having worked on the construction of the Apollo 13 moon lander, Stark displayed his homemade steam engine in part "to show where this technology came from."[10] Today his son is retired and uses his father's little steam engine to cut shingles at the fair.

As time passes, however, fewer demonstrators have the firsthand experience of traditional crafts and skills that the village originally aimed to convey to fair attendees. Second-generation volunteers are not uncommon, but the future of the Pioneer Village at the Indiana State Fair is precarious. Administrators wonder what will happen when the current generation of demonstrators can no longer volunteer. Will a new generation of craftspeople keep the village going? What talents and skills will they bring to the event? Will future generations remain interested in rural art and agricultural practices? Given the demographic changes that Indiana is experiencing, can the village become more inclusive of traditions beyond white settler culture? What will be lost if the Pioneer Village goes away?

While the village offers a valuable portrayal of Indiana's agricultural past and a family-friendly experience for fairgoers, it has another very important benefit: the sense of community it engenders in the lives of these older adults. Many of the demonstrators meet year-round for potluck dinners and ice-cream socials. They

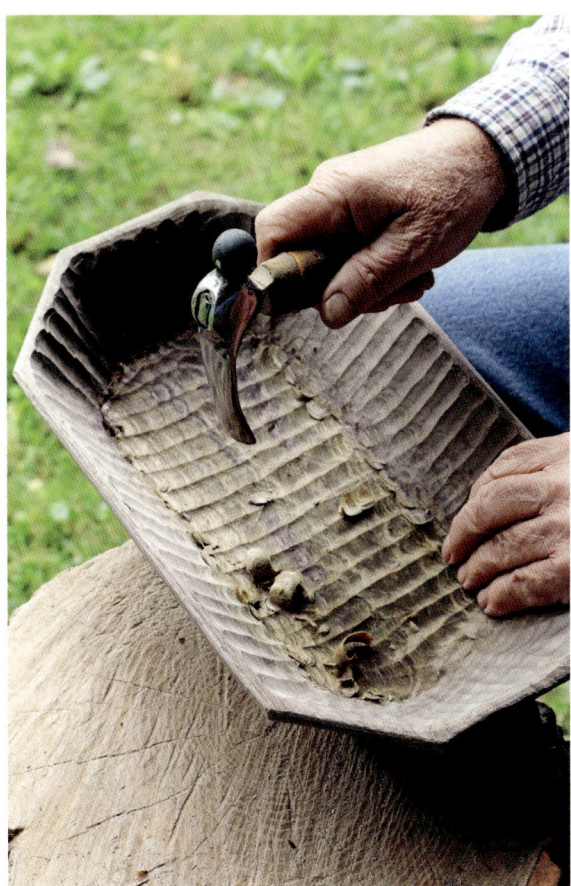

Keith Ruble hewing furrows in the bottom of a walnut bowl with a handmade adze in 2015.

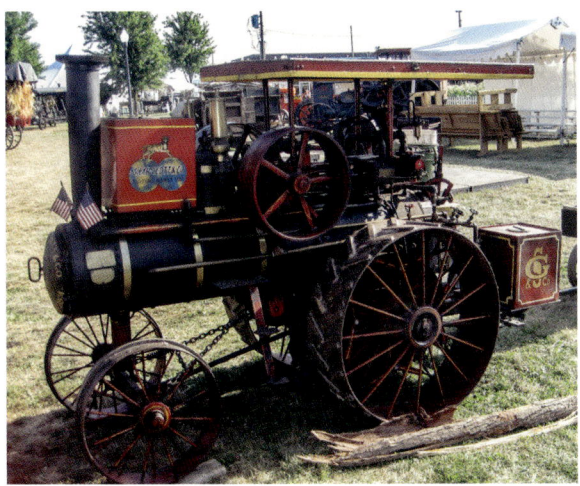

Harold Stark's half-scale steam engine, patterned after Gaar, Scott, and Company's 1909 model.

help one another when they face health problems or bereavement. They commonly speak of their fellow participants as their Pioneer Village family. Many of them have spent most of August together for decades, sleeping in dorms together and describing the event as a kind of summer-camp experience.

The Pioneer Village at the Indiana State Fair allows elders to share their traditional knowledge and personal experiences with thousands of attendees each year. Heritage events, pioneer villages, and fairs in general create opportunities for participants to build social connections, engage in meaningful practices, and feel a sense of mastery, all the while providing a fun and educational event for attendees of all ages.

Indigenous Fashion and Cultural Exchange in Native Gatherings

AMBER-DAWN BEAR ROBE

At the first state fairs in the nineteenth century, Native American contributions to the regional culture and economy were largely overlooked. When Indigenous cultures were featured at all, displays often took the form of ethnographic exhibits or Wild West shows, showcasing Native people as stereotypes and curiosities.[1] Rather than being recognized for their diversity, creativity, and innovation, Native societies were marginalized and misrepresented, reinforcing colonial narratives that ignored their rich diversity and significance to the fabric of America. Native American groups eventually began to take part in the programming of state fairs. In addition, Indigenous peoples have long held their own celebrations and community gatherings. In the twentieth century, non-Native entities such as the Bureau of Indian Affairs also began organizing tribal fairs and juried art markets, which

evolved into key venues for art, performance, fashion, and cultural exchange.

The first official state fair, held in 1841 in Syracuse, New York, took place during the era of federal laws and policies that centered on Indian removal and the establishment of reservations. Native American practices, including art and clothing, were viewed as a threat to American progress. At the start of the twentieth century, when Native Americans were confined to reservations and undergoing significant lifestyle changes, anthropologists, collectors, traders, curators, and government agencies shifted their focus to "preserving" the so-called vanishing Indian and "authentic" Indian art. Cultural practices were seen not as high art or fashion but as ethnographic artifacts. This mindset laid the groundwork for Indian fairs, which often featured parades, powwows, pageants, and rodeos.

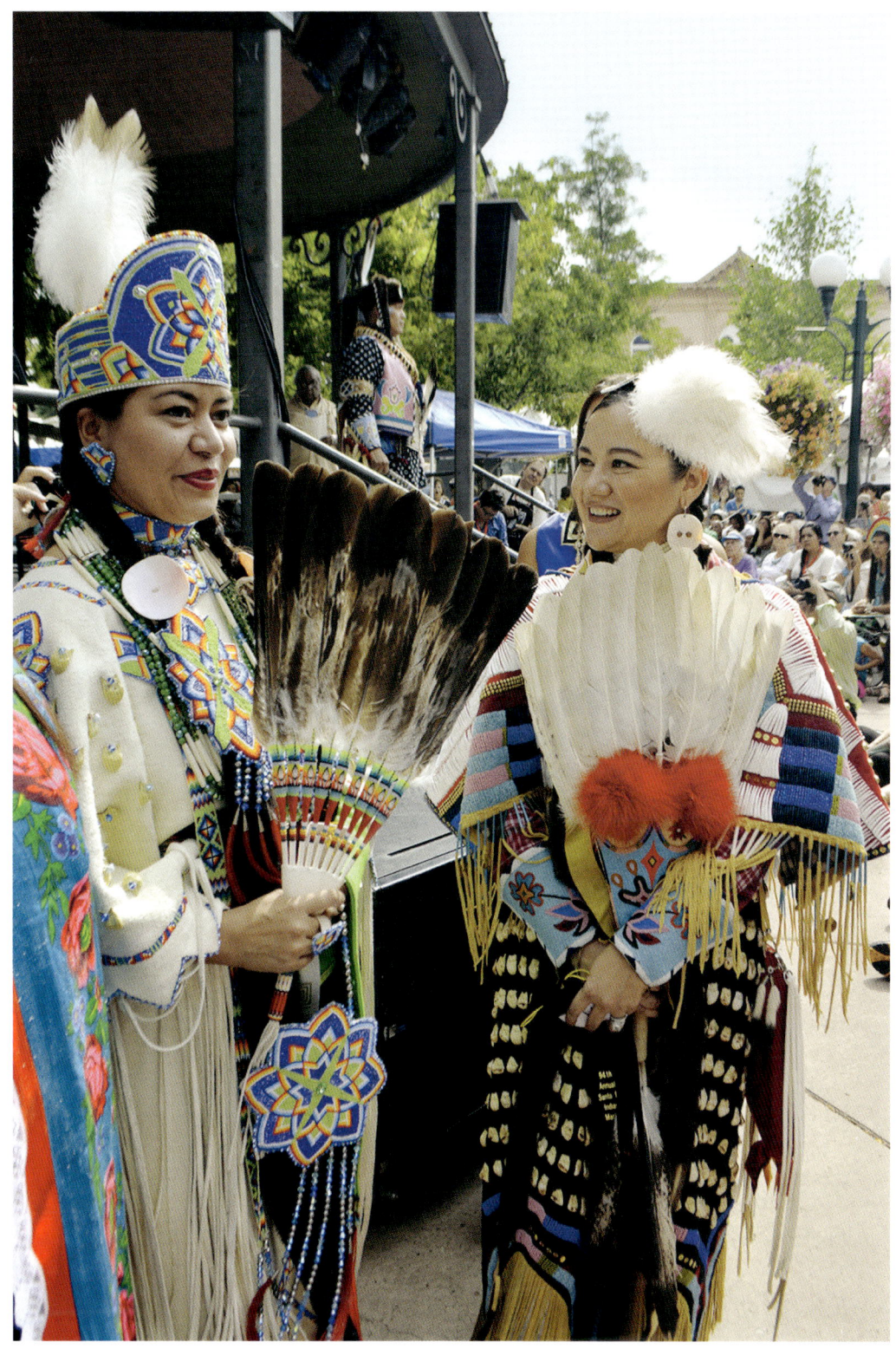

Jamie Okuma and Michelle Flying Man at the 2015 Fashion Challenge of the Native American Clothing Contest at SWAIA, 2015.

Indigenous Fashion and Cultural Exchange in Native Gatherings **63**

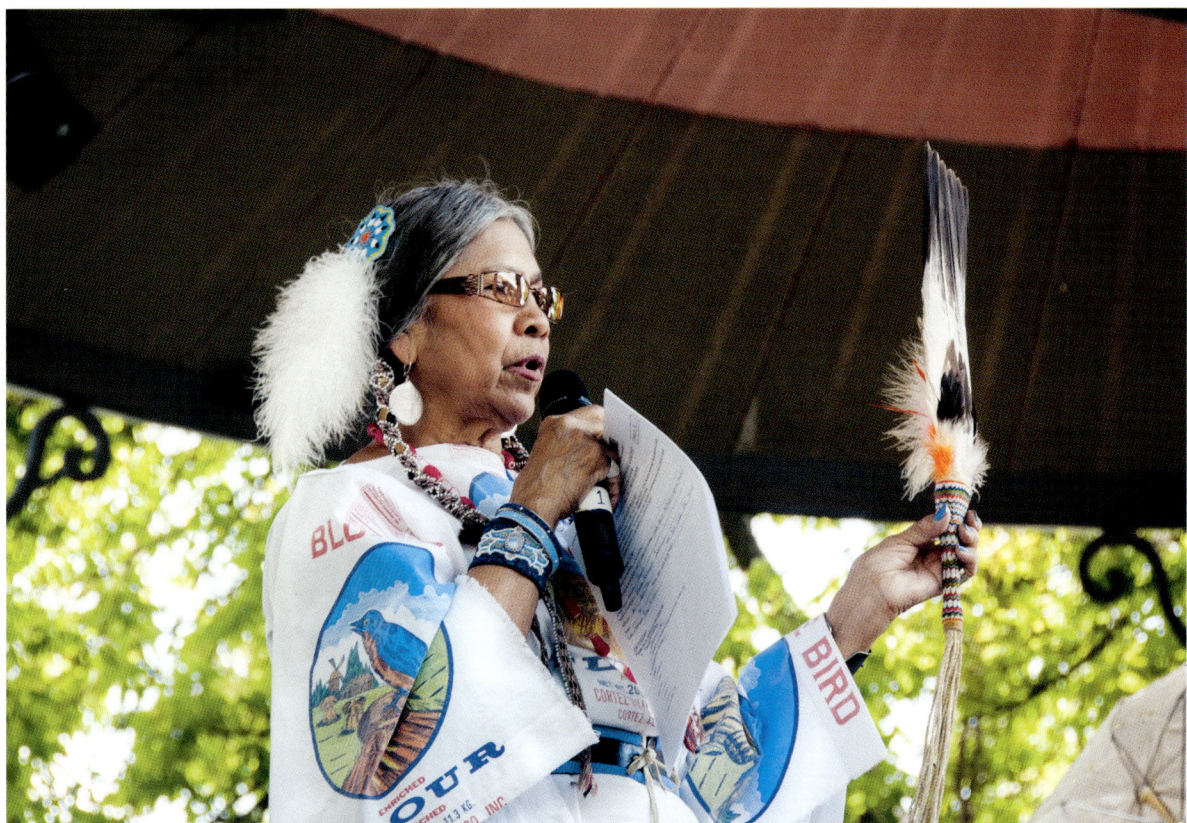

Jeri Ah-be-hill (1934–2015), pictured in her Blue Bird Dress, served as MC for the Santa Fe Indian Market Clothing Competition on the Santa Fe Plaza in the late 1990s. Ah-be-hill, a dedicated member of the SWAIA board of directors for over a decade, played a pivotal role in expanding the Indian Market Clothing Competition.

In 1922, a pivotal chapter began for Native artists with the establishment of the first Santa Fe Indian Fair by the Museum of New Mexico as a part of the Santa Fe Fiesta.[2] The first fairs were indoors, and admission was charged, but free admission was offered to Pueblo people wearing their customary clothing. The fairs focused on representing Indigenous cultures from before European colonization and settlement. Eventually, the indoor fairs morphed into an outdoor weekend market that became the annual Fiesta Indian Market. Most Pueblo people who attended the market camped in areas designated by the city and the market's organizers.[3] Fiesta attendees were encouraged to wander through the campground to see and experience "Indian life."

When the museum's organization and oversight of the Indian Fair ended in 1926, a group of interested citizens formed the Independent Fair Committee. In the 1930s, organization of the fair passed to the New Mexico Association on Indian Affairs (NMAIA), an Anglo-led Indigenous rights organization. The NMAIA allowed artists and craftspeople to sell their own work, such as woven belts and cotton shirts. In the late 1950s the NMAIA was renamed the Southwestern Association for Indian Affairs (SWAIA).

During the 1960s and 1970s, a renewed interest in Southwest Pueblo and tribal peoples brought new vitality and audiences to the Santa Fe Indian Market.[4] The market and its artists recognized historical and traditional clothing as a vital aspect of Indigenous culture, and the event became an incubator for Native American fashion. In addition to granting free admission to those attending the event in traditional clothing, the fair offered awards to Native artists who dressed in traditional attire.

The fairs enabled Indigenous designers to reach broader audiences and to highlight both historical and contemporary fashion. Cultural pageant competitions became the mainstays of the Crow Fair in Montana, the Navajo Nation Fair in Arizona, and the Choctaw Indian Fair in Mississippi. As interest in Indigenous fashion grew, tribal fairs began to host "Indian Princess" competitions for young women. Today, contestants are expected to give presentations on the history of their garments and adornment. Competition winners often serve as tribal ambassadors, visiting schools, community centers, and powwows. The acclaimed beadwork artist Terri Greeves notes that an Indigenous pageant contestant has a huge responsibility to educate others, as "she represents their entire Nation as a diplomat … through fashion and beauty."[5]

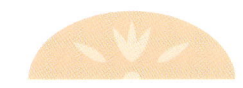

"This knowledge in the clothing is linked to all the aunties and mothers."

TERRI GREEVES

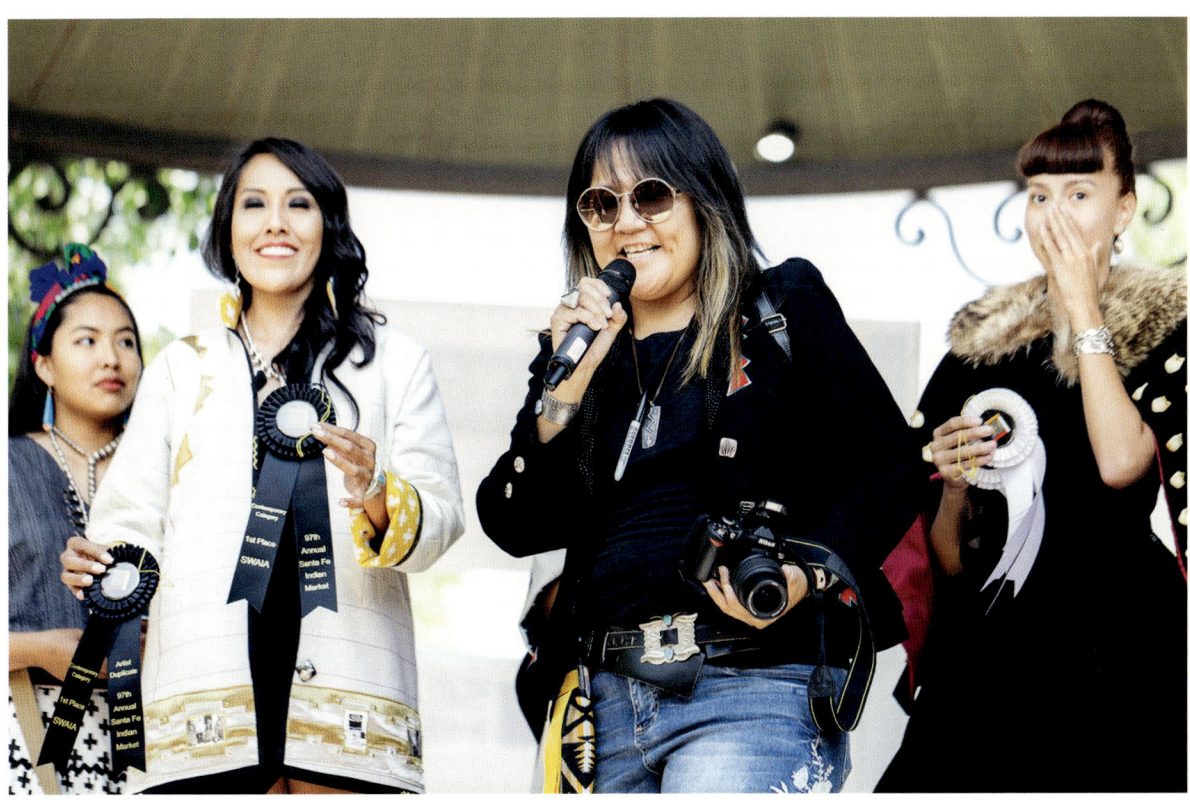

Designer Penny Singer (front, with microphone) won first prize in the 2018 Traditional Clothing Contest (contemporary category) at SWAIA with her Betty Belen jacket, modeled by Sheena Begay. The jacket was made in memory of and as an homage to Singer's grandmother, Betty Belen.

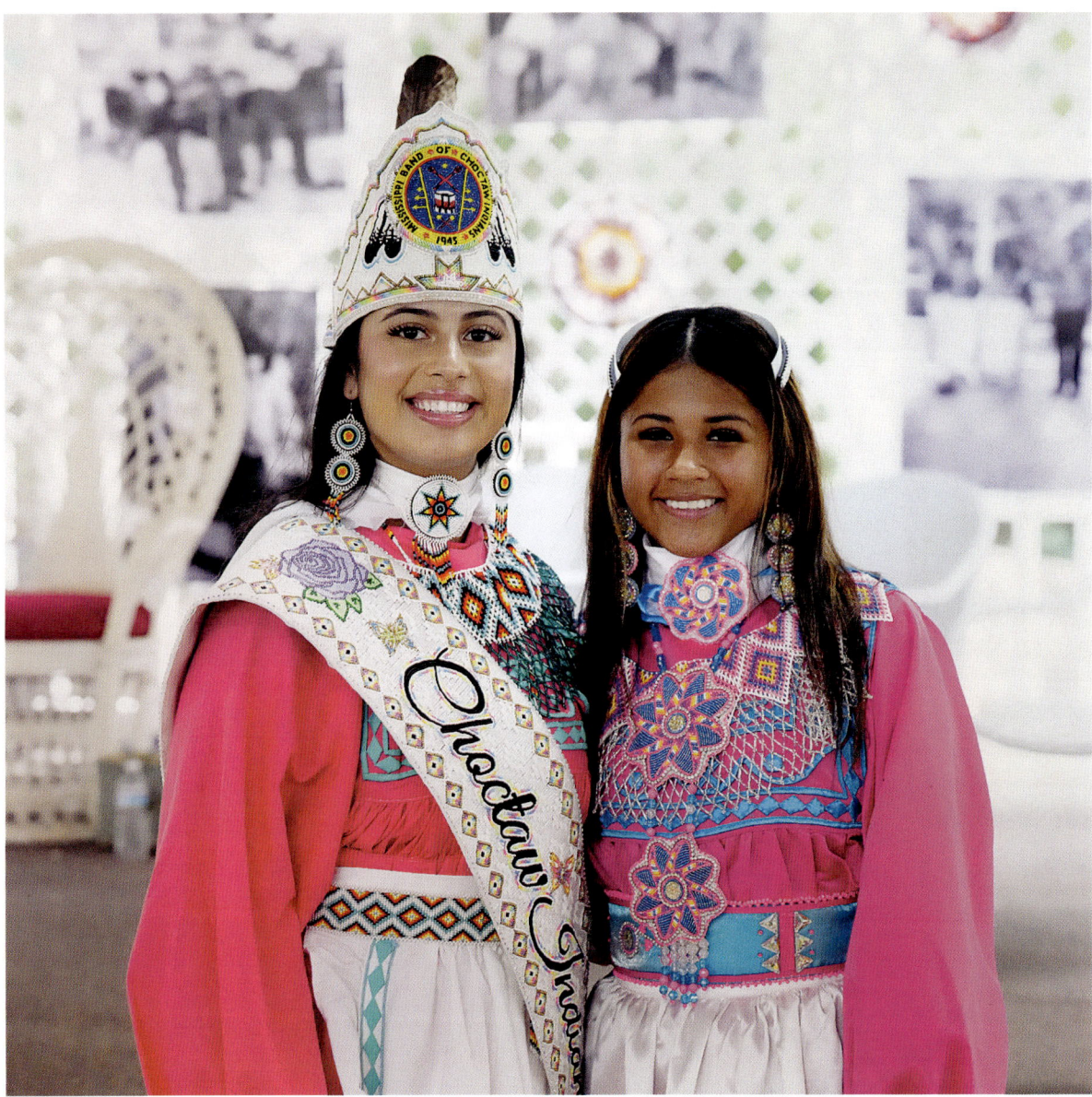

Top: The 2023 Choctaw Indian Fair Princess, Nalani LuzMaria Thompson (Mississippi Band of Choctaw Indians), poses with Alaysa Clemmons. The Choctaw Indian Princess has been crowned on the first night of the annual Choctaw Indian Fair since 1955.

Greeves also notes that the competitions require Navajo women to understand and demonstrate other traditional practices, such as sheep butchering, in addition to clothing.

The fashion designer Virginia Ballenger, who started her design career by winning pageant titles at the Gallup Inter-tribal Fair in New Mexico, made her way to Santa Fe in 1985 to participate in the clothing competition at the SWAIA Market. Few Indigenous fashion makers were sharing their work at that time. "Broomstick skirts were all the rage when I first started," Ballenger recalled, and "only about five of us were traveling around showing at powwows, Indian and art fairs."[6] By selling at SWAIA, she hoped to connect with other Native artists and the Native community.

The Fashion Contest was renamed the Indian Clothing Contest in 1990 and the Traditional Clothing Contest by 1992, and the SWAIA rebranded itself as the Southwestern Association for Indian Arts (using the same abbreviation) to better reflect its cultural focus. Jeri Ah-be-hill (1933–2015), a Kiowa-Comanche fashion connoisseur and advocate for Native fashion who had served as the Kiowa Tribal Princess in 1953–54, was elected to the SWAIA board of directors in 1992 and quickly started running the fashion/clothing competitions.[7] Teri Greeves, Ah-be-hill's daughter, observed that with her mother's involvement, the SWAIA fashion contest "became a real big thing. She started pulling in the media people, asking prominent people to be a judge. She knew how to promote."[8]

Ah-be-hill pointed out that Native fashion is not "costumes" but culturally significant clothing, often handmade, in tribally specific styles.[9] The Traditional Clothing Contest included both "traditional" and "contemporary" categories, in which contestants were required to speak about the techniques and materials they used. "This was mom's lifelong pursuit, clothing, fashion, learning and sharing this knowledge," Greeves commented. "I think she helped SWAIA mature into understanding how important things are that we wear. This knowledge in the clothing is linked to all the aunties and mothers."[10]

Indigenous women who have contributed to the celebration of Native fashion through Indian fairs and markets include Kay Bennet (1922–97). Known first for her doll making, she started on her fashion path by entering beauty pageants at the Gallup Inter-tribal Fair. In 1953, she was named queen of the Flagstaff Indian Powwow, and in 1954 she represented Navajo women as a finalist in the Miss Indian America contest in Sheridan, Wyoming.[11] In the Gallup community, according to Ballenger, Bennet "was known for her style, a beautiful lady, outspoken, classy, confident."

Margaret Roach Wheeler, a pathbreaker in Native American fashion, was active in fashion shows, though not at SWAIA, in the 1980s. Since

Native designers are no longer viewed as mere artisans: instead, they are celebrated as innovators whose contributions enrich both fashion and art.

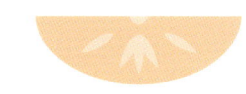

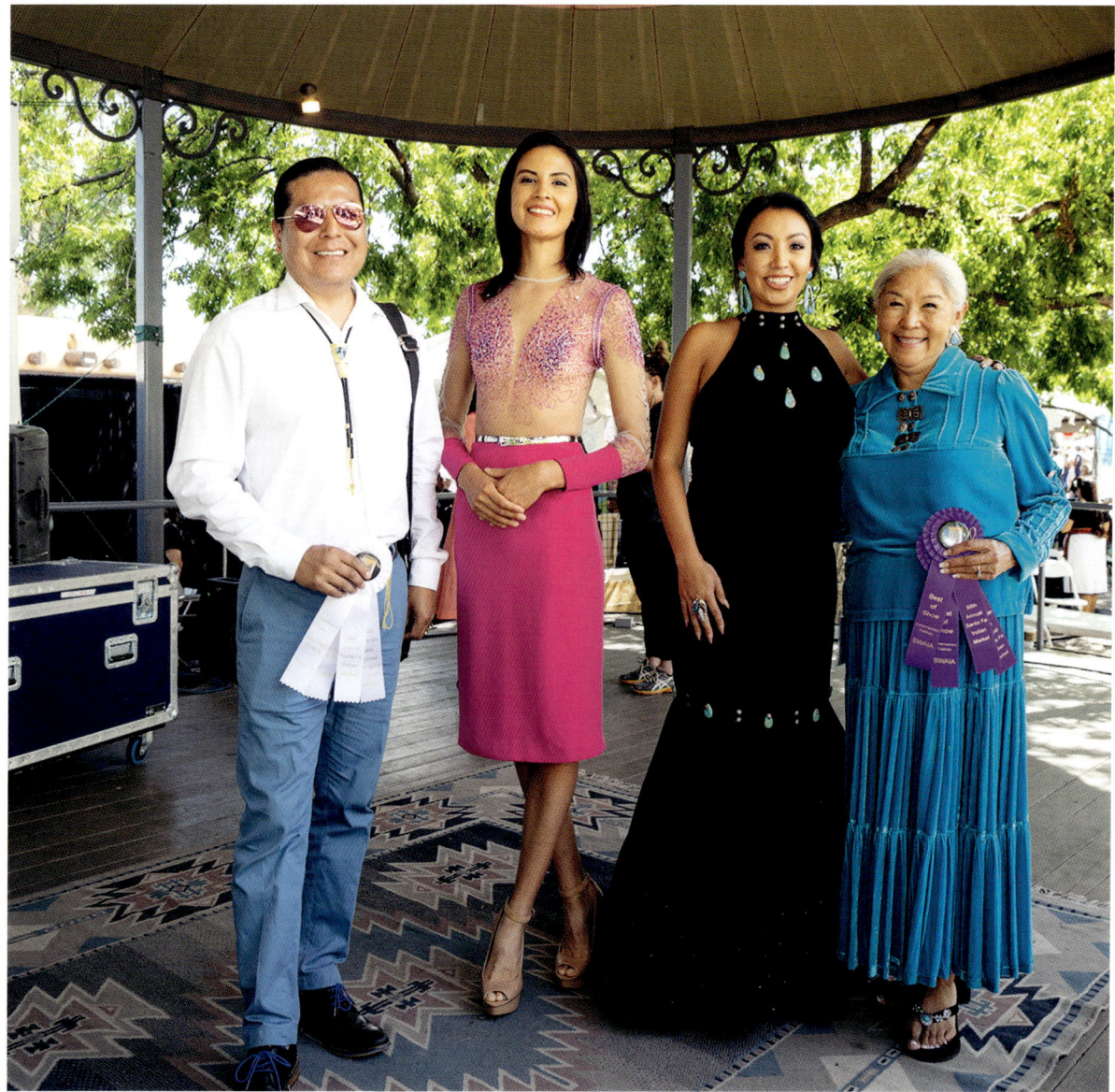

Left to right: *Fashion designer Orlando Dugi, models Mona Bear and Courtney Ballenger, and fashion designer Virginia Ballenger. Orlando Dugi and Virginia Ballenger won second place and "Best in Show," respectively, at the 2019 Sante Fe Market Contemporary Clothing Competition.*

then she has won many ribbons from the Eiteljorg Indian Market and Festival in Indianapolis; the Chickasaw Arts Festival in Sulphur, Oklahoma; the Oklahoma Red Earth Festival in Oklahoma City; the Heard Museum Indian Fair and Market in Phoenix, Arizona; and SWAIA.[12]

Patricia Michaels made her design debut at the Santa Fe Indian Market in 1996 and has since showcased her work at markets, fairs, and venues such as New York Fashion Week.[13] Renowned for her hand-painted textiles, Michaels gained broader recognition as a finalist on season 11 of *Project Runway*. Penny Singer, known for her contemporary geometric appliqué work and shirts, began competing at Indian fairs and markets in the mid-1990s.

Dorothy Grant, a leading figure in Indigenous fashion, began participating in SWAIA in the early 2000s and is renowned for integrating formline design—a distinctive design language and artistic style found among the Indigenous peoples of the Pacific Northwest—into high fashion.[14] Her solo retrospective exhibition, *Dorothy Grant: Raven Comes Full Circle,* organized by the Haida Gwaii Museum at Kay Llnagaay in British Columbia, was launched in 2024.[15]

Jamie Okuma is another designer who established a thriving fashion brand through Indian fairs and markets. In an interview with the *Vogue* writer Christian Allaire, she commented that the SWAIA Market has been her life since she was fifteen. In 2000, she became the youngest artist to win the "Best of Show" award and has since become the first Native designer invited to serve on the Council of Fashion Designers of America. Okuma has rocked the Indian market world with her one-of-a-kind beadwork creations, and her creations are worn by Native and non-Native attendees.

Indian clothing exhibits, once seen as an exotic attraction for white fair visitors, have evolved into a recognition of Indigenous fashion as a powerful and sophisticated form of artistic expression. The Santa Fe Indian Market has become a dynamic and organic platform for showcasing fashion, and its reach continues to grow. Native designers are no longer viewed as mere artisans: instead, they are celebrated as innovators whose contributions enrich both fashion and art. The evolution of Indigenous fashion at SWAIA and other venues represents a significant cultural shift, one that honors the past while paving the way for a bold and dynamic future.

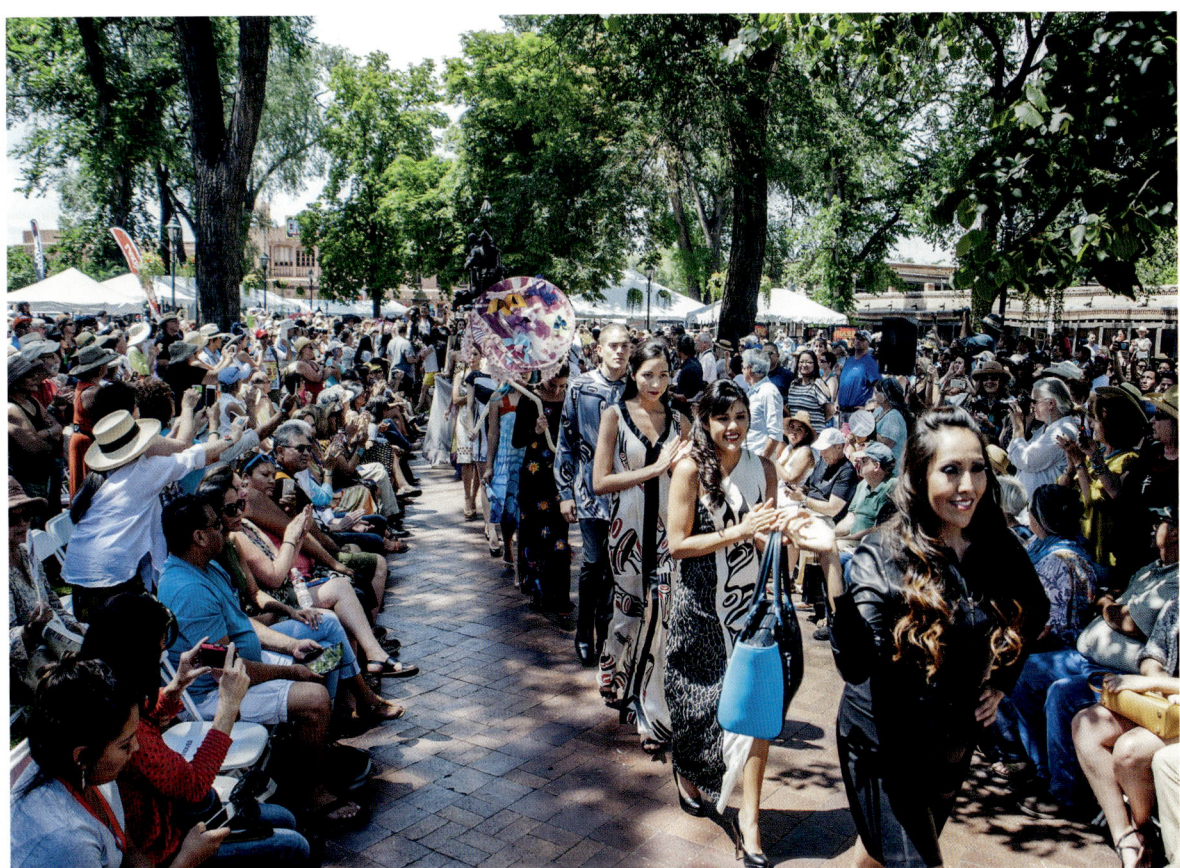

Designers Dorothy Grant, Patricia Michaels, Jamie Okuma, Orlando Dugi, and Bethany Yellowtail walk through the crowd at the 2015 SWAIA Fashion Show.

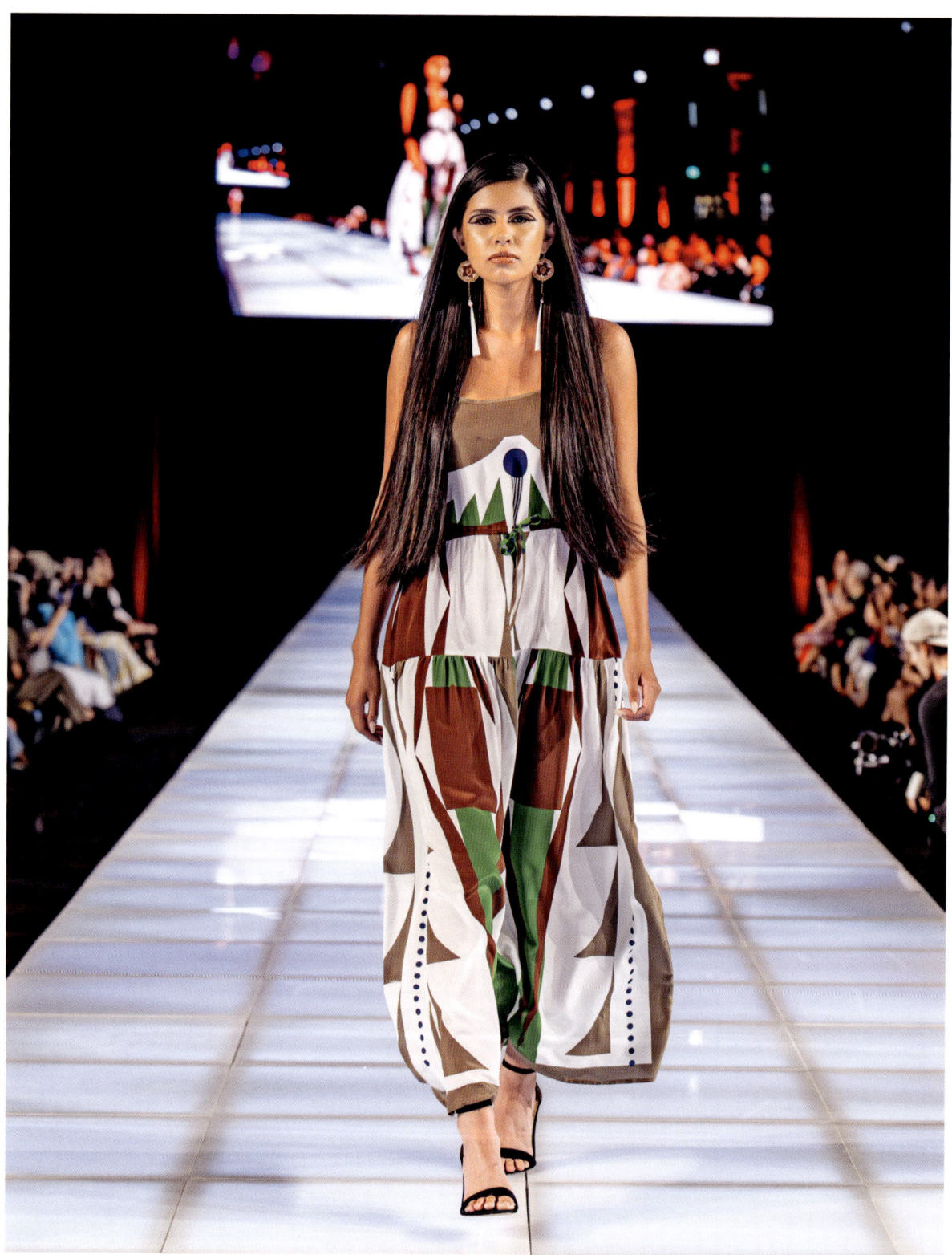

Designer and model Jamie Okuma (Luiseño, Wailaki, Okinawan, and Shoshone-Bannock) walks the runway at the 2024 SWAIA Fashion Show.

BLUE RIBBON GALLERY

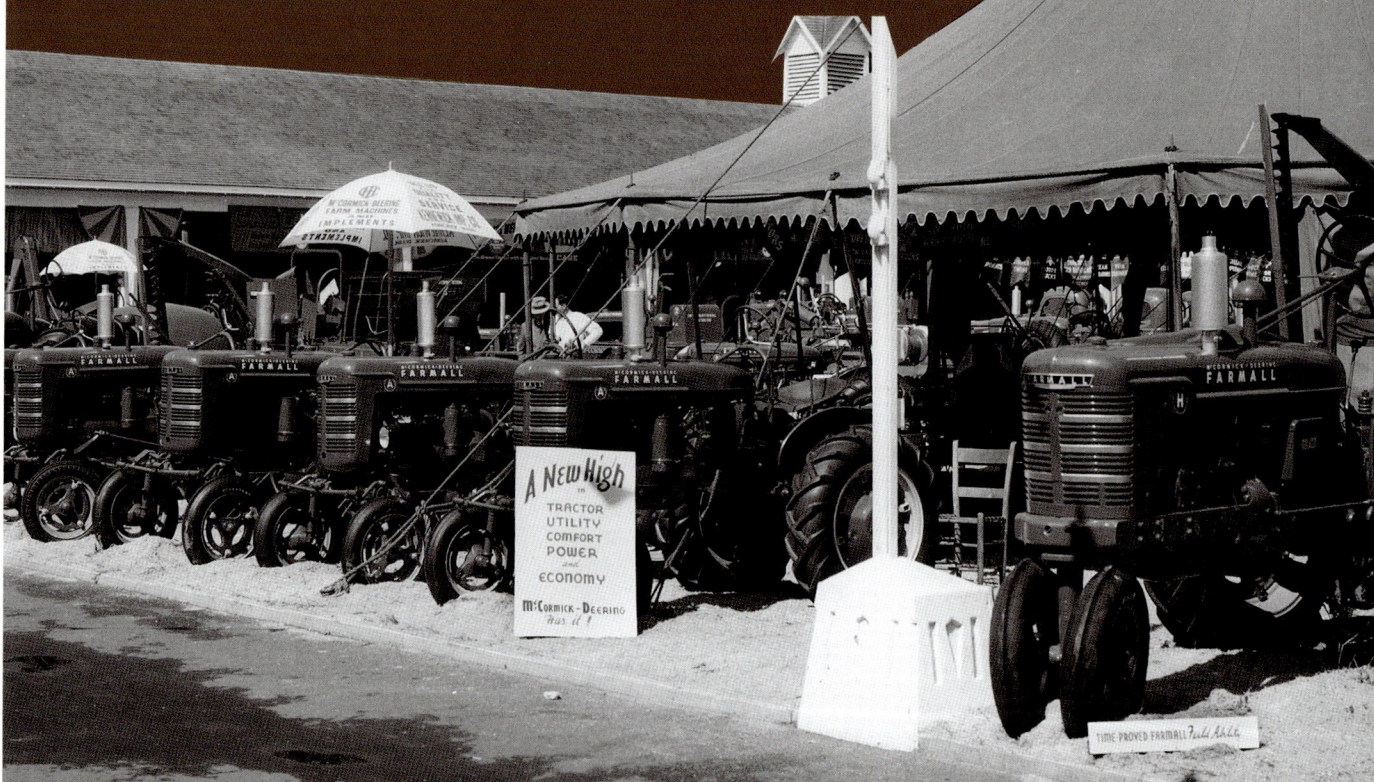

Row of Farmall tractors on display at the Oregon State Fair on September 2, 1940.

Tractor Rows
and Machine Halls

At state fairs, agricultural manufacturers touted their machinery directly to farmers and also scouted out each other's progress.

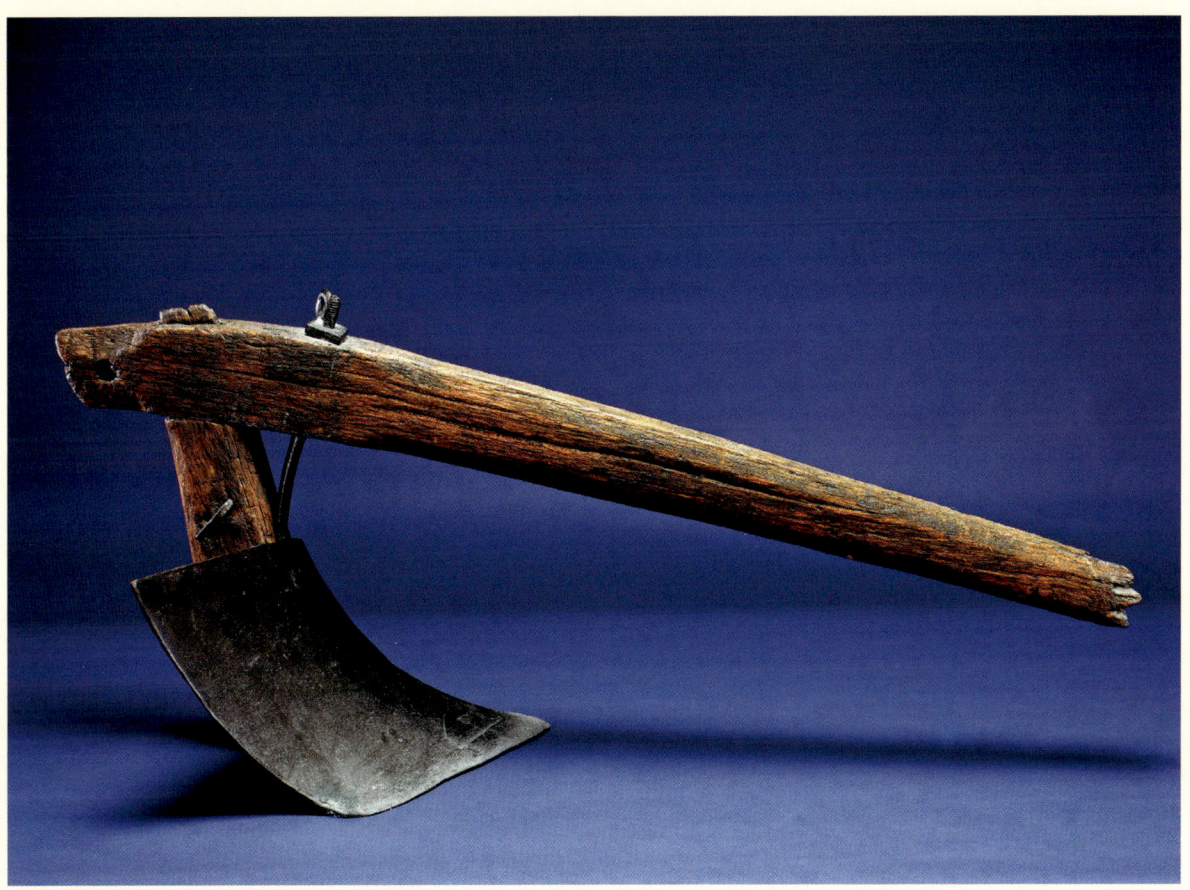

John Deere, plow, 1838

Wood, iron, steel, 14^{15}⁄$_{16}$ × 18⅛ × 48^{7}⁄$_{16}$ in.

In the mid-nineteenth century, millions of Americans (mostly white) migrated to the Midwest in pursuit of land and farming opportunities. Although tilling the fields was initially easy, it became increasingly difficult over successive seasons as the prairie soil became depleted, compacted, and more resistant to plows designed for sandier Eastern soils.

John Deere, a blacksmith, moved from his home state of Vermont to Grand Detour, Illinois, in 1836, and invented a new kind of plow for the sticky soil. By 1840, Deere listed his occupation in the national census as an "agricultural manufacturer" and was building a booming business. He traveled to state and county fairs to advertise his new products. Deere & Company won the prize for "Best and Greatest Display of Plows in Variety" at the 1869 Illinois State Fair, earning a $10 premium, a silver medal, and positive press. The pictured plow is missing its handle.

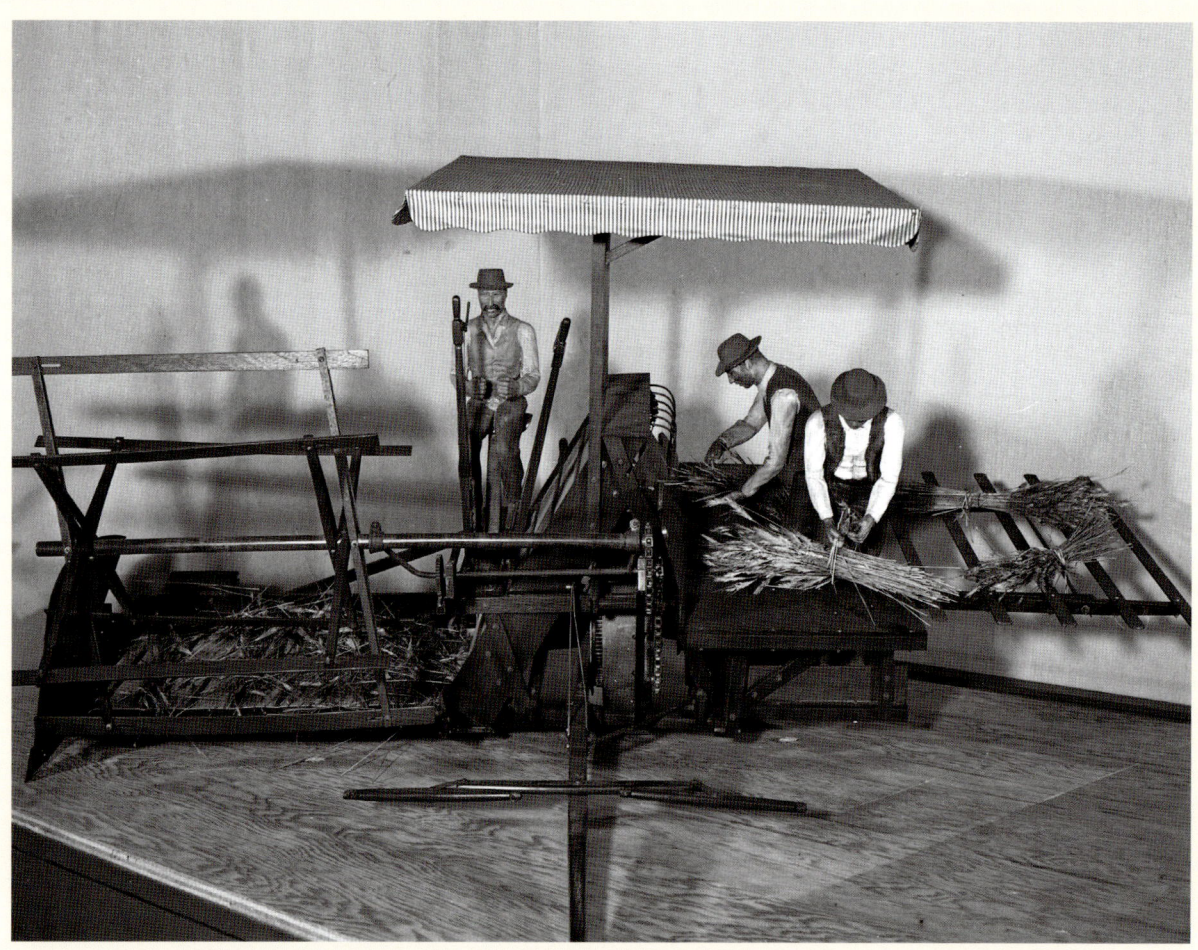

Scale model of the Marsh Harvester of 1882

Designed in 1868, the harvester was manufactured from 1869 through 1890.

The McCormick Harvesting Machine Company, founded by Cyrus Hall McCormick, crafted models of their equipment to demonstrate at fairs. Farmers, horses, and even small sheaves of wheat showed fairgoers the modern equipment in use. Mechanization would eventually outpace many forms of manual farm work and craft at the start of the twentieth century.

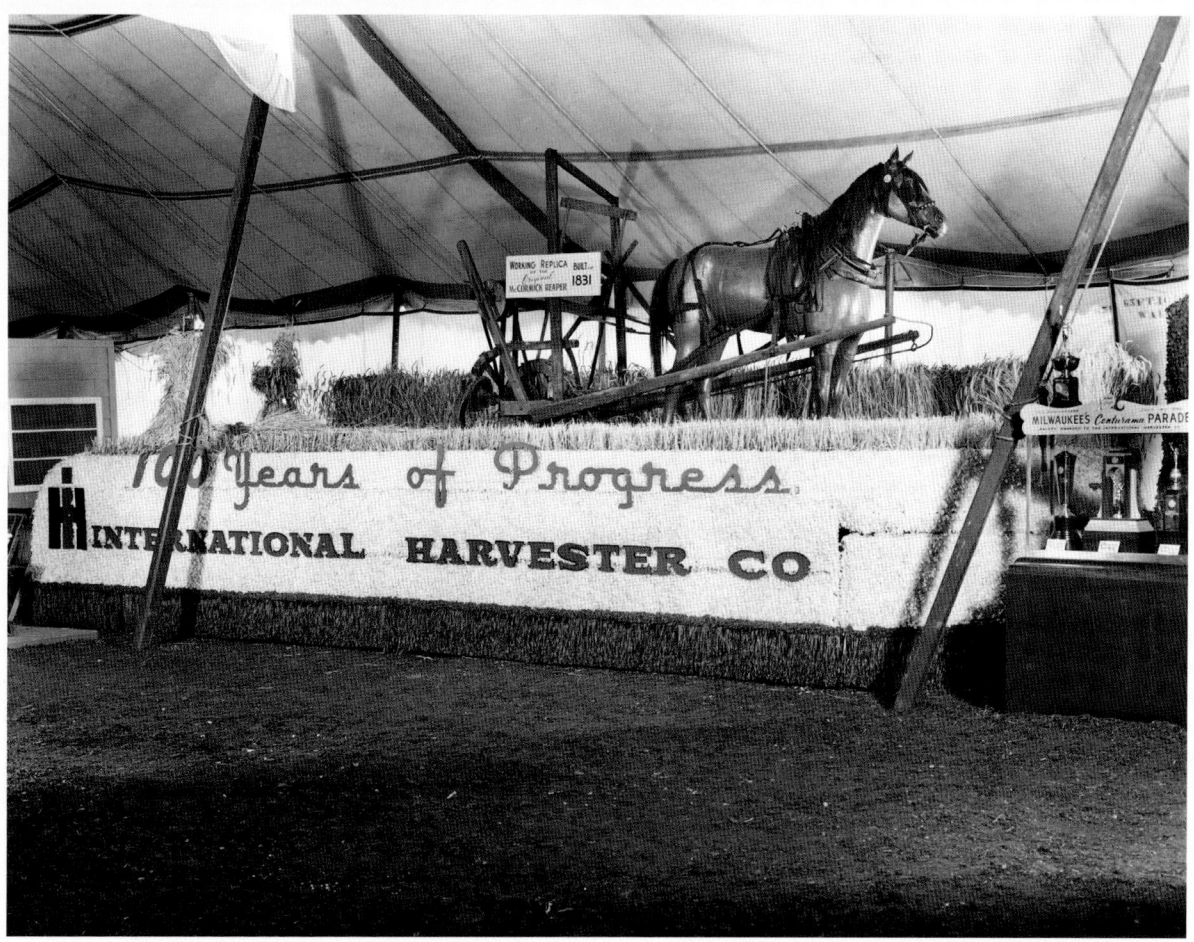

International Harvester Company "100 Years of Progress" float with reaper

Wisconsin State Fair Dairy Parade, August 23, 1946.

At the 1946 Wisconsin State Fair, the International Harvester Company (formerly the McCormick Harvesting Machine Company) won first prize for its float in the Dairy Parade. It displays a working replica of the revolutionary McCormick reaper, invented in 1831 by Cyrus McCormick in his family's blacksmith shop in Virginia. The mechanized reaper harvested grain far faster than manual workers could, enabling farmers to produce more grain with fewer laborers.

Fair parades have historically invited nostalgia and retrospection. The 1811 Berkshire Agricultural Fair hosted an elaborate parade of sixty pairs of oxen pulling a wooden plow and the country's two oldest men. A century later, steam- and gasoline-powered agricultural equipment would replace hand tools and ox-drawn implements. As tool makers evolved from small rural blacksmiths' shops to large urban factories, fair parades celebrated these dramatic changes.

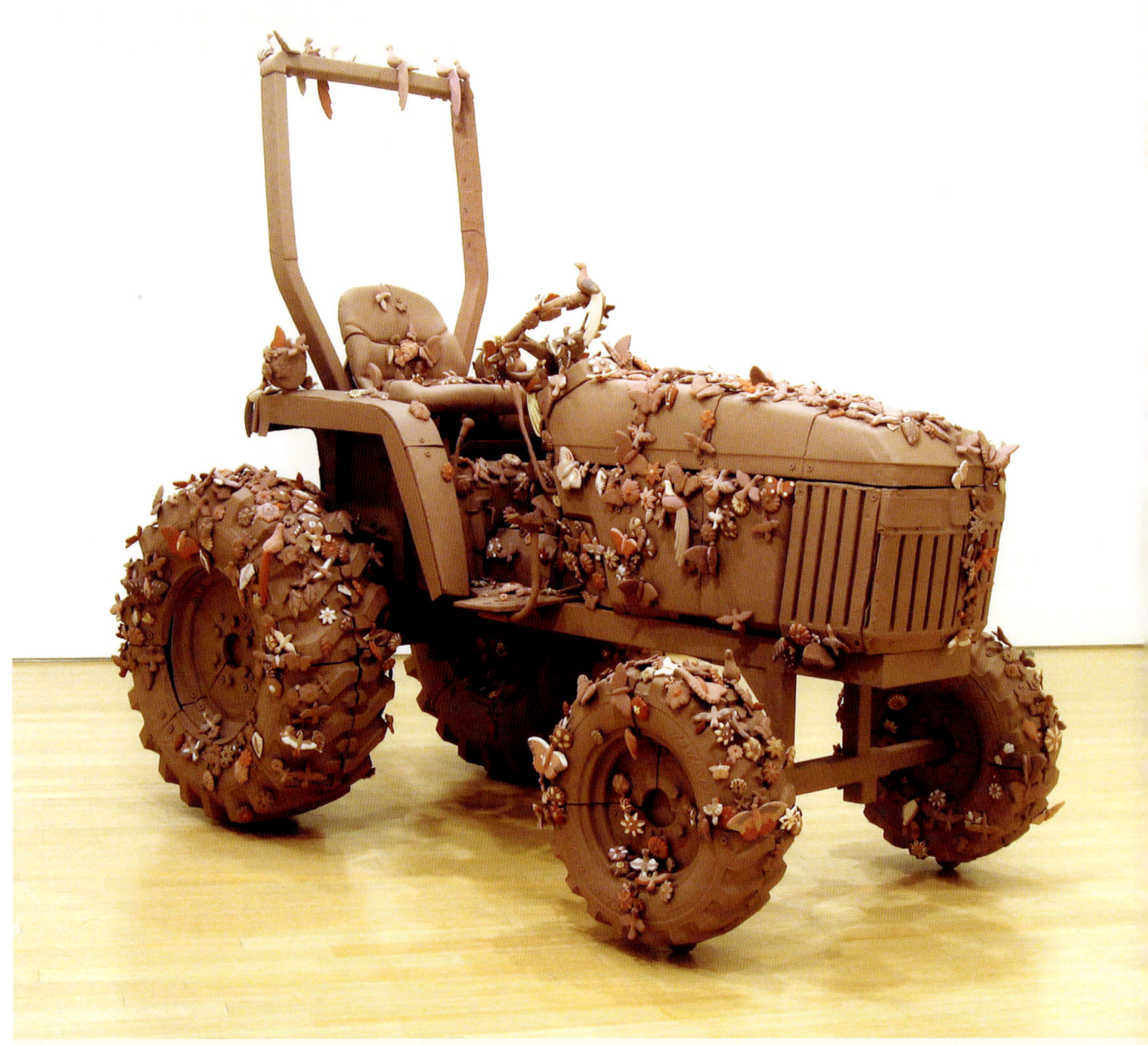

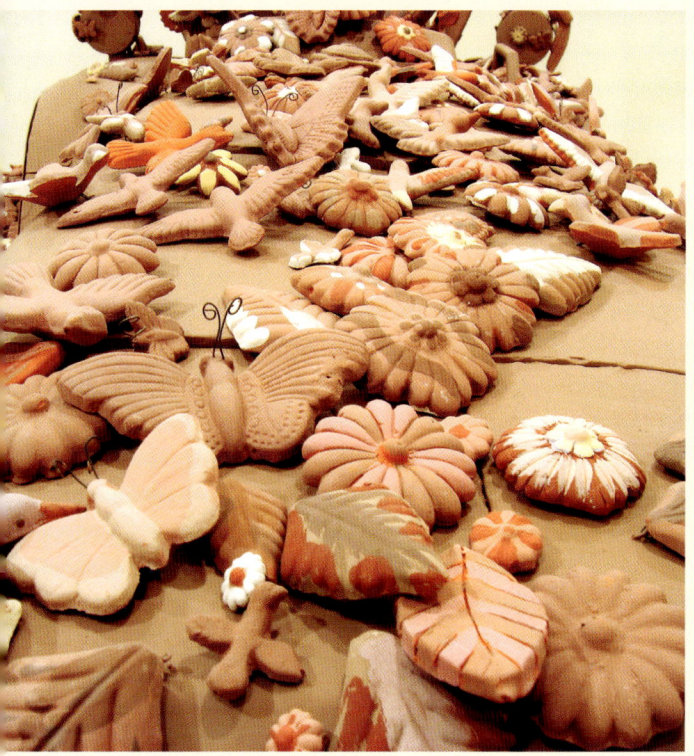
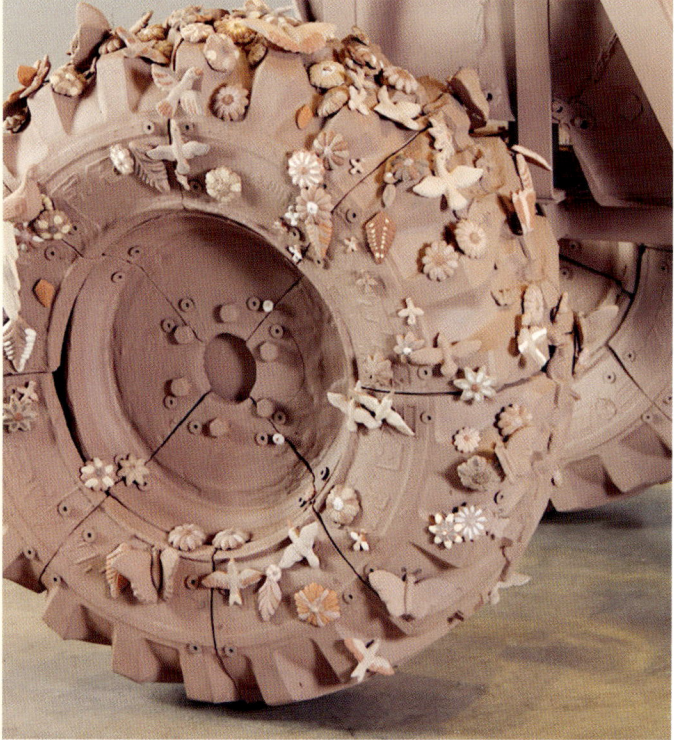

Margarita Cabrera, *Arbol de la Vida—John Deere Tractor Model #790*, 2007

Clay, slip paint, latex acrylic, and metal, 96 × 60 × 100 in.

Though state fair tractor displays celebrate the technology that drives the agricultural industry, they often neglect the contributions of the immigrant farmworkers who help feed the nation. Artist and activist Margarita Cabrera used one of the most iconic symbols of American agriculture, the John Deere tractor, to draw attention to these vital workers. Her use of clay references Arbol de la Vida (Tree of Life) sculptures, a Mexican ceramic tradition developed by the ancient Olmec civilization, which conveys the story of creation. Cabrera then added the flowers, birds, and butterflies that traditionally decorate these sculptures. By merging the American tractor with an Indigenous Mexican craft practice, Cabrera highlights the reliance of American food production on immigrant labor.

Horticultural Hall

Horticultural buildings have long exhibited the fruits of agricultural labor while extolling the potential of the agricultural industry.

The Agriculture Horticulture Building at the Minnesota State Fairgrounds in 1947, shortly after its opening.

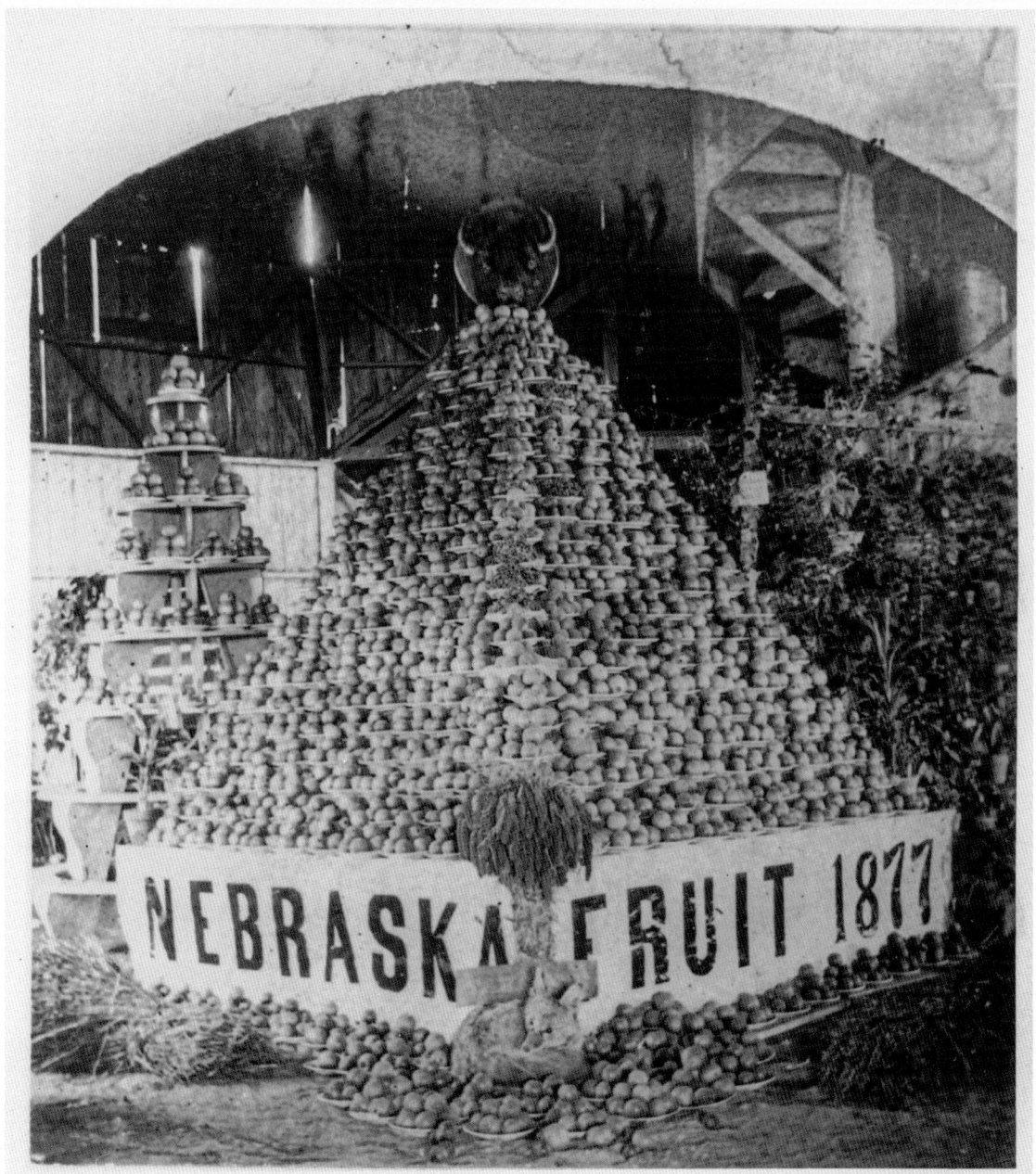

Fruit exhibit at the Nebraska State Fair, 1877

In this display, thousands of apples and other produce from Nebraska form a pyramid topped with a stuffed bison. Extravagant displays like this emphasized how US farmers were improving on nature. Farmers introduced apple trees to the Nebraska Territory around 1850, when millions of bison still grazed on the prairie. Horticulture in Nebraska thrived, partly as a result of improved transportation networks and industry. But these interventions on the land separated and weakened the great herds of bison. By the 1880s, the American bison was nearly extinct.

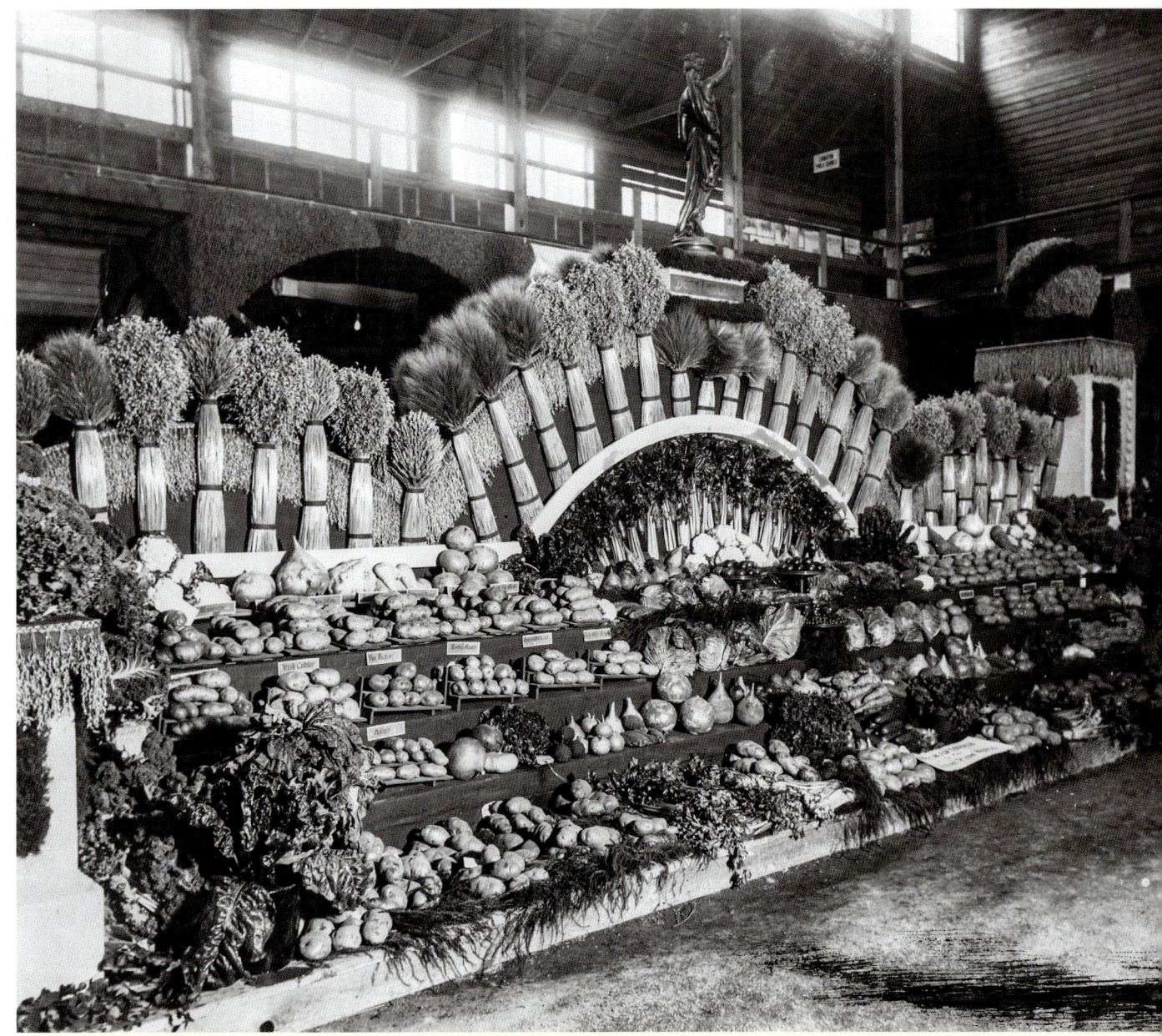

Exhibit of produce and grains at the Montana State Fair, 1894

arge horticultural installations followed the trends established at world's fairs, radiating optimism and celebrating progress. In the words of the historian Pamela H. Simpson, "The idea of having so much food that sculpture can be made of it or buildings can be covered in it speaks of a place of plenty where dreams and hopes can prosper and where everyone has a chance for a better life."[1]

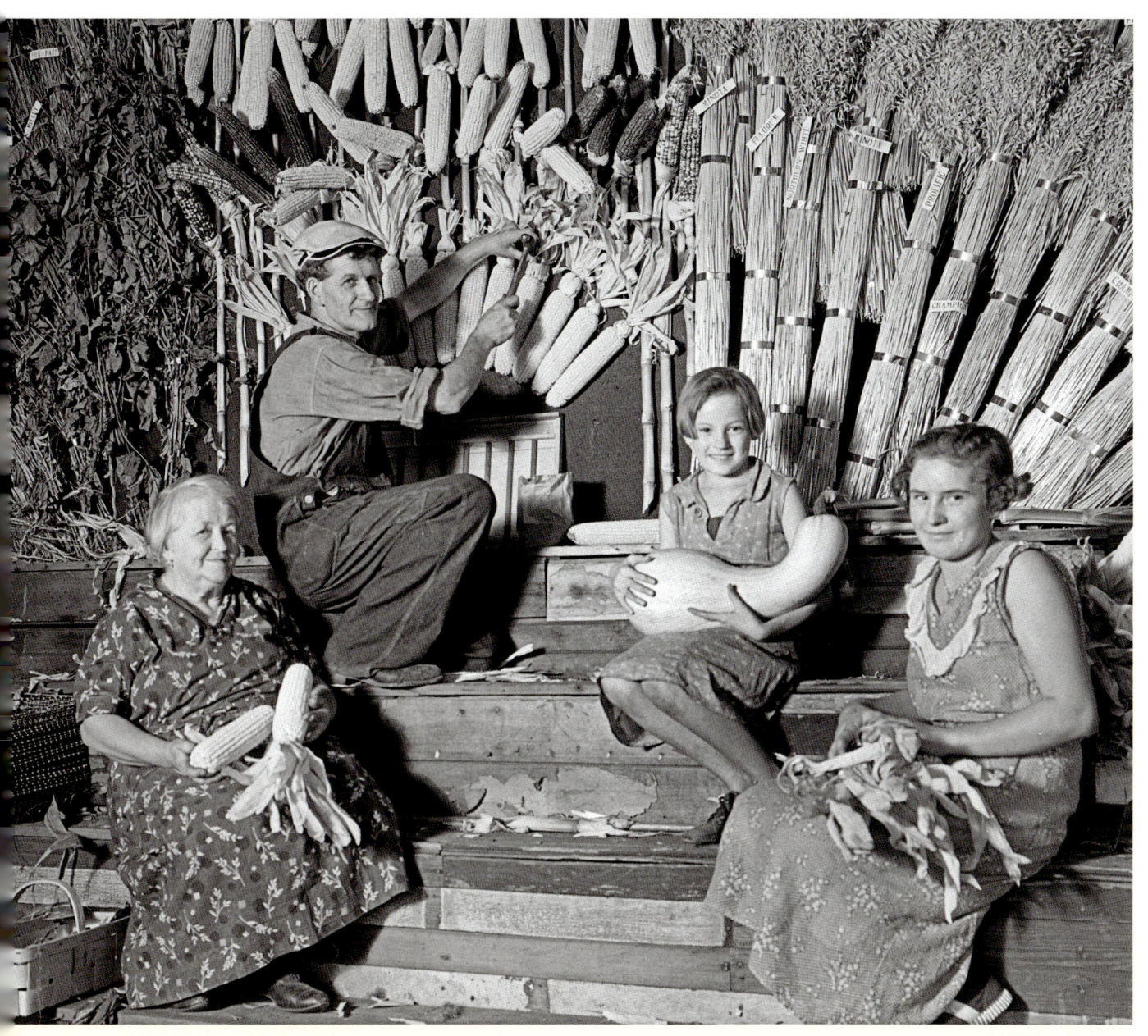

**Workers setting up a wheat and corn display
for the Indiana State Fair, 1934**

Lillian Colton and Linda Paulsen, crop art portraits

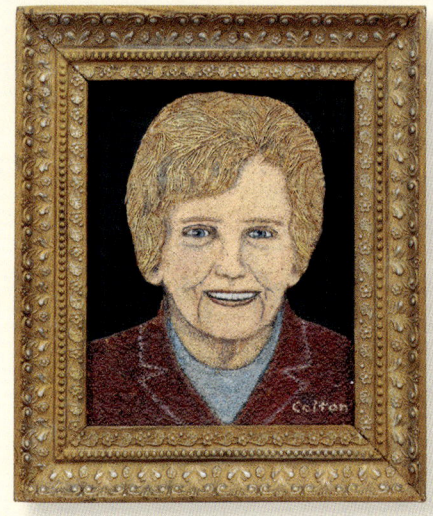

Lillian Colton singlehandedly revolutionized crop art. In 1965, the Minnesota State Fair started a competition to promote the state's crops through art. For a few years Colton, a hairdresser in Owatonna, used crop seeds of different sizes and colors to create fancy floral motifs, as did most other participants. But in 1969, a magazine cover photograph of Richard Nixon piqued her interest, and she wondered if she could re-create the portrait with seeds. The portrait won a blue ribbon and the "Best of Show" award at the Minnesota State Fair.

Colton's portraits popularized the entire category. She selected well-known subjects in order to make her work accessible and familiar to fairgoers. In 1967, Colton encouraged her daughter, Linda Paulsen, to compete in the fair with her. Colton retired from competitions in 1984 to make room for new competitors, though she continued to demonstrate her precise intricate techniques.

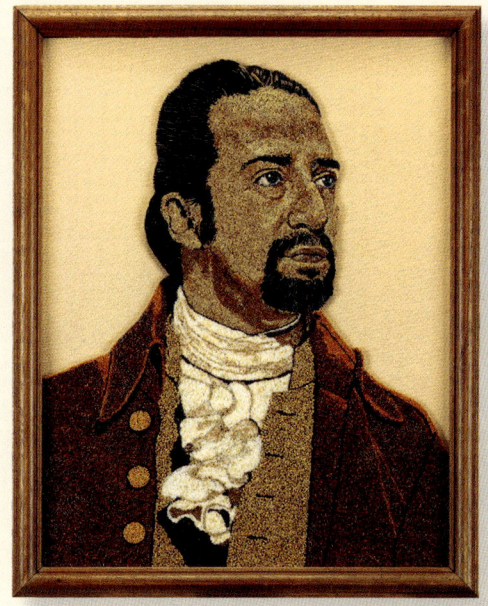

Clockwise from top left:

Lillian Colton, Self-Portrait, 2004, birdsfoot trefoil, canola, timothy grass, poppy, brome grass, grits, cream of wheat, salsify, 9½ × 7½ in.

Lillian Colton, Grandma Moses, 1975, brome, salsify, clover, cantaloupe, watermelon, hollyhock, 18½ × 12½ in.

Linda Paulsen, Barack Obama, 2009, poppy, trefoil, Japanese millet, timothy grass, alfalfa, canola (rapeseed), rutabaga, onion, balloon plant, canary grass, white millet (hulled), amaranth, ground corn, 19¼ × 11½ in.

Linda Paulsen, Betty White, 2022, timothy grass, amaranth, cream of wheat, salsify, lettuce, trefoil, alyssum, red millet, camelina, lily, 13¾ × 10 ¾ in.

Linda Paulsen, Dolly Parton, 2007, alfalfa, alsike clover, amaranth, balloon plant, canary grass, canola, corn husk, cream of wheat, eats, German millet, pearl barley, poppy, sorghum, trefoil, 16 × 12 in.

Lillian Colton, Elvis Presley, 2005, poppy, grits, pine needles, timothy grass, brome grass, 15½ × 12 in.

Linda Paulsen, Lin Manuel Miranda, 2019, timothy grass, Japanese millet, celery, trefoil, poppy, camelina, clover, amaranth, alyssum, cream of wheat, German millet, sudan pods, ground, balloon plant, rutabaga, wildrice, salsify, 21 × 17 in.

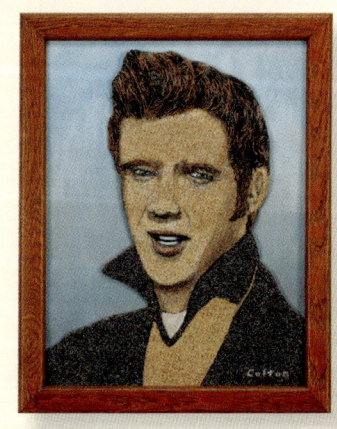

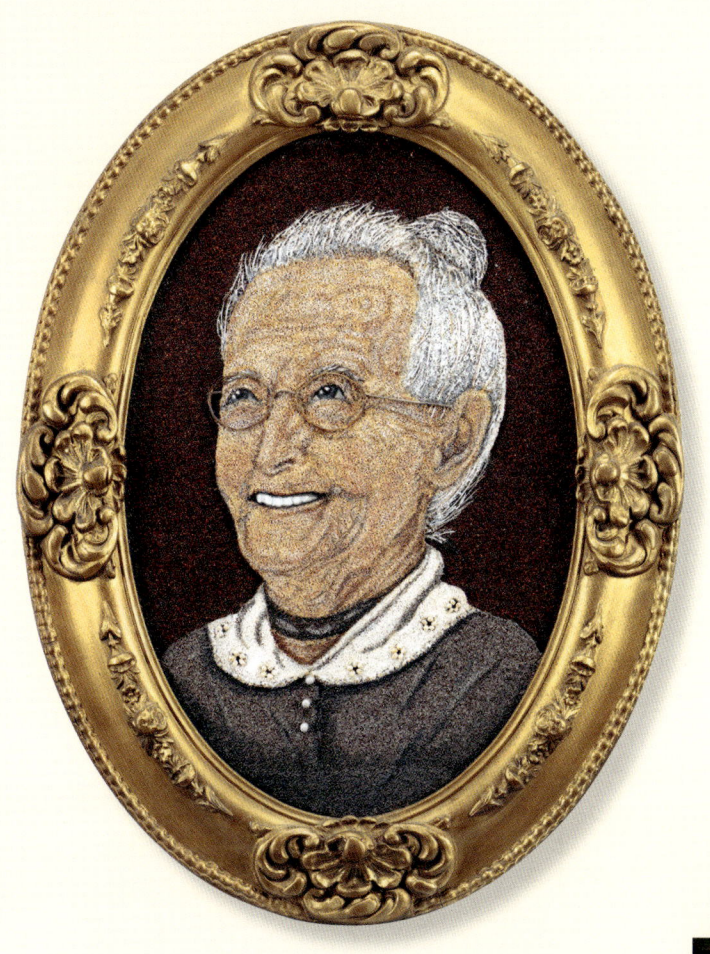

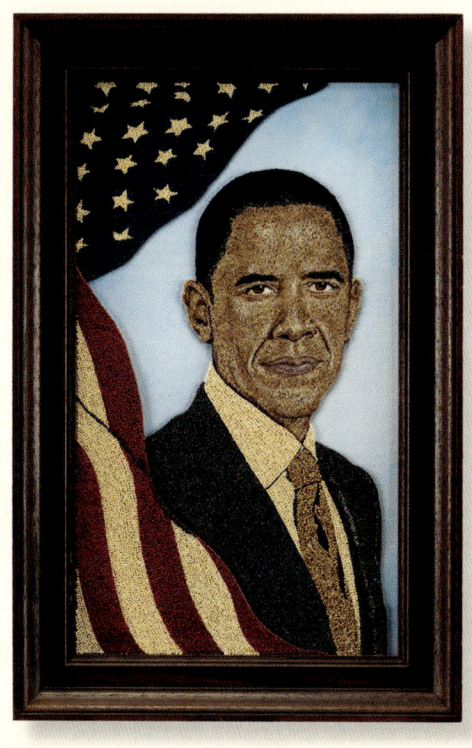

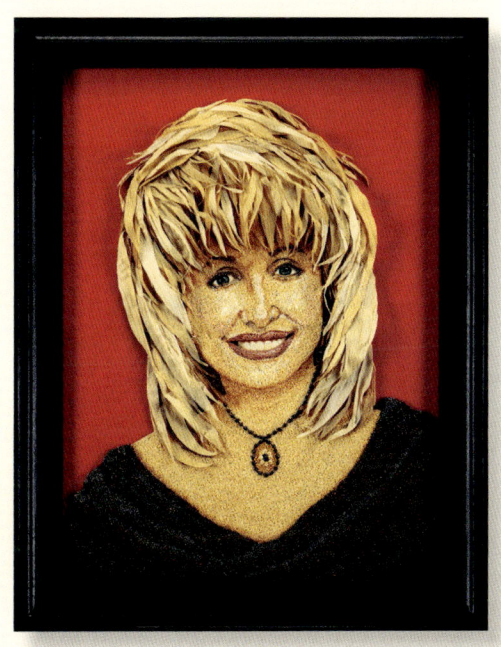

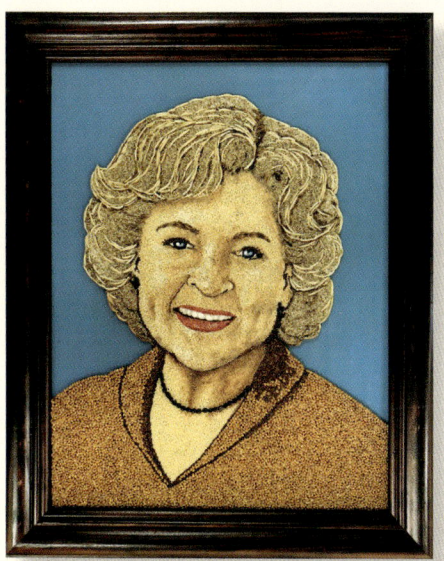

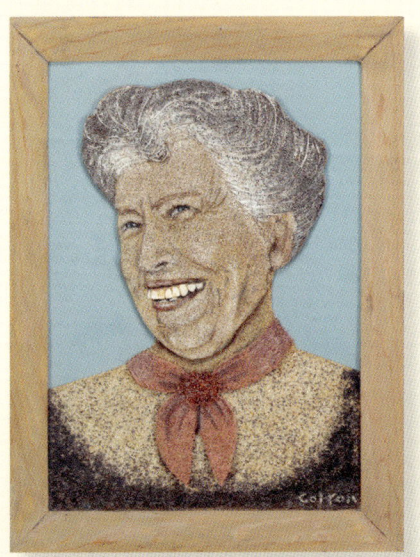

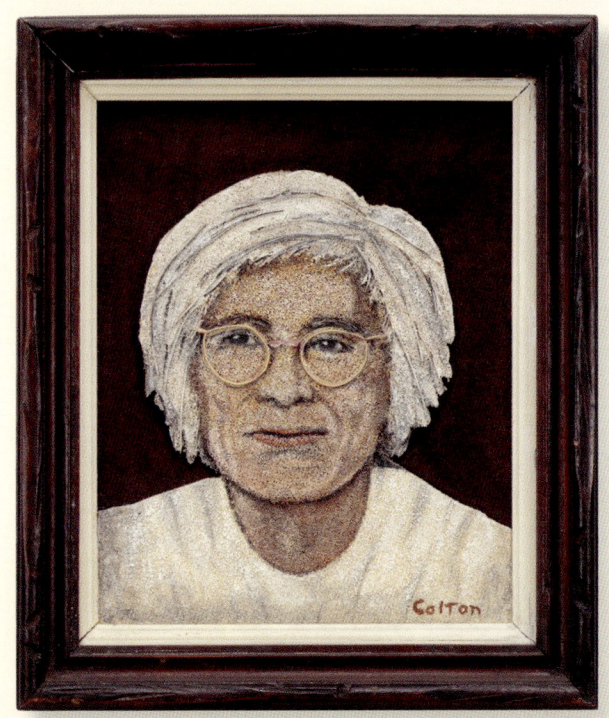

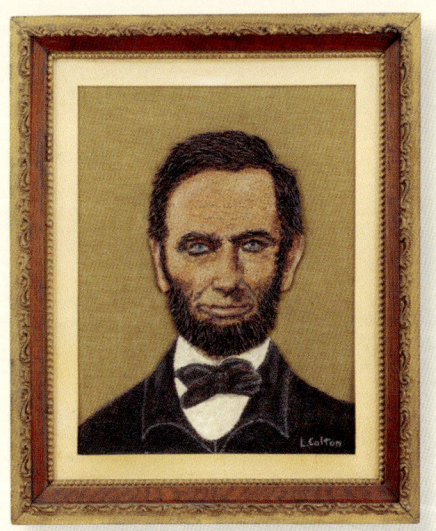

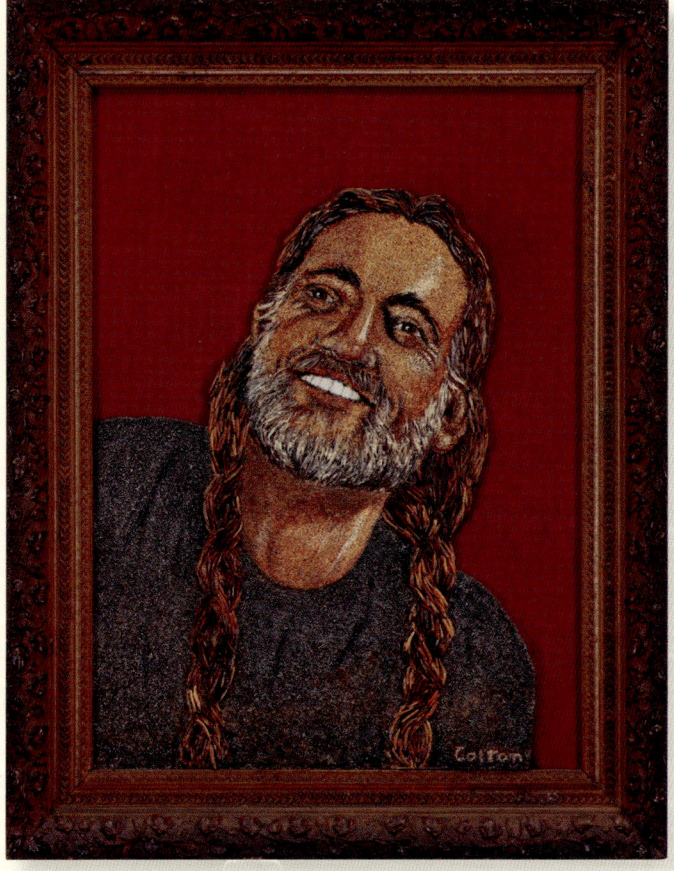

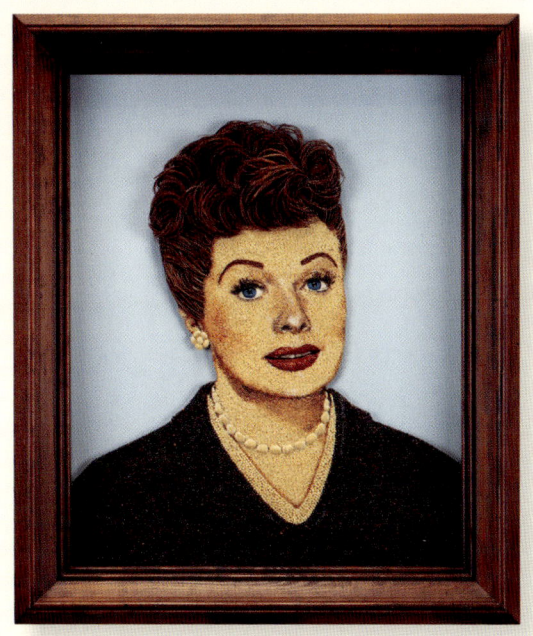

Clockwise from top left:

Lillian Colton, Eleanor Roosevelt, 2004, birdsfoot trefoil, canola, timothy, poppy seeds, brome grass, grits, cream of wheat, salsify, 15½ × 11½ in.

Lillian Colton, Andy Warhol, 1992, cream of wheat, grits, pine needles, timothy, poppy seeds, 11½ × 9½ in.

Linda Paulsen, Lucille Ball, 2006, African cosmos, alfalfa, amaranth, balloon plant, canary grass, canola, cream of wheat, hulled white millet, lima beans, poppy, red pine needles, white pine needles, balsam pine needles, wheat noodles, Sudan grass, trefoil, 16¼ × 13½ in.

Lillian Colton, Prince, 1987, timothy, canola, poppy seed, grits, brome grass, 11 × 14 in.

Lillian Colton, Barbra Streisand, 1974, ground white corn, grits, timothy, poppy seeds, peas, safflower, 16¼ × 12½ in.

Lillian Colton, Willie Nelson, 1983, timothy, canola, alsike, bromegrass, birdsfoot trefoil, salsify, 15½ × 11¼ in.

Lillian Colton, Abraham Lincoln, 1973, timothy, canola, wild rice, clover, brome grass, 17 × 13½ in.

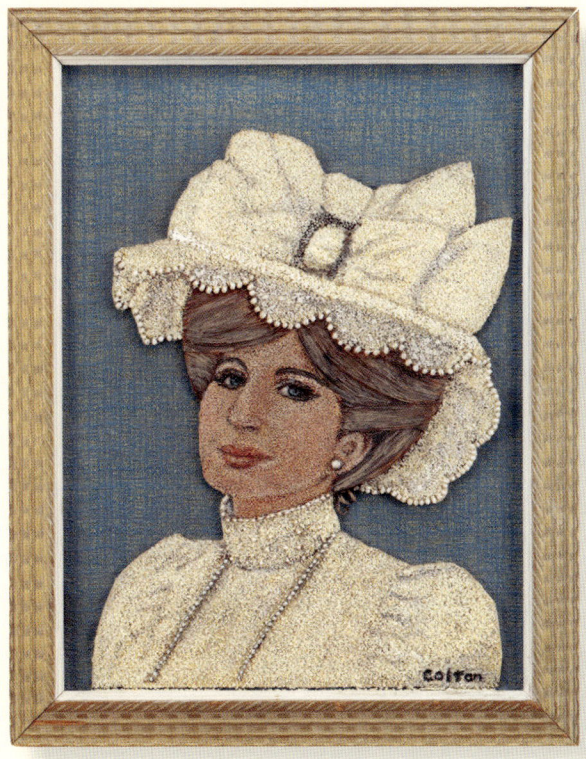

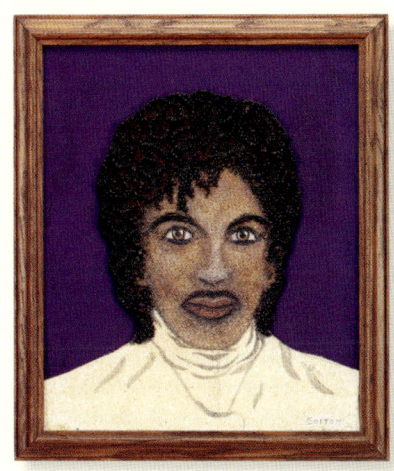

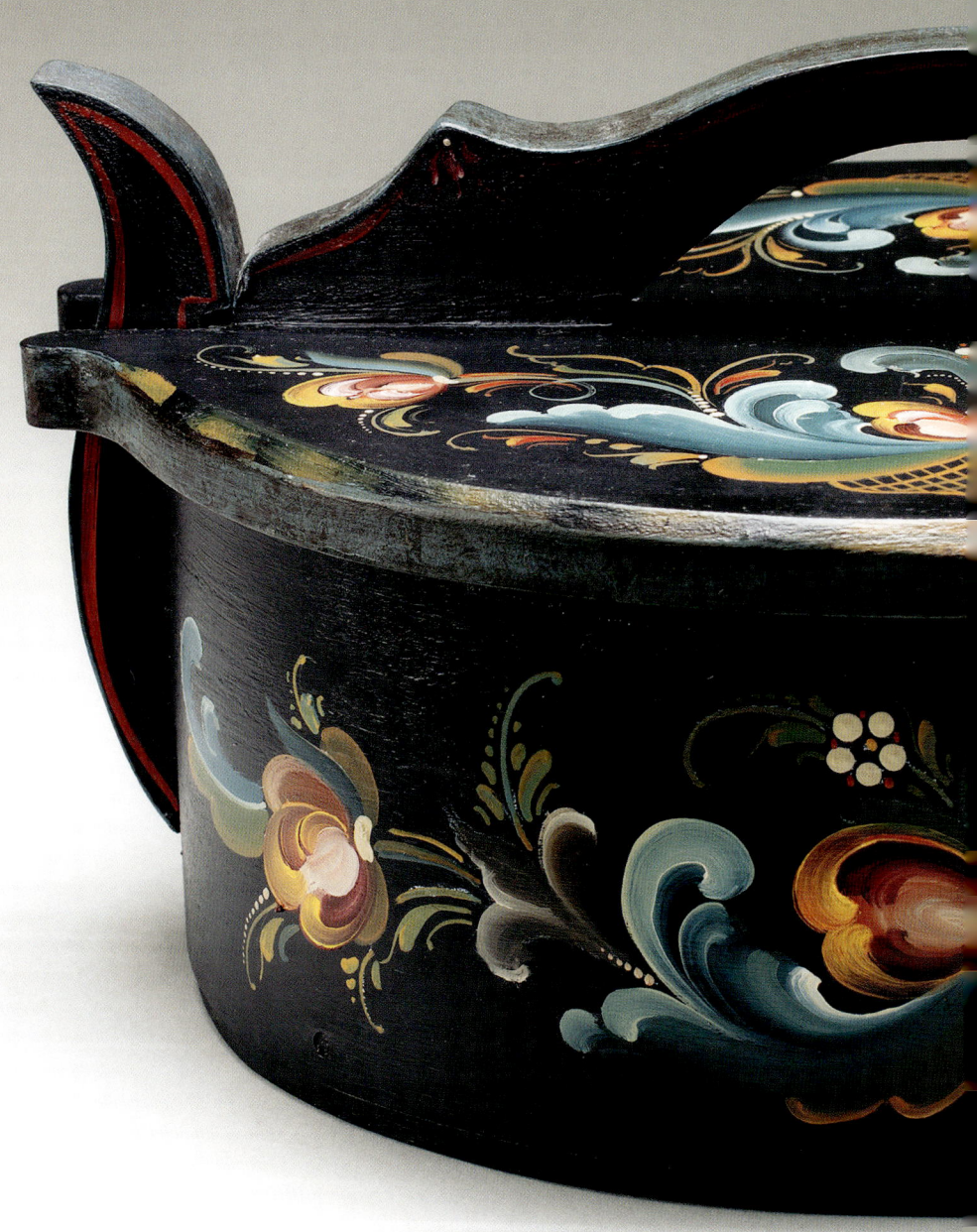

Ronna Thorson, *Tine*, 2023

Oil paints on wood, 8 × 10 × 14 in.

Rosemåling, a decorative freehand painting style, originated in rural Norway in the mid-1700s and was brought to the Upper Midwest by Norwegian immigrants in the mid-nineteenth century. Rosemålers have competed at the Minnesota State Fair since the 1930s.

Ronna Thorson grew up in a small town in Minnesota, where an artist named Karen Jenson had

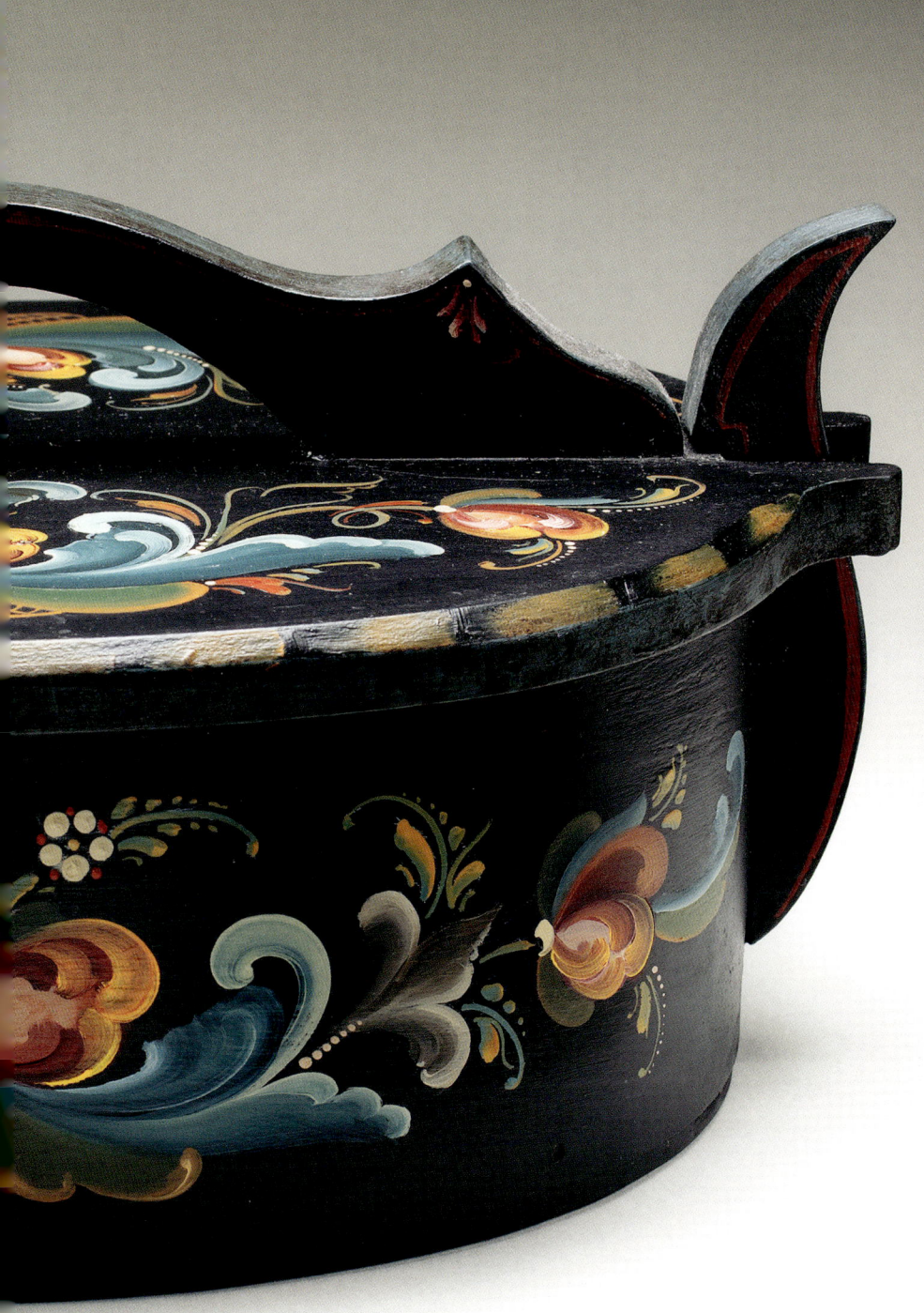

rosemåled the wall of a local bank. Thorson was interested, but did not take a class until she was recovering from cancer and motivated to check an item off her bucket list. After one class, she was swept away. Thorson has entered her rosemåling in the Minnesota State Fair's creative activities competition for more than twenty years, and many of those entries have won ribbons. In 2021, Thorson won a first-place ribbon for her rosemåling on a *tine,* a Norwegian box used to carry lunches and other provisions that is popular with rosemålers. Thorson paints in the Telemark style, characterized by overlapping scrolls.

Dairy Barn

Dairy buildings and displays have competed for the attention of fairgoers since the late nineteenth century.

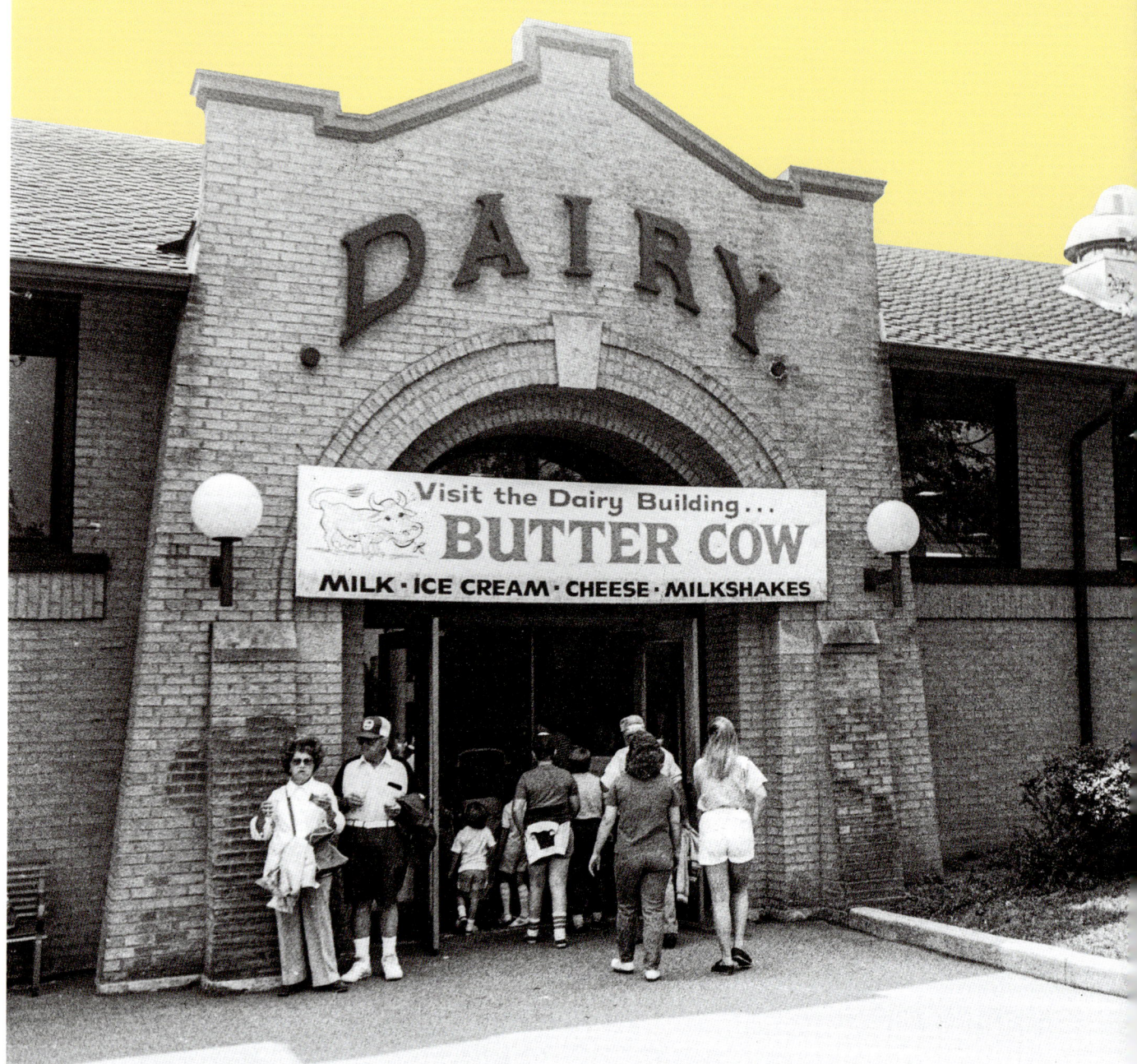

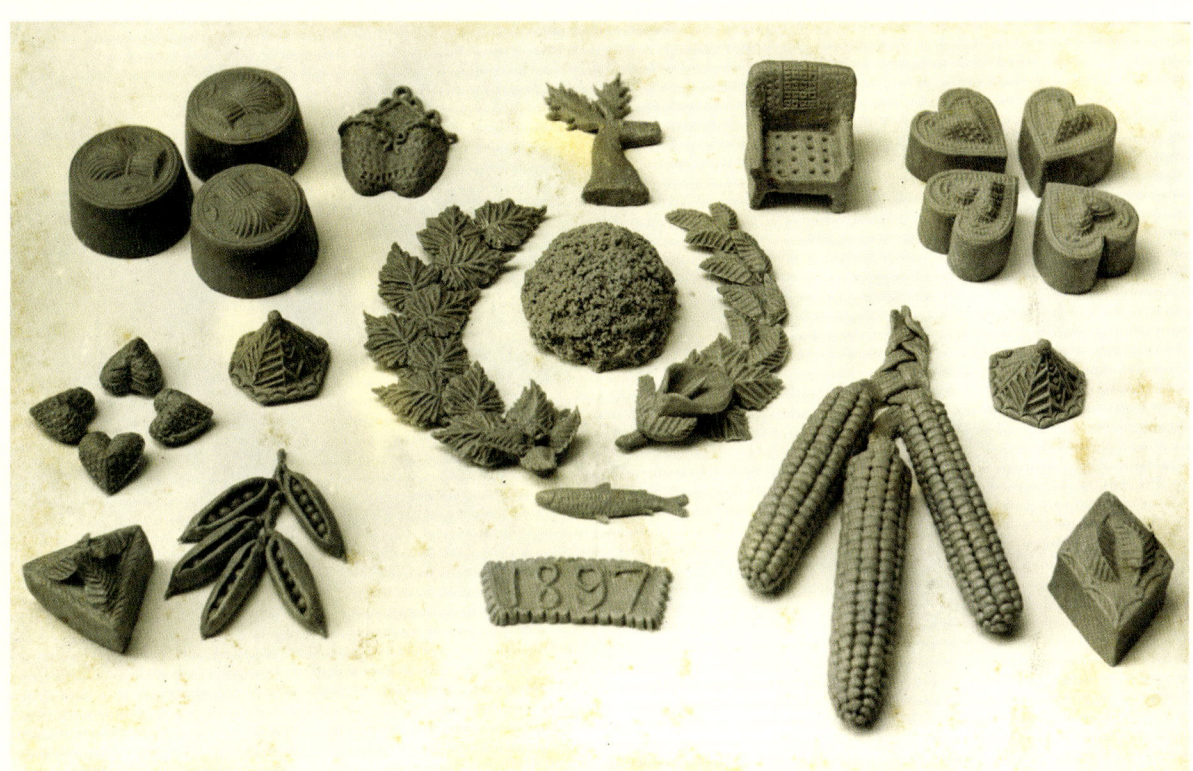

Minnie Casey, display of molded butter at Northeastern Maine State Fair, Presque Isle, Maine, 1897

In the nineteenth century, women managed the dairy operations on family farms and sold extra butter to sustain their families. They taught their daughters many facets of dairy production, including butter art, in which chilled butter is molded into decorative shapes. This became a competitive category at state fairs. In 1897, Minnie Casey won a premium for her molded butter art.

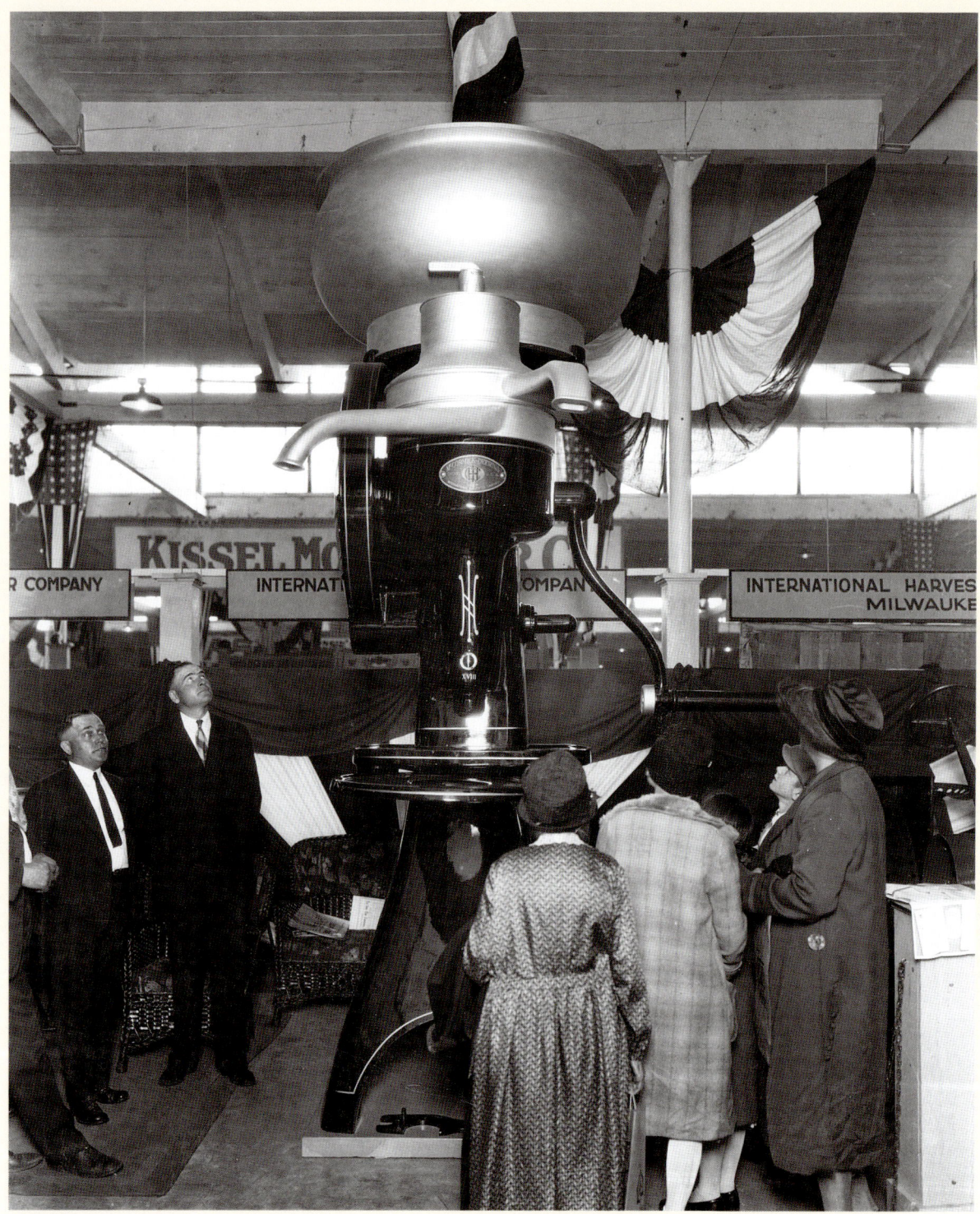

Giant cream separator model, possibly at the Wisconsin State Fair, 1928

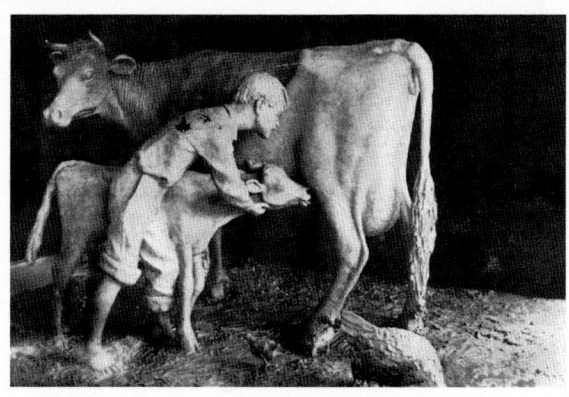

John K. Daniels, butter sculpture of a boy, cow, and calf, Iowa State Fair, 1904

In the late 1880s, technical and scientific advancements like centrifugal cream separators and pasteurization transformed the domestic dairy industry—previously managed by women—into an industrial enterprise.

To promote the industry, professional artists were commissioned to sculpt life-size vignettes of dairy operations. At the 1911 Iowa State Fair, the artist John K. Daniels exhibited a butter sculpture showing a young boy tending a dairy cow and her nursing calf. The sponsoring company, Beatrice Creamery Company, produced this souvenir postcard for fairgoers. Though the butter industry was reducing its reliance on small, family-owned dairy farms, the butter cow communicated agrarian family values. As the historian Pamela Simpson observes, "The cow is literally a mother, and her milk provides nourishment for other mothers' babies."

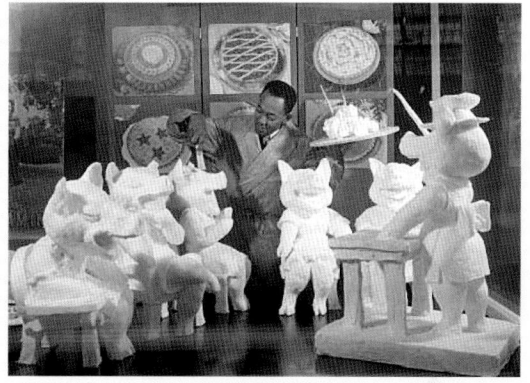

Artist preparing sculptures for the lard exhibit at the Indiana State Fair, 1941

When butter was in short supply during World War II, the lard industry attempted to steal the spotlight. The National Livestock and Meat Board organized a lard sculpture display at the Indiana State Fair, with renditions of jolly pigs supplanting butter cows. Lard sculptures, however, did not win the public's affection, and butter cows continued to rule the fairground dairy barns.

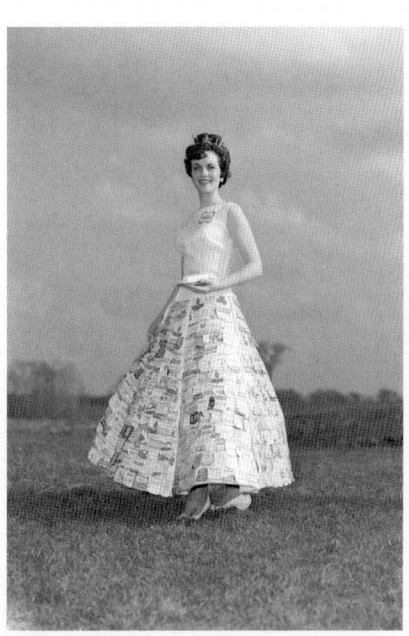

Karen Bracken, Princess Kay of 1964, in a butter carton skirt prototype, 1965

Ethel Meehan Ryan and Mary Ann Titrud, butter carton dress for "Princess Kay of the Milky Way," 1965-1966

Paper (butter cartons) and fabric, 41 × 22 × 10 in.

In the 1950s, women began to reclaim butter culture. Dairy producers and cooperatives staged dairy princess competitions at state fairs. Teenage dairy farmers competed for the titles of Alice in Dairyland in Wisconsin and Princess Kay of the Milky Way in Minnesota, among others. The reigning Princess Kay continues to visit local schools and organizations, connecting consumers to Minnesota dairy farms. These days Princess Kay also addresses issues of sustainability as they affect both the environment and small family farms.

At the 1965 Minnesota State Fair, Princess Kay winner Mary Ann Titrud modeled this butter carton dress to promote the state's many creameries. The idea for the dress was conceived by Howard Ryan, public relations director for the American Dairy Association of Minnesota. His mother, Wilma Ryan, helped Mary Ann Titrud make the dress. They sewed together approximately 475 squares cut from butter cartons into a skirt, capelet, and shift dress. Titrud placed a carton from Clarissa Creamery, located in her hometown, on the breast of the capelet.

Such a dress would not look the same today because many state creameries and cooperatives have been consolidated. The US Department of Agriculture reports that the number of US dairy herds halved between 2002 and 2019, even as butter production rose. In 2023, the United States produced more than 2.3 billion pounds of butter, an increase from 1.4 billion pounds in 2005.

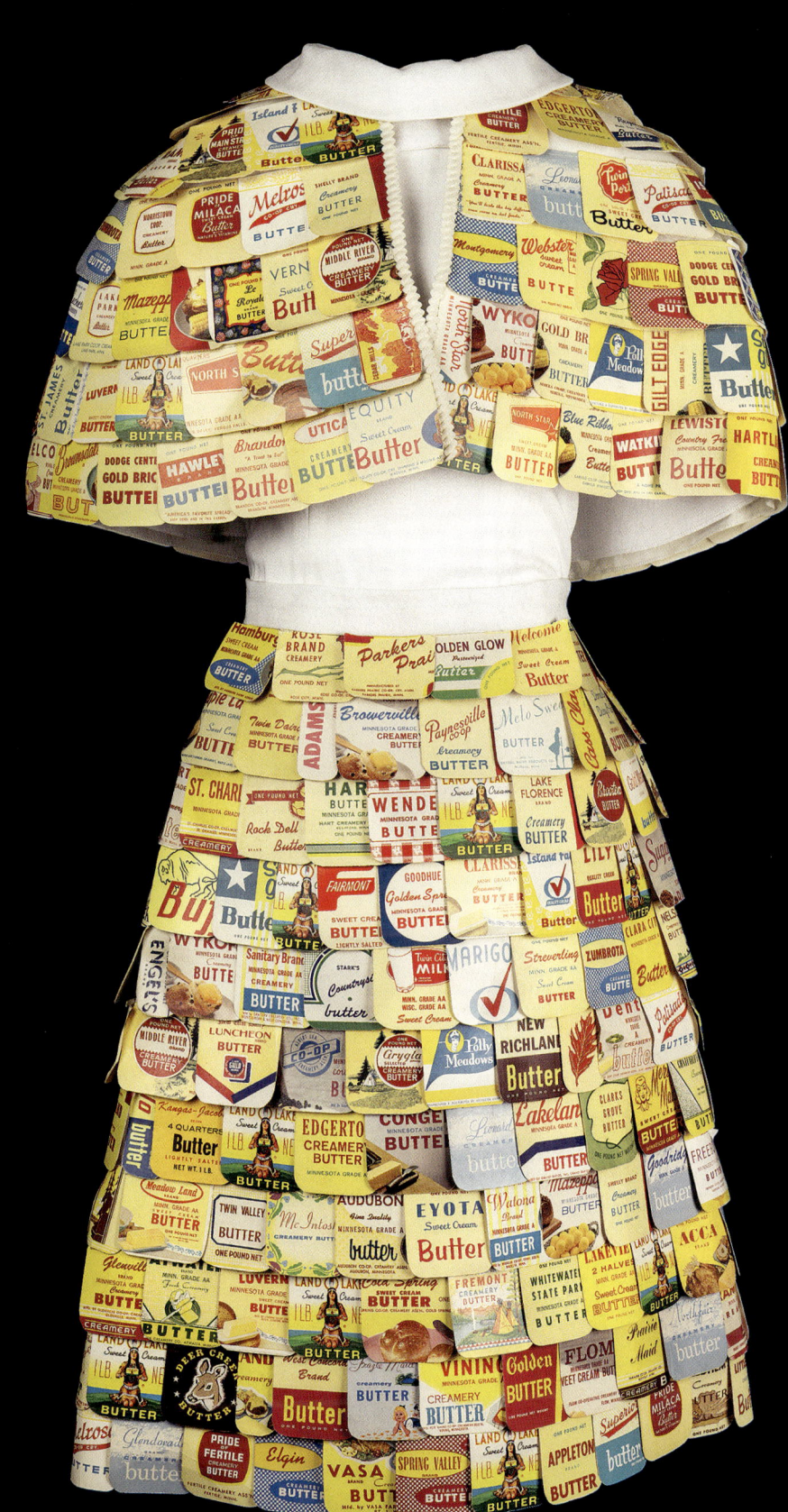

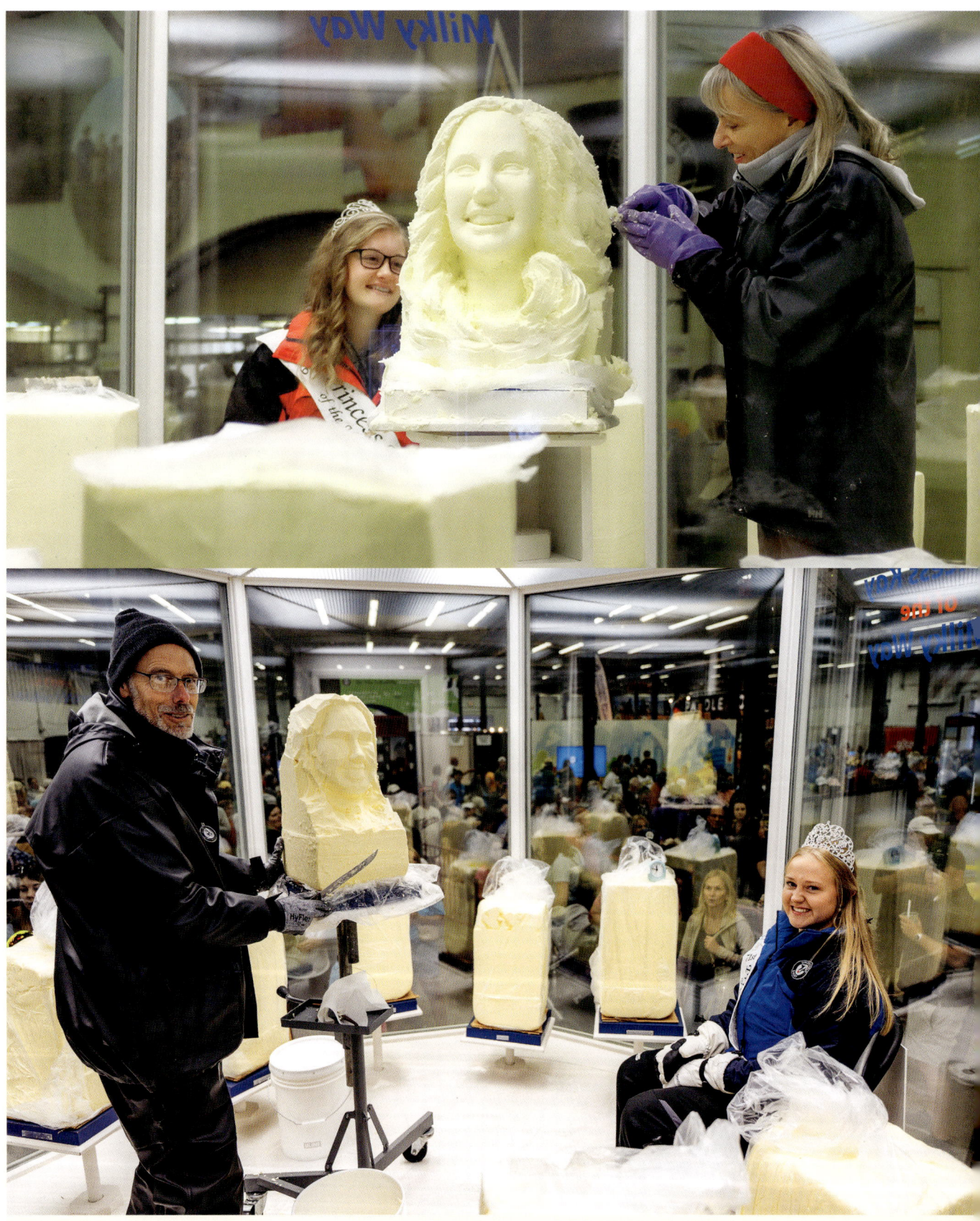

Linda Christensen and Gerry Kulzer carving butter portraits, Minnesota State Fair, 2024

Since 1965, every contestant for the title of Princess Kay at the Minnesota State Fair has had her portrait carved for display in a chilled revolving butter booth. The likeness of the winner commands the center pedestal.

For fifty years, the artist Linda Christensen *(top)* carved busts of butter princesses in front of thousands of spectators, shaping an estimated 41,500 pounds of butter into five hundred sculptures. In an interview, Christensen observed: "There are people who have art in galleries and have gallery showings, but I have tapped into an audience that is entirely different with this butter sculpting. I had people outside the butter booth who came in from rural areas from all over the state. They loved watching what I do and are involved with it in ways that people don't normally get involved in art—because that's their hometown girl in there, or family member." When Christensen retired in 2021, she was succeeded by Gerry Kulzer *(bottom)*, a public school art teacher. As an aspiring sculptor, he visited the state fair specifically to see the butter carving demonstrations.

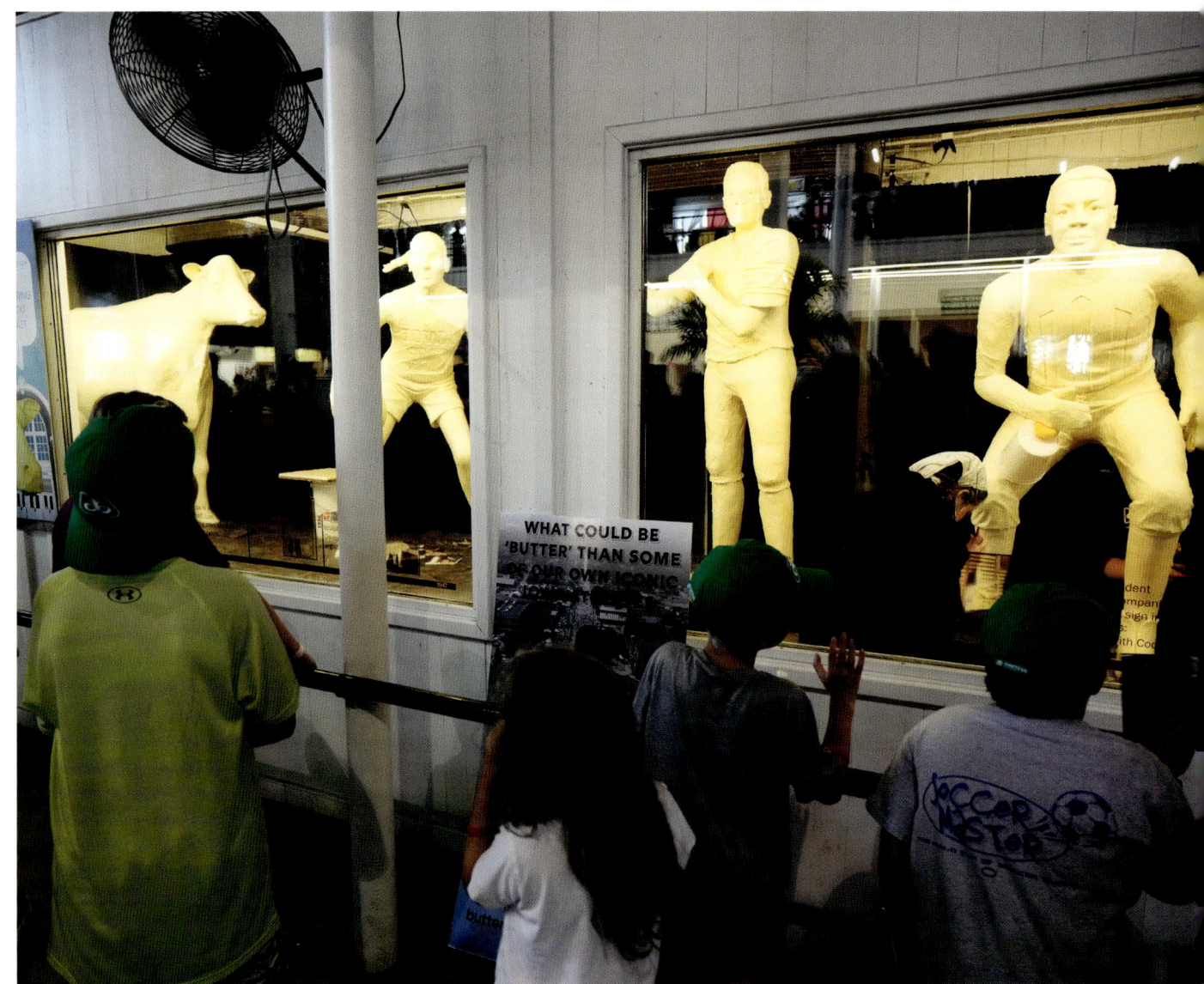

Sarah Pratt, butter cow and sculptures of Caitlin Clark, Jack Trice, and Kurt Warner, Iowa State Fair, 2023

Butter

Butter art became a women's tradition in part because rural women did not have the same opportunities as men to attend art school. As a teenager, Sarah Pratt apprenticed with the long-time Iowa State Fair sculptor Norma "Duffy" Lyon, a dairy farmer's wife who originally aspired to be a veterinarian. She studied animal science and took art classes at Iowa State University. At the 1956 Iowa State Fair, Lyon was unimpressed with the butter cow sculpture and said as much to the state dairy association. They allowed her to assist the following year, and in 1960 she became the head sculptor. In 2006, Lyon passed on her butter knife—and some of her butter—to Pratt, who brings a present-day

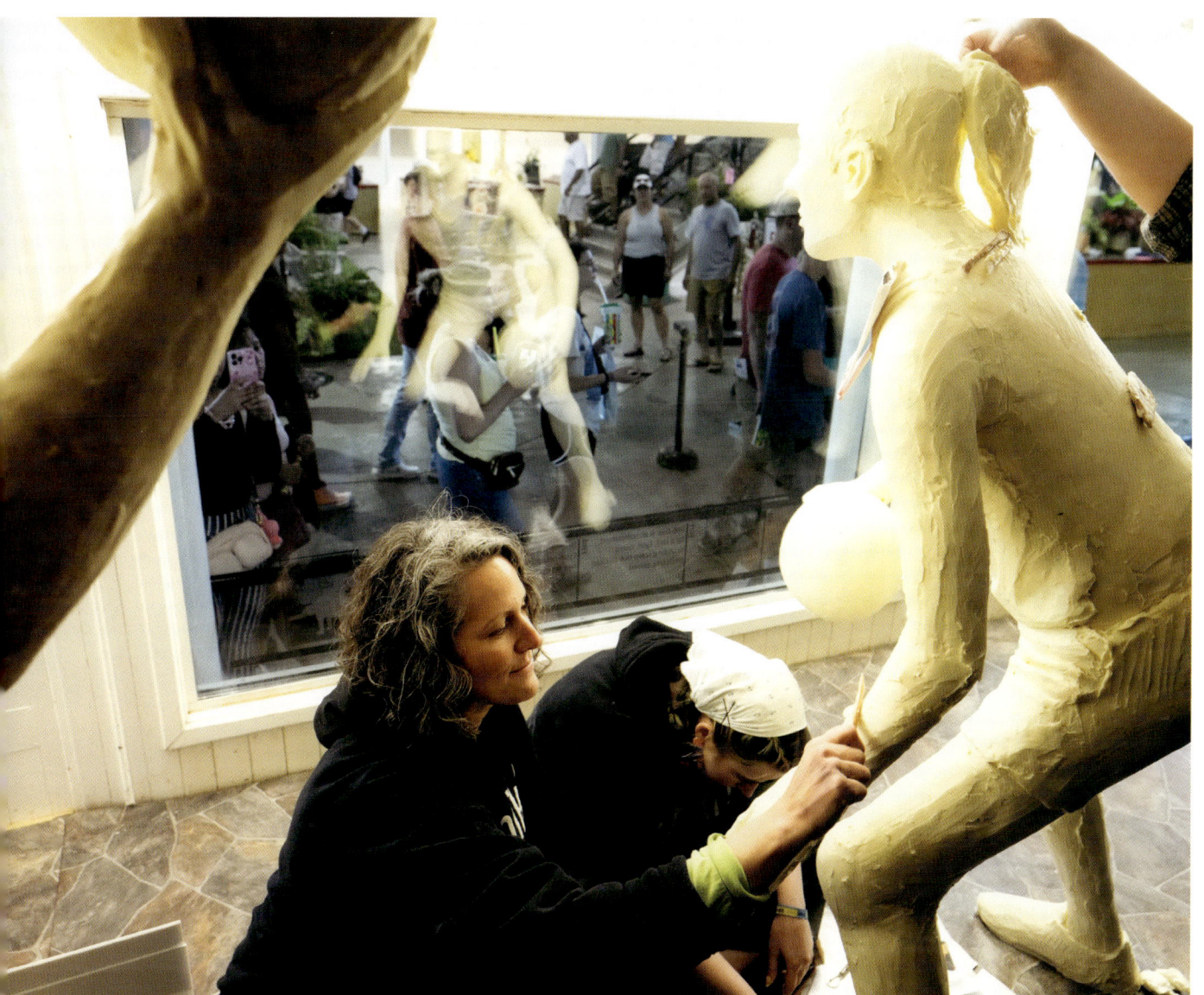

vantage point to her work while building on the state fair tradition of entertaining and educating fairgoers about the dairy industry.

In 2023 Pratt sculpted three portraits of famous Iowa athletes: Kurt Warner, Jack Trice, and Caitlyn Clark. Warner, who played football for the Northern Iowa Panthers, would eventually lead the Arizona Cardinals to the Super Bowl in the "greatest Cinderella story in NFL history." Trice was the first Black football player at Iowa State College. He majored in animal science, with ambitions to improve Black farming in the South after graduation. He died during a game in 1923 against the University of Minnesota after being tackled and trampled by three players. Alongside Trice, the college and WNBA basketball superstar Caitlyn Clark dribbles a basketball. These portraits resonate with the history of exclusion, showing how culture can change over time, but not by accident—it must be molded. In 2023, Clark broke scoring records—for both men and women—at the NCAA tournament while playing for the University of Iowa and earned the title Big Ten Female Athlete of the Year.

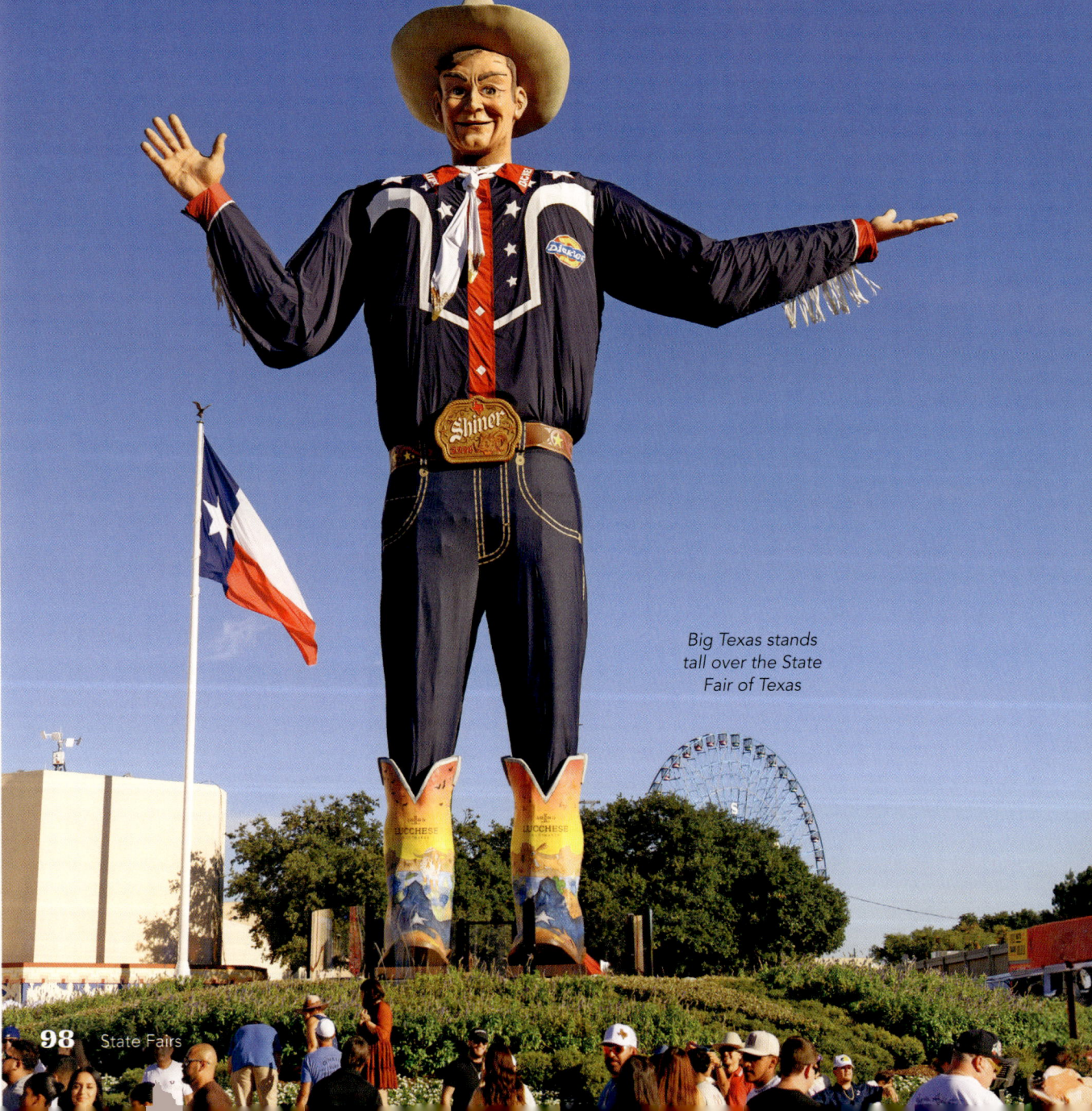

Craft's Rural Roots

Artists embed their memories of farm life
and family histories in blue-ribbon artworks.

Big Texas stands
tall over the State
Fair of Texas

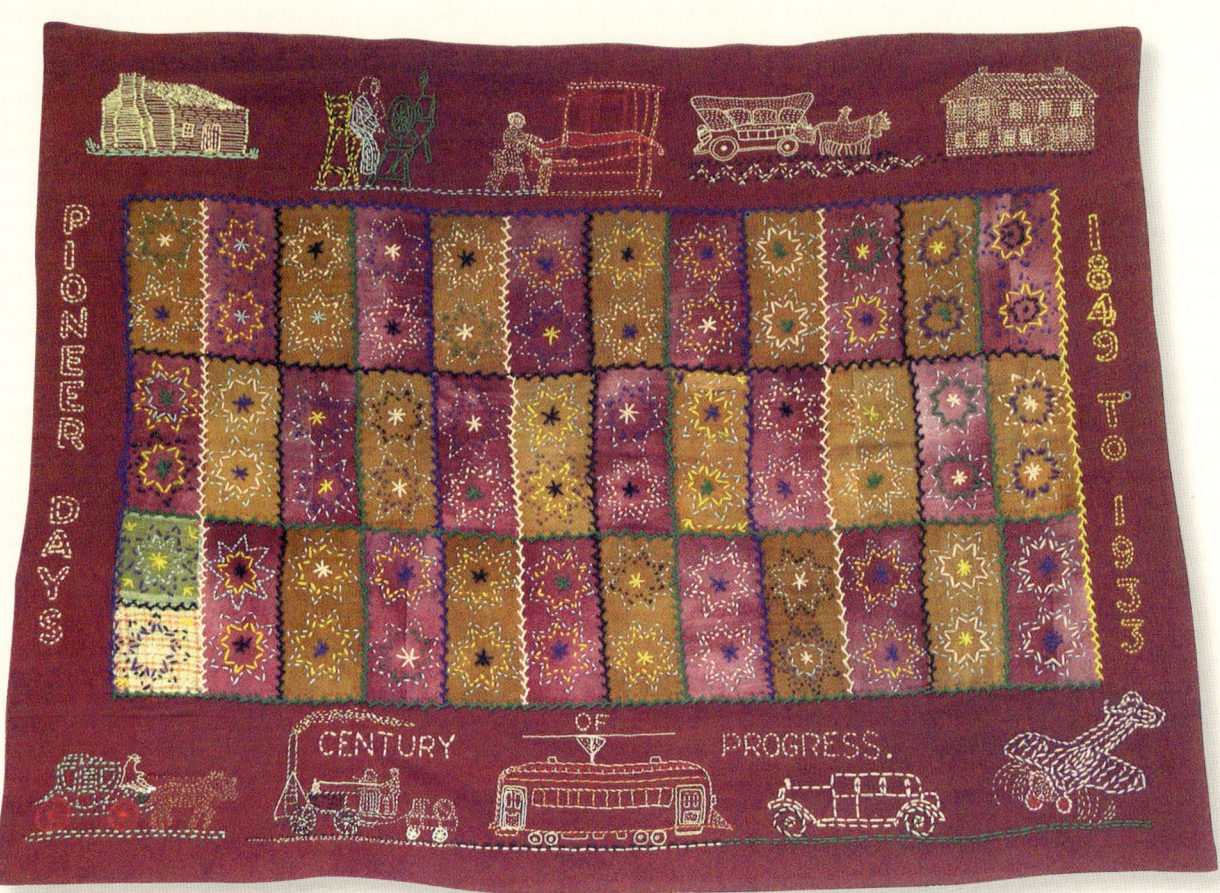

Katie Goar Maze, *Century of Progress*, 1925–1933

Wool, 44 × 57 in.

The Nebraska artist Katie Goar Maze stitched this blanket at the age of seventy-two for the 1933 Chicago's Century of Progress Fair. The blanket depicts technological advancements from 1849 to 1933. The central panels were made from wool produced on her parents' Illinois farm in 1849, before the family migrated to Nebraska as homesteaders. Their story is embroidered in the top border, which shows a rustic cabin, a spinning wheel, a loom, and a buggy. But then life grew somewhat easier: the bottom border features a train, a bus, a car, and an airplane. Maze's quilt tracks the obsolescence of once-essential household objects like looms and spinning wheels and also expresses the nostalgic and nationalist attitudes about pioneers and progress common in the 1930s.

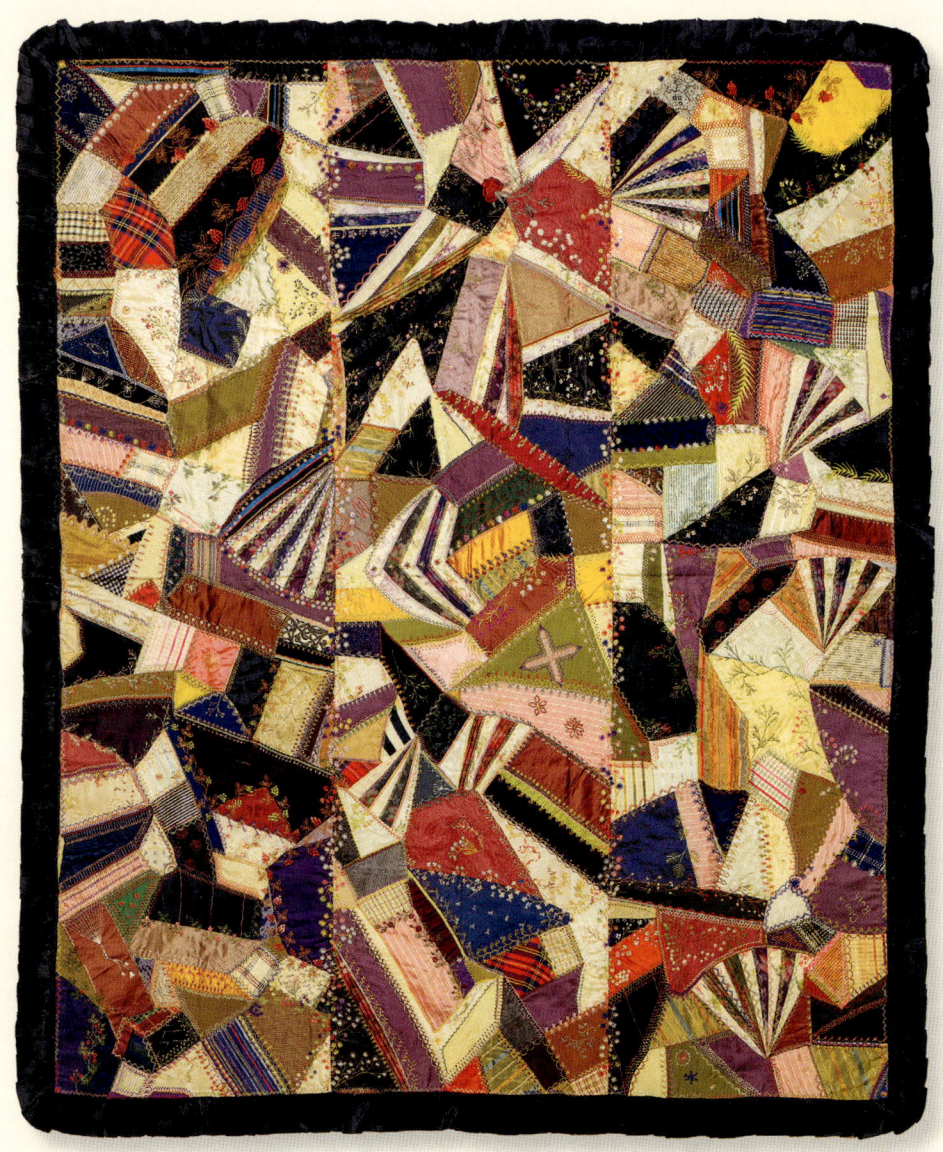

Margaret J. Gilman (1860–1925), Quilt, 1903

Silk, 58 × 68½ in.

Margaret J. Gilman was a seamstress in Penacook, New Hampshire, at the start of the twentieth century. Like many rural women, she sewed to earn a respectable living outside of farm work. Gilman made clothing for local families and saved the scraps for her own textile projects. She made this exemplary crazy quilt by piecing together irregularly shaped pieces of bright silk and adorning them with embroidered feathers, vines, fronds, and berries. She added the names of her children, Ruth and Charles, at the request of young Ruth, who watched her mother at work. The quilt won second prize at the 1903 Concord State Fair. Ruth Gilman recalled that a fairgoer offered her mother $100 for the quilt, but Gilman refused, already considering her quilt a family heirloom.

Grace Snyder, *Flower Basket Petit Point Quilt*, 1942–43

Cotton, quilted, 94 × 92 in.

G rowing up in a homesteading family in Sand Hill, Nebraska, Grace Snyder learned to quilt at the age of six to keep herself occupied during long days of watching cattle. After marrying a rancher in 1903, she raised four children but always found time to stitch. She loved seeing her quilts on view in state fairs. In 1944, this quilt won the "Sweepstakes Award" (Best in Show) at the Nebraska State Fair, and Snyder took home a prize of $2.50.

The quilt is one of the best known in American quilting history. Snyder handstitched approximately eighty-seven thousand tiny triangles into this quilt over the course of sixteen months. She adapted the pattern from a porcelain design produced by the Salem China Company in Ohio, which itself imitates the petit point embroidery technique. In this way, Snyder created the illusion of needlepoint on a quilt. The president of the Salem China Company not only approved her use of their pattern but sent her a set of the china and put her in touch with the German designer.

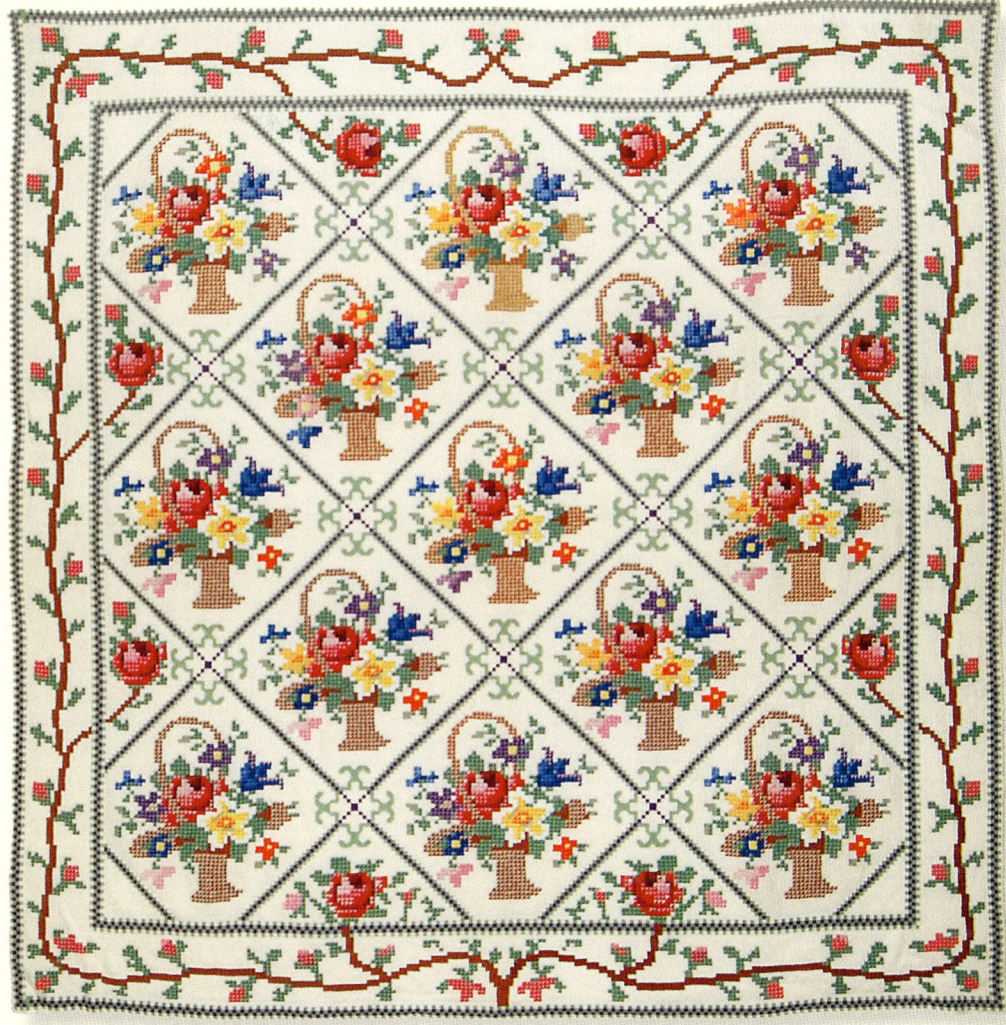

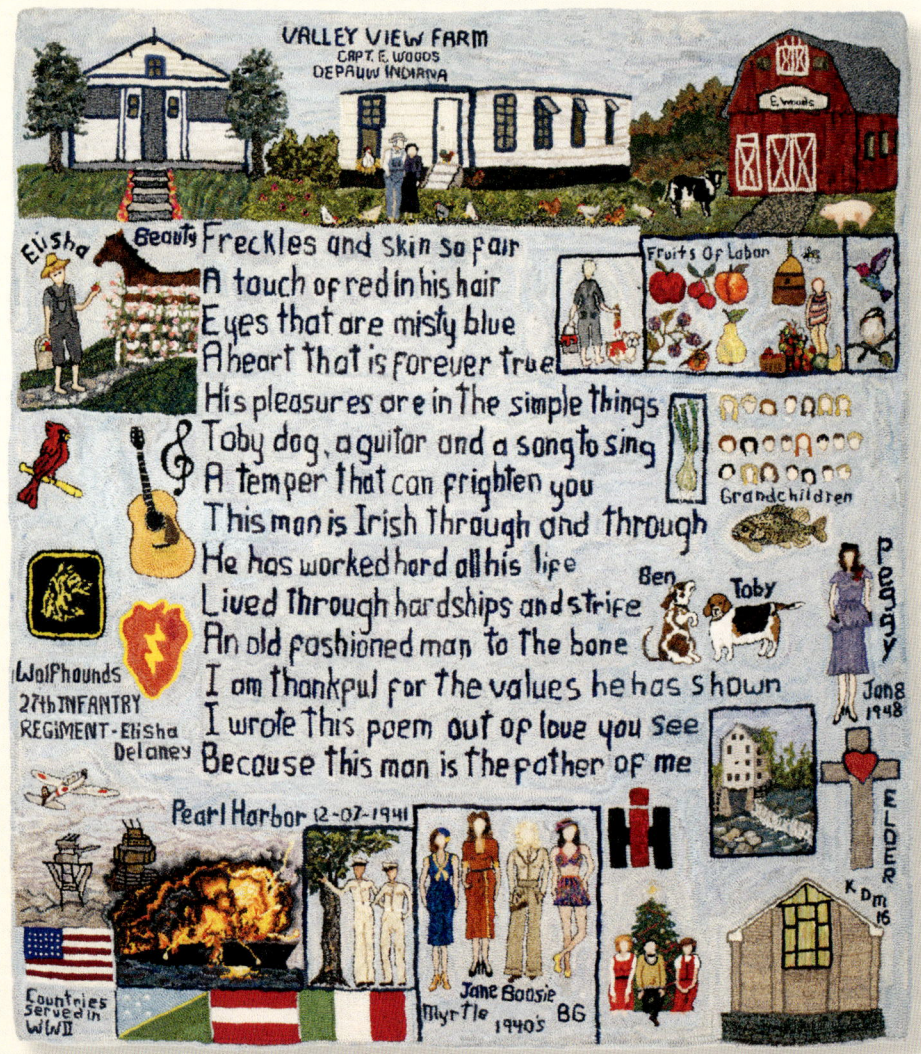

Kaye D. Miller, *Hooked Rug*, 2019

Wool and backing, 46 × 52 in.

In this hooked rug, Kaye D. Miller illustrated colorful scenes from the life of her father, Elisha Delaney. Raised on a farm by his grandparents, he later developed PTSD from his experience during the bombing of Pearl Harbor on December 7, 1941. Miller began hooking this rug before her father died as a way to help him see the value and beauty in his life. On the left border she included a portrait of young Elisha in an outfit made by his grandmother, feeding his horse, Beauty. Miller also lovingly illustrated his favorite guitar, his beloved dogs, all of his grandchildren, and a green onion—because he ate one every single day.

Miller became intrigued by rug hooking while viewing rugs on display at the Kentucky State Fair. She wanted to purchase one but soon realized she could make one herself. Miller spent about a year making this rug, which won the "Best in Show" award at the 2019 Kentucky State Fair.

Beth Grabau, *The Pump House*, 2023

Wood, various other elements, 13½ in. high × 9¼ in. diameter.

Displays of miniatures draw massive crowds at the Iowa State Fair, where viewers peek into the windows of tiny dollhouses and rooms. Beth Grabau started this project with a miniature kit purchased at a Halloween sale. As a child, Grabau watched her grandmother doing the laundry in the pump house on her grandparents' farm, a small space with a dirt floor. In her model of that space, Grabau included miniature representations of embroidered tea towels, fresh farm eggs, jars of canned food, and braided rugs made from scraps, all emblems of her grandmother's daily life. She even included one of the plump toads that frequented the farm's cellar. Grabau's *Pump House* won "Best in Show" at the 2023 Iowa State Fair.

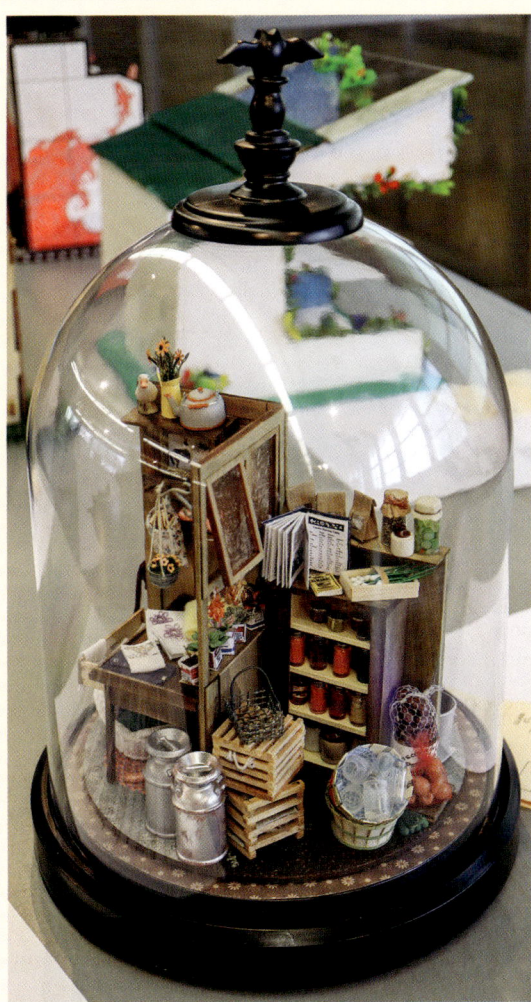
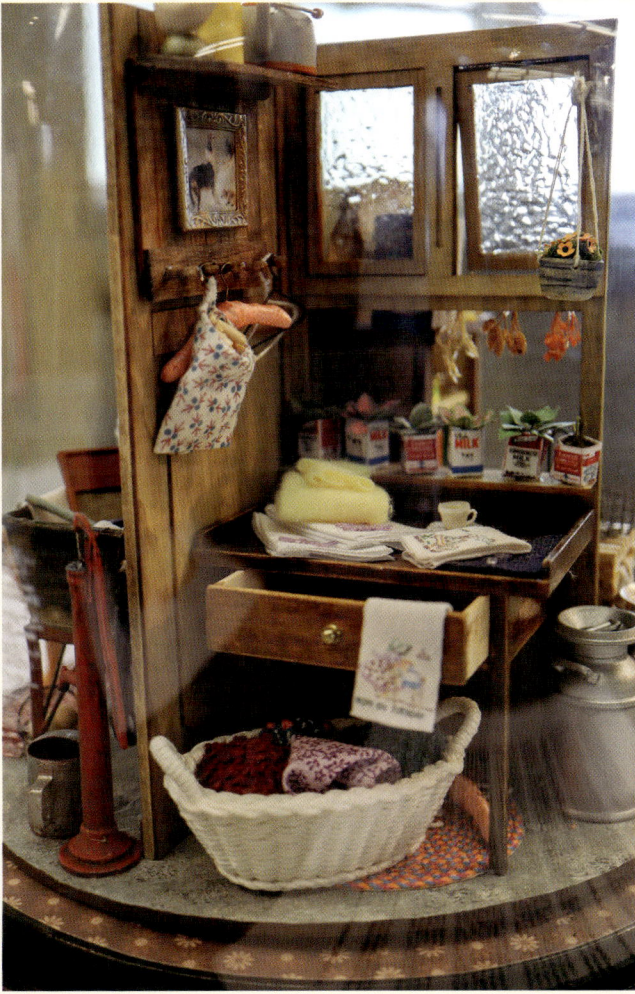

Robbie LaFleur,
The Farmer's Daughter's Yggdrasil (Tree of Life), 2019

Norwegian spelsau wool yarn, synthetic dyes, 21½ × 43 in.

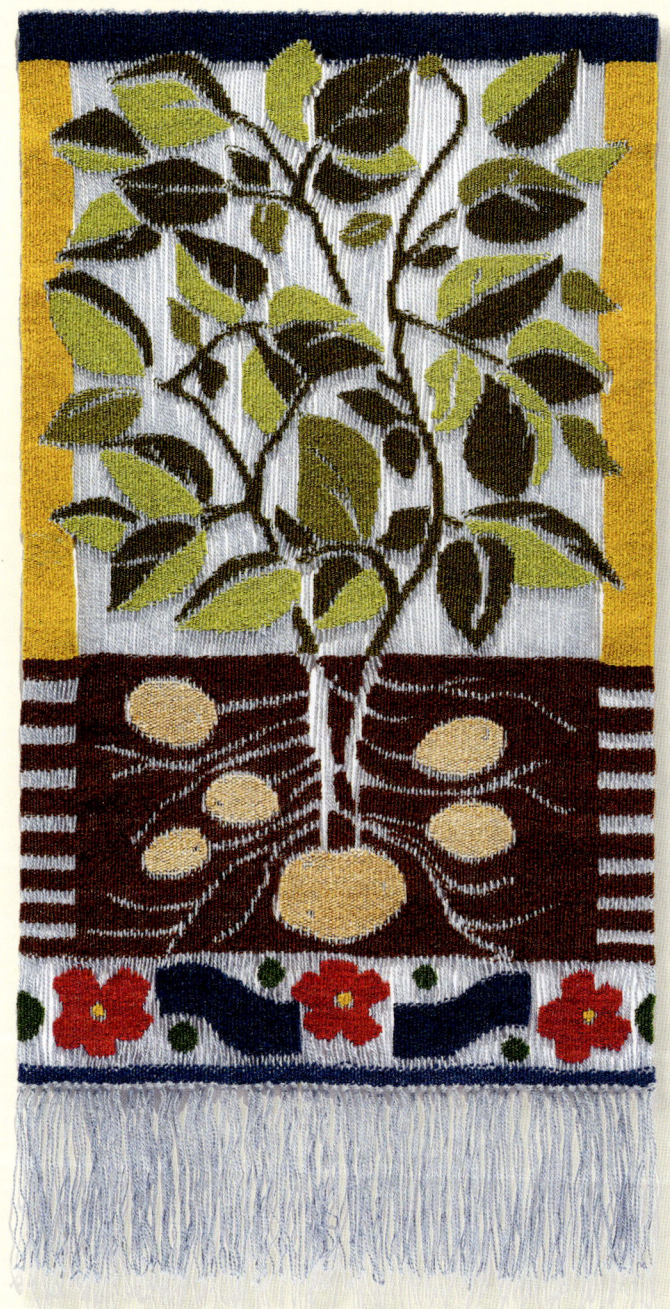

Robbie LaFleur is a farmer's daughter. Yggdrasil, the tree of life in Norse mythology, is represented here as a potato plant. LaFleur's father and grandfather farmed potatoes in the Red River Valley, a fertile farming region extending through North Dakota and northern Minnesota. A particularly successful harvest in 1952 enabled LaFleur's father to build the family home.

LaFleur was inspired to make this work during a weaving fellowship in Stavanger, Norway, where she studied the open-warp technique of the famed weaver Frida Hansen. The space left between the warps (the vertical threads) gives a sense of transparency, conjuring the appearance of natural sunlight through the verdant leaves in the top half of the tapestry. In the bottom half, the light-colored warp threads delineate the potato root system. LaFleur also added a stylized row of prairie rose blossoms. "There are prize-winning potatoes at the Minnesota State Fair each year," she commented, "but generally not in the Creative Activities Building. This year, mine are."

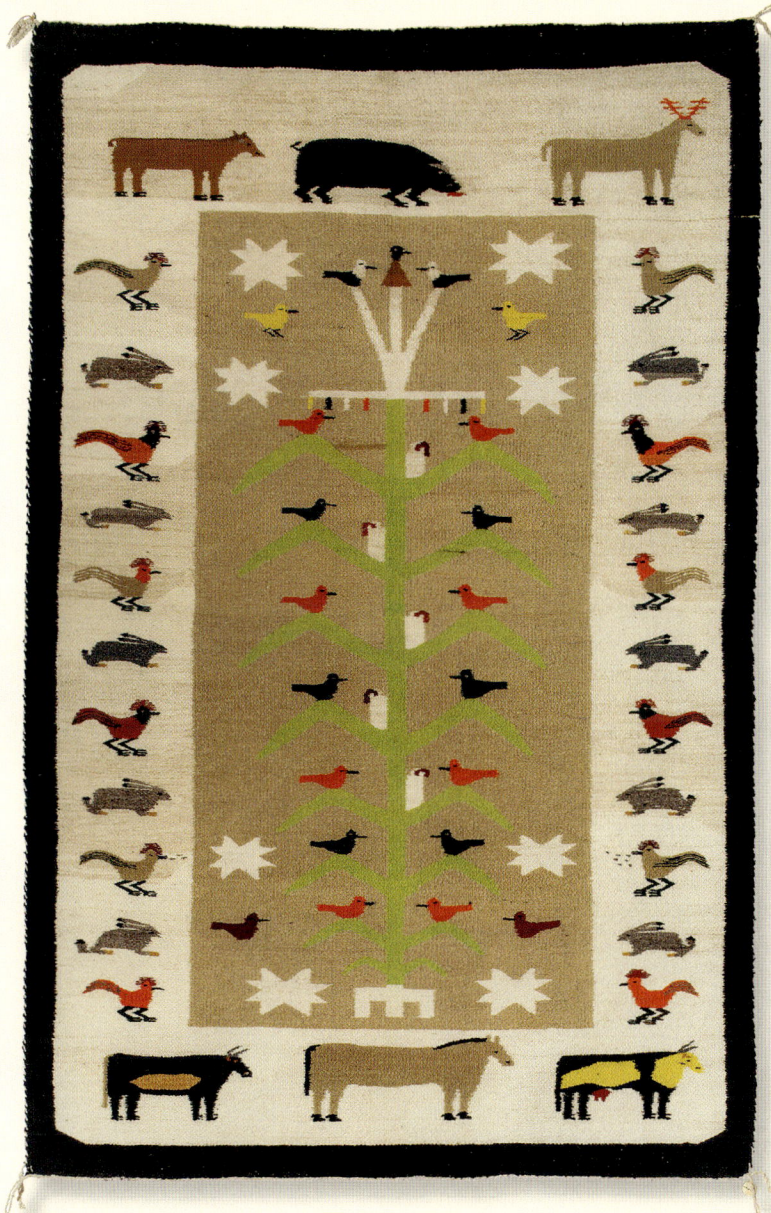

Alice Ray (Diné), *Tree of Life, 1962*

Wool, natural and aniline dyes, 84 × 54 in.

Alice Ray was a Diné (Navajo) weaver, farmer, and mother in Arizona. Her woven rug *Tree of Life* won second place at the 1963 Arizona State Fair. The weaving offers a window into her world. The tree is a motif that became popular in the Diné market in the late 1800s. At the center, a cornstalk rises from the earth, surrounded by birds and farm animals. The weaving symbolizes the connection of all beings. Using wool spun from sheep that she would have raised and sheared herself, Ray created textiles whose sale would support her family and the farm.

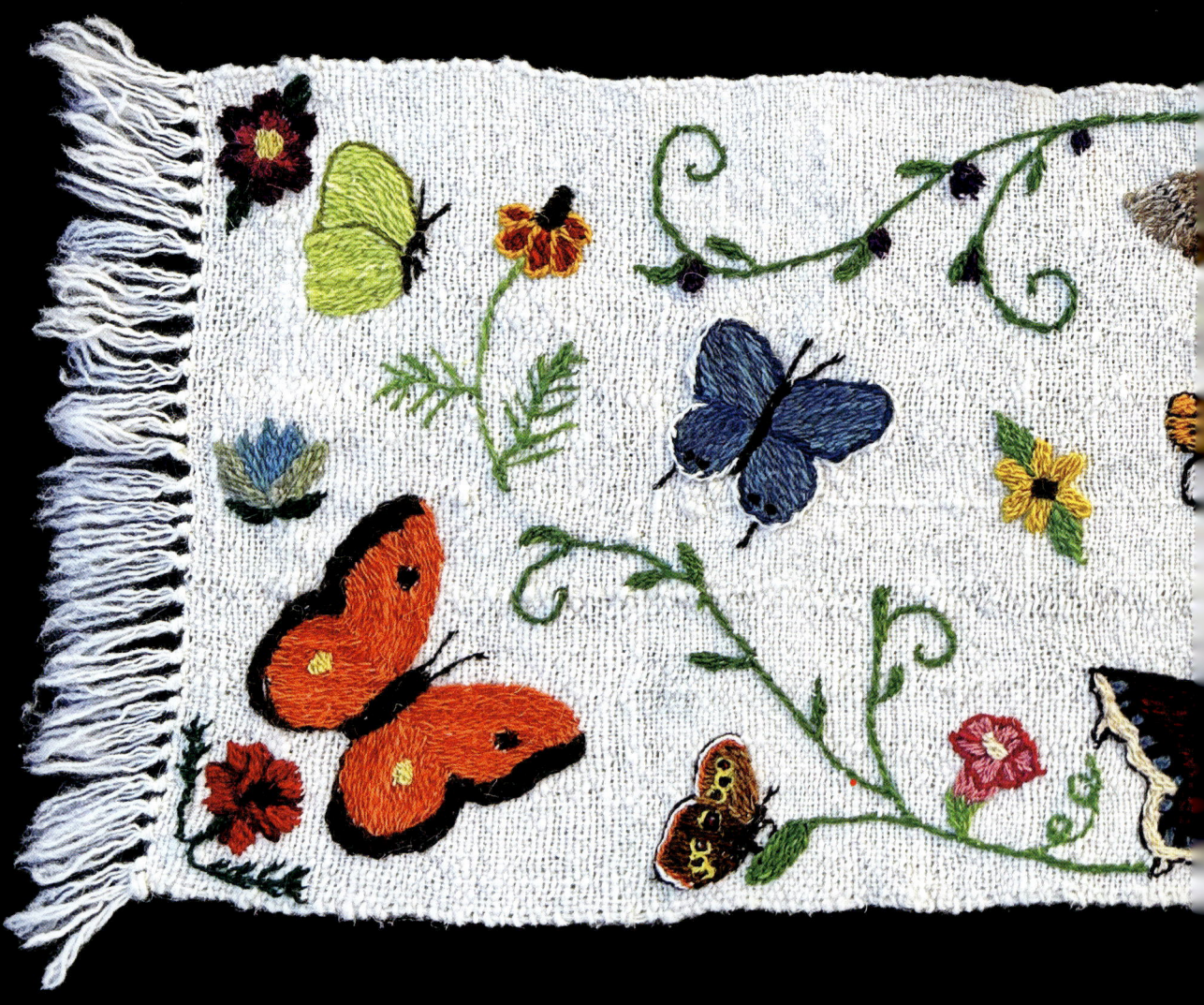

Julia Gomez, *Butterflies of New Mexico*, 2024

Colcha embroidery, wool, and natural dyes, 38 × 13⅛ in.

J ulia Gomez began practicing colcha, a traditional style of hand stitching used in the American Southwest, more than forty years ago. In addition to teaching classes and leading workshops on the technique, she has shown her work at the New Mexico State Fair and the Traditional Spanish Market in Santa Fe. In the eighteenth century, Spanish colonists used the efficient couching stitch that features in Gomez's work to repair utilitarian textiles such as blankets, known as *colchas*. They also imported to New Mexico the Churro sheep, whose thick, coarse wool gives colcha embroidery its distinctive texture.

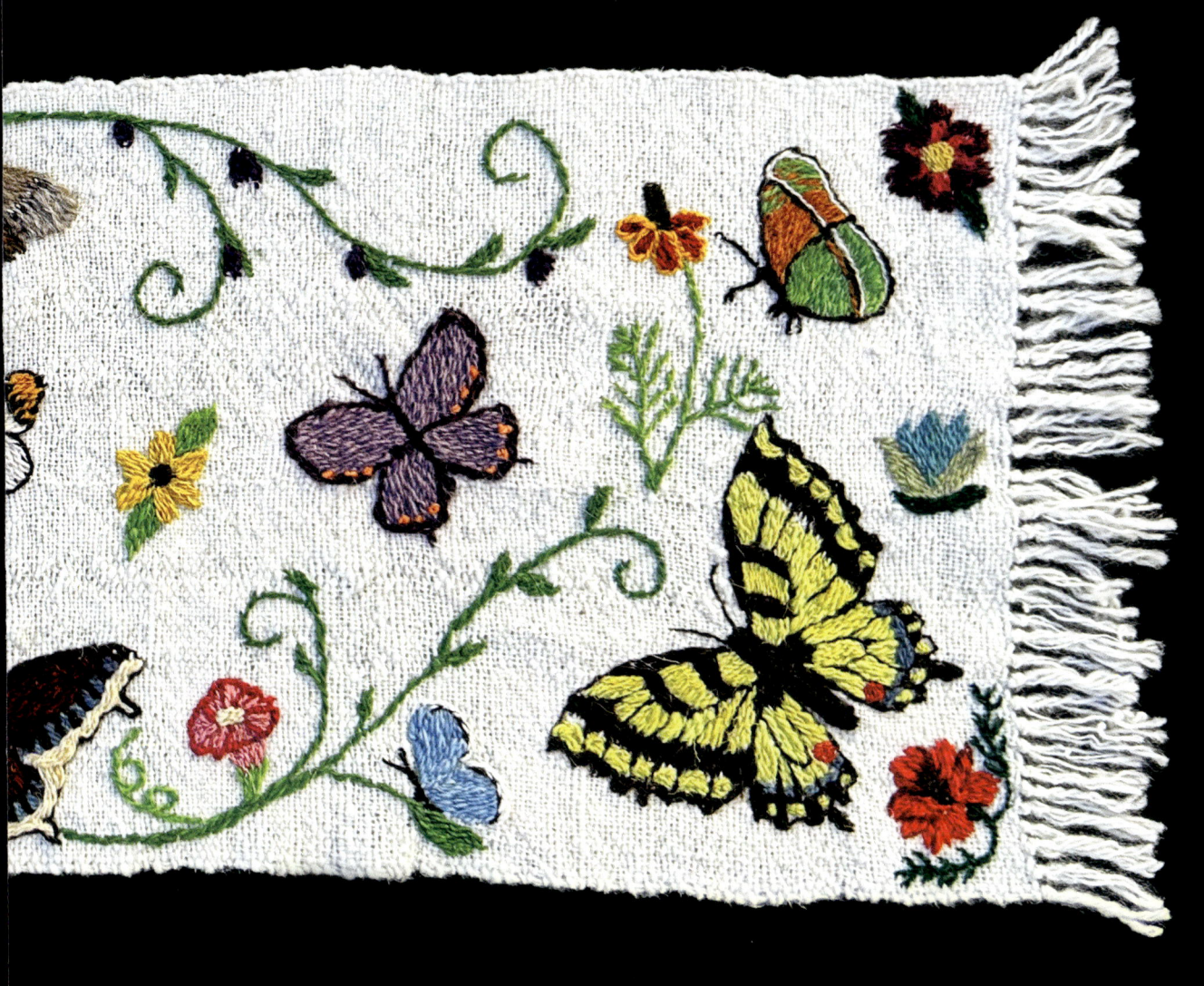

For *Butterflies of New Mexico*, Gomez drew on nineteenth-century entomological surveys to render local butterfly species in vivid color. In addition to shearing, carding, spinning, and weaving the wool used in the work, the artist prepared the natural dyes that give this piece its prismatic effect. The yellow of the large swallowtail butterfly at the lower right is derived from the cota herb, also known as Navajo tea, which Gomez harvested from her own garden. The diminutive white and orange butterfly that anchors the center of the textile, a Sara orangetip, carries special meaning for the artist, whose daughter shares a first name with the species. For Gomez, colcha is a way of connecting with both her personal history and that of the region. Through her demonstrations at fairs, it is also a means of sustaining a tradition into the future.

Carol St. Clair Johnson, *O Fair New Mexico—41 Fair Years*, 2023

Ribbons, 96 × 106½ in.

After unexpectedly winning her first blue ribbon in 1981, Carol Johnson developed an enduring love for the New Mexico State Fair. The quilt *O Fair New Mexico—41 Fair Years* incorporates more than six hundred of the ribbons that she won at the fair every subsequent year except 2020 (when the fair was canceled because of the COVID-19 pandemic). Johnson earned ribbons in several categories, including needlework, knitting, crochet, pies, cookies, cakes, canning, jewelry, flowers, vegetables, and potted plants. The title of the quilt is a reference to the state song, and the design places the state's Zia sun symbol at the center. The quilt earned Johnson yet another ribbon: "Best in the Miscellaneous Quilt Category" at the 2023 New Mexico State Fair.

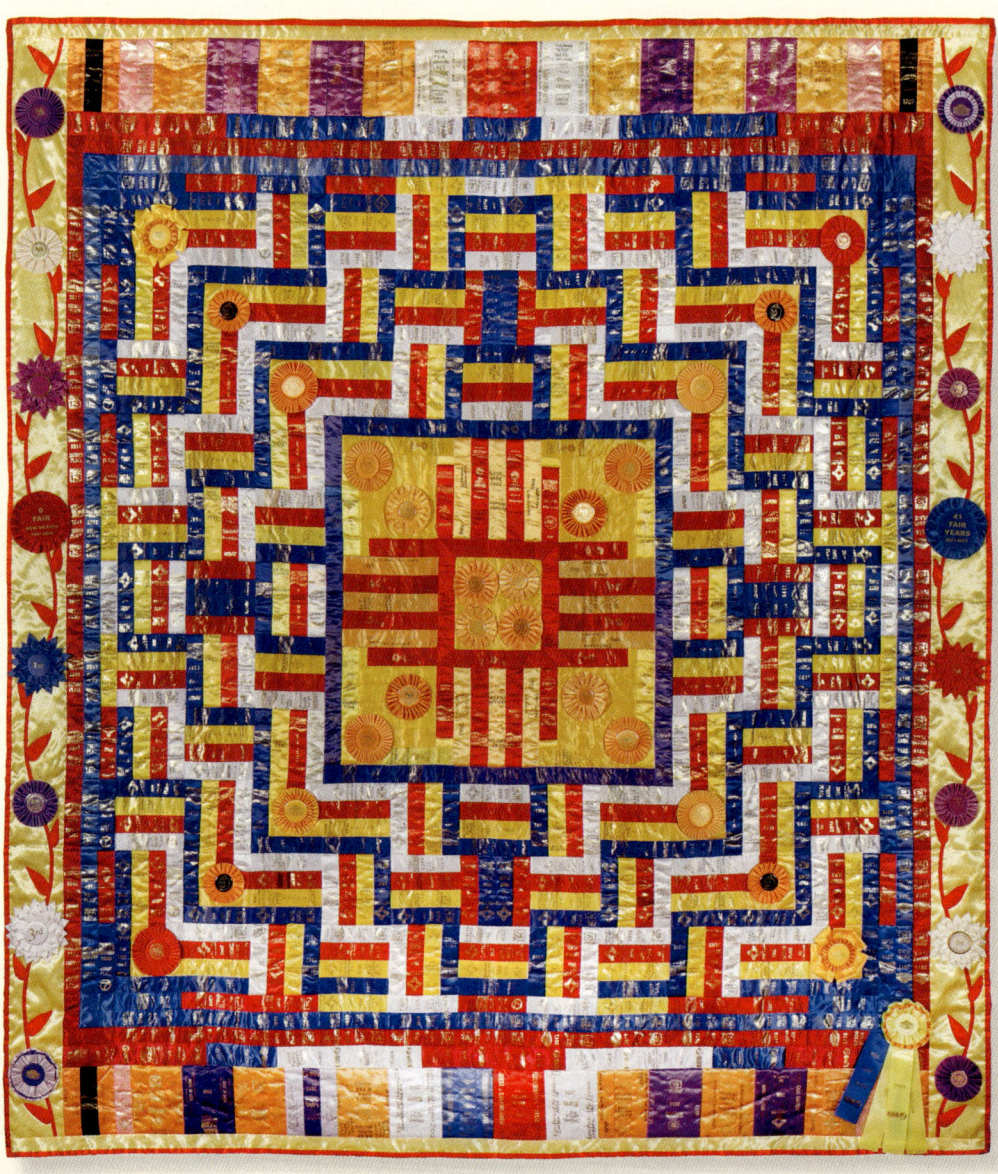

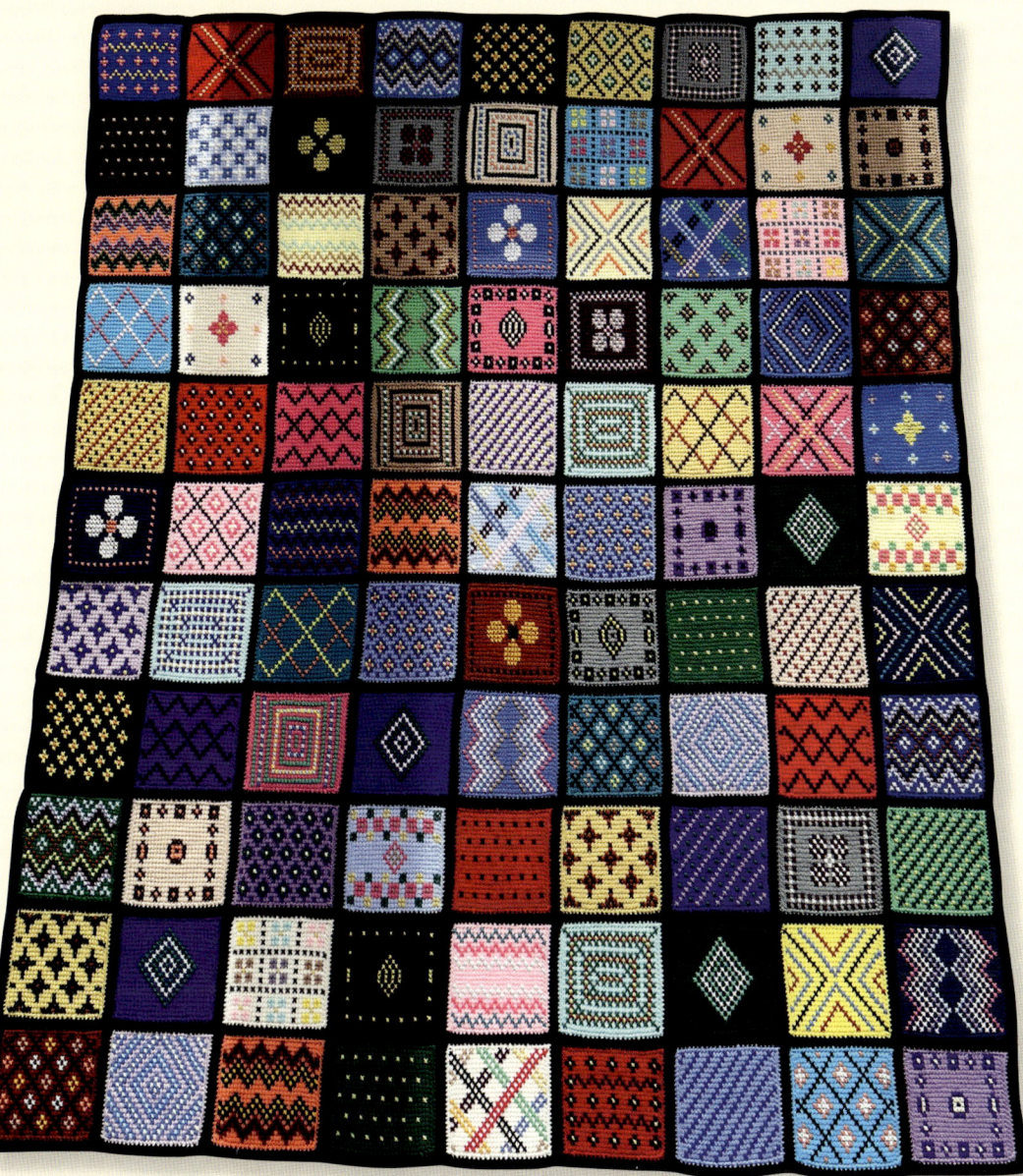

Ruth Ellen Klug, *Blue-Ribbon Afghan*, 2001

Yarn, 84 × 68 in.

T his colorful crocheted afghan won a rare perfect score from the needlepoint judge at the Minnesota State Fair, exceeding all the established criteria for workmanship, condition, design, and color. The judge simply remarked, "My *pleasure* to judge your afghan!"

Klug was surprised to win the highest "Sweepstakes Award" in the Afghan division at the fair because she had previously enjoyed more success at county fairs in southern Minnesota than at the State Fair. Klug first learned needlework from her mother. This afghan was made for her grandson, Weston, who, at 6 feet 4 inches, found her existing blankets to be too small.

Morgan Hill, *Smorgasbord*, 2024

Holly, resin, silk thread, paint, steel, sterling silver, 23 × 11 × 1¼ in.

The jewelry maker Morgan Hill finds inspiration in the small pleasures of daily life: campy horror films, '80s and '90s pop culture, and nostalgia for her childhood. She made this elaborate necklace in honor of her great-grandmother, Frankie, who won hundreds of ribbons for her crafts at the St. Francis County Fair in Eastern Arkansas and influenced Hill's artistic ambitions. The necklace was inspired by Templeton, the greedy rat in the 1973 animated movie *Charlotte's Web*. When Templeton visits the fair at night, he and Goose sing that a fair is "a veritable smorgasbord-orgasbord-orgasbord." Hill's arrangement of fairground finds reminds us that sometimes there is pleasure in excess.

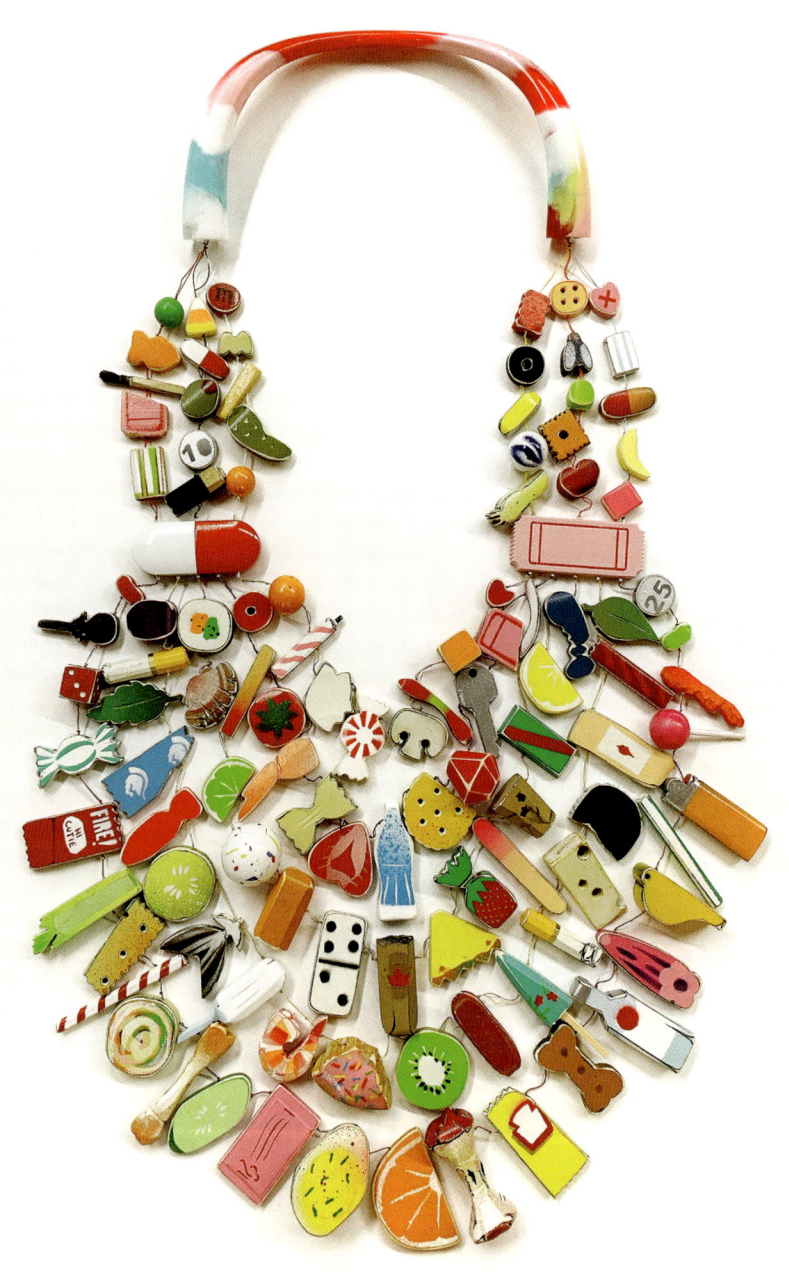

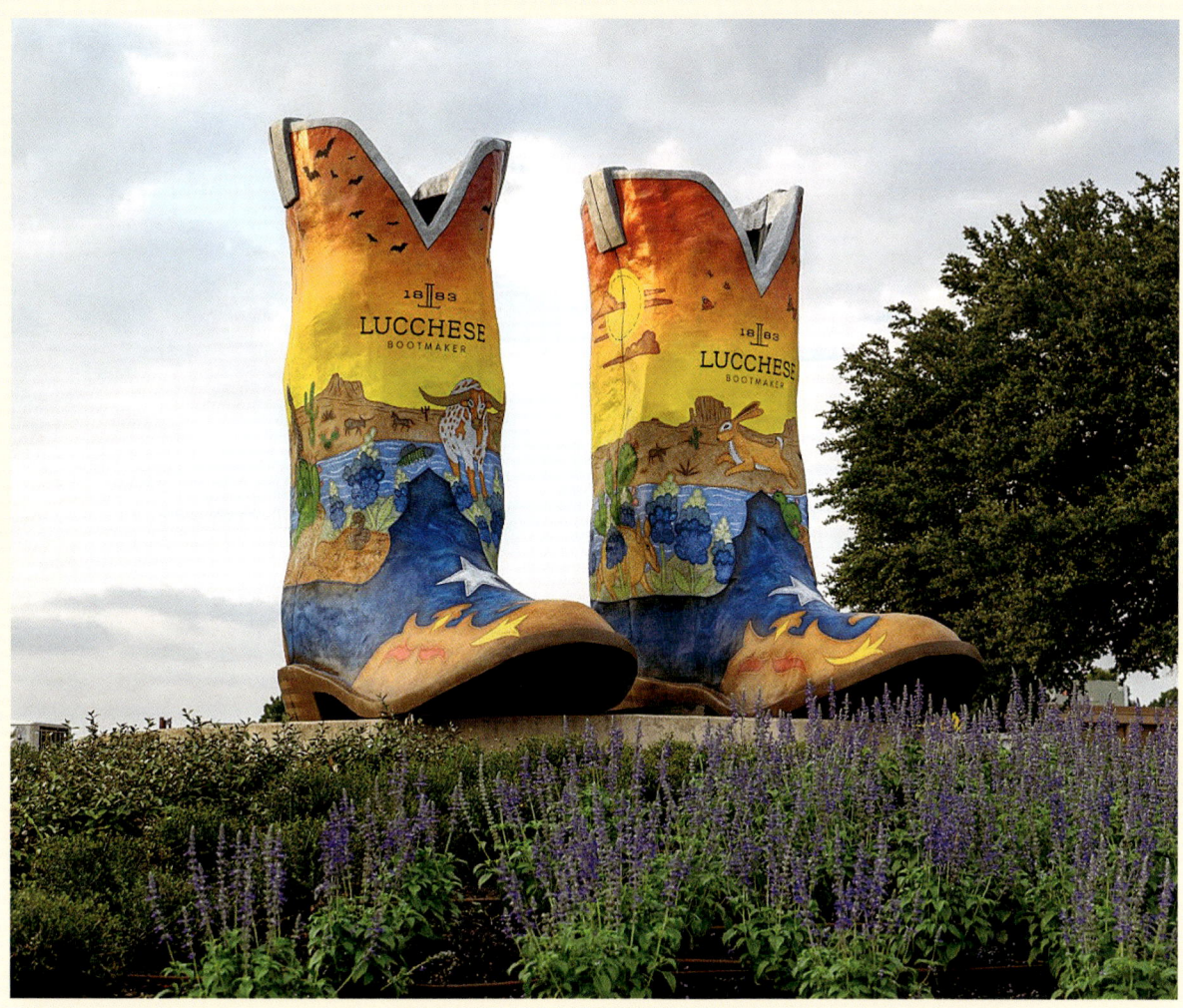

Jessica Bonilla, *Big Tex Boots*, 2023

Fiberglass, 144 in. high, weighing 400–500 lb. each.

Since 1952, Big Tex has presided over the State Fair of Texas in his size 96 boots. The original fiberglass boots were hand sculpted. In 2023 the fair partnered with Lucchese Bootmakers to sponsor a contest for a new Big Tex boot design. The winner, Jessica Bonilla of Irving, Texas, grew up attending the fair. Her design features a golden sunset illuminating the unique Texas landscape, reflecting her pride in the Lone Star State.

A Flourishing Field

Many professional artists participate in fair competitions to gain recognition and advancement. State fair art exhibitions offer public platforms for sharing works that express personal values, cultural traditions, and expansive definitions of craft.

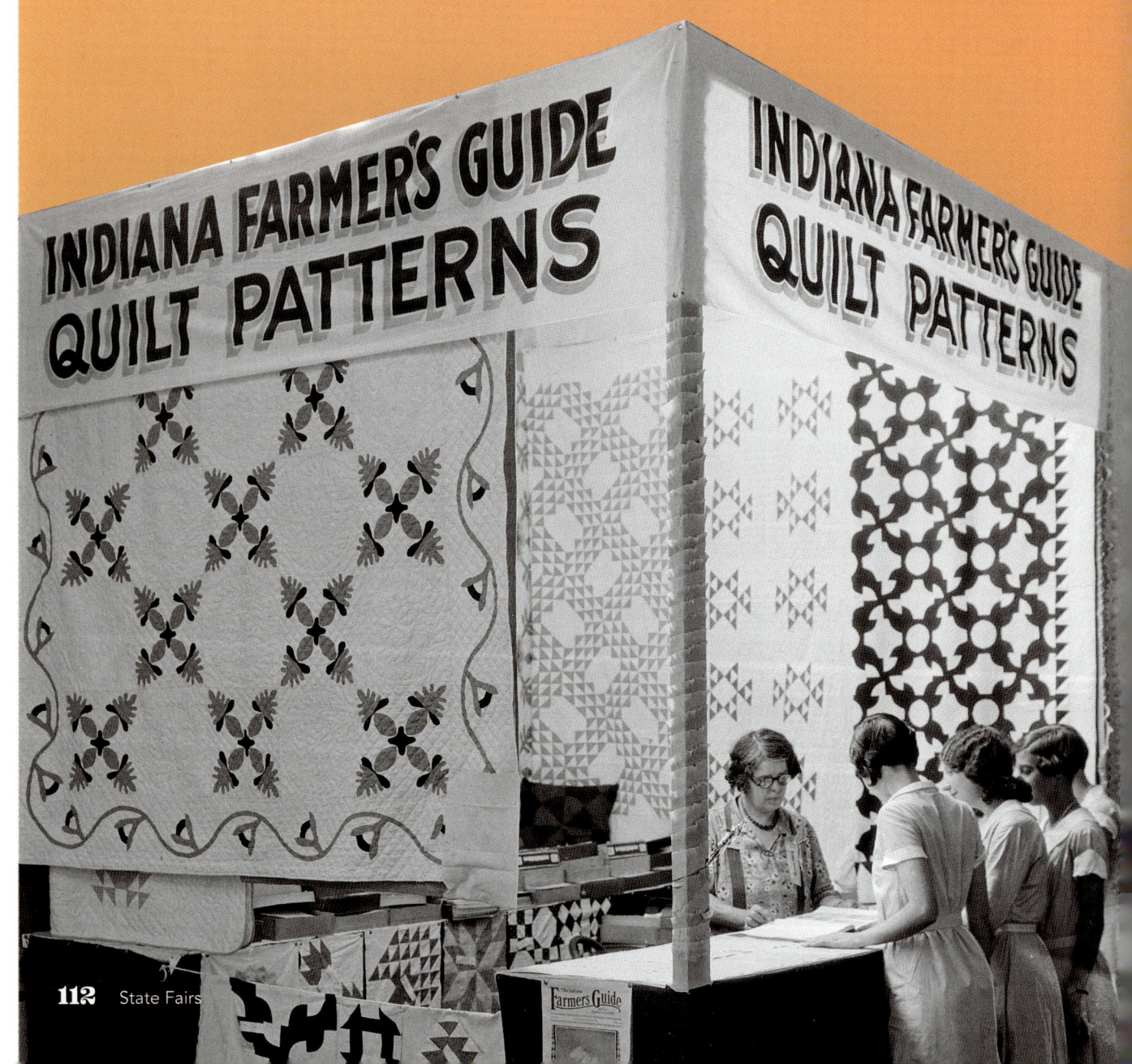

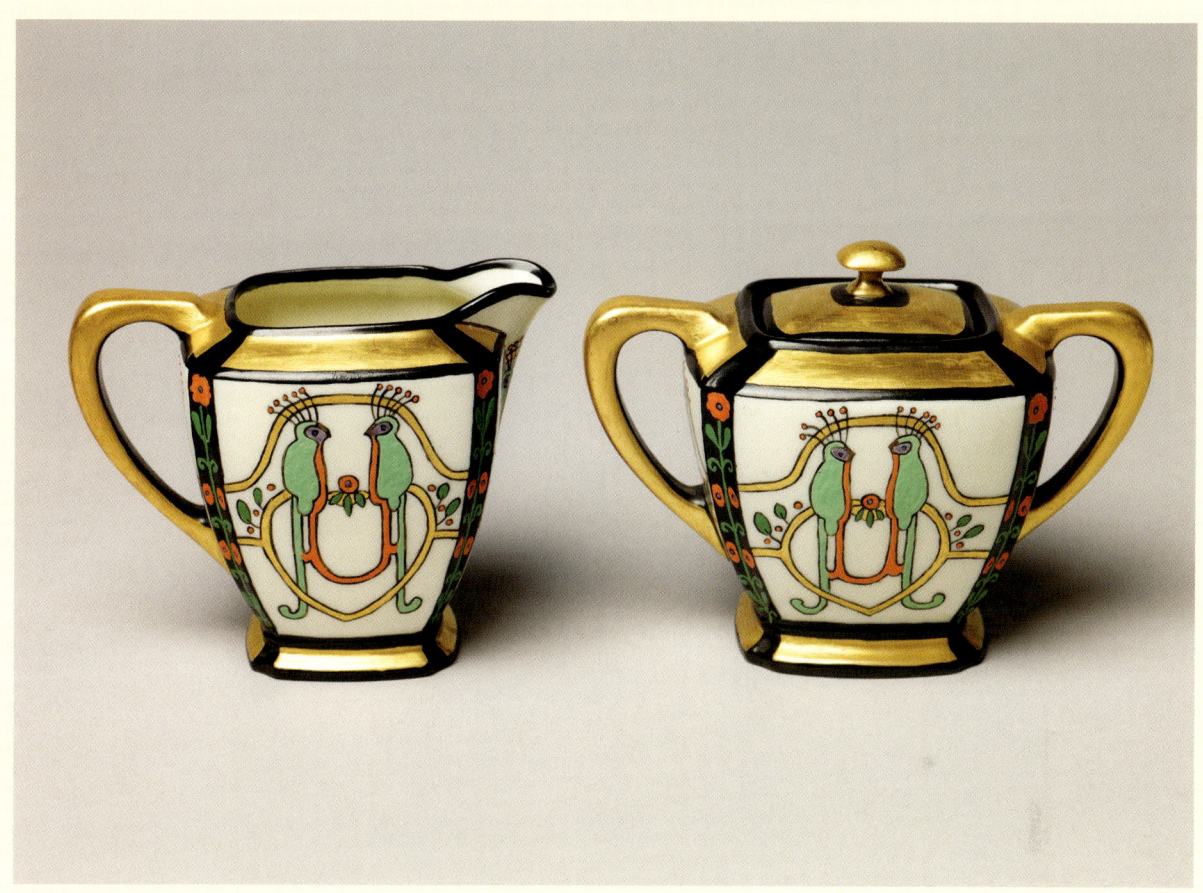

Gertrude M. Anderson Armantrout, *Sugar and Creamer,* 1906–26

Hand-painted porcelain. Creamer: 8¾ × 7 × 12 in. Sugar bowl: 10 × 14¾ × 8¼ in.

Among the porcelain painters of the early-twentieth-century Arts and Crafts movement was Gertrude Anderson Armantrout of Topeka, Kansas. She was one of a generation of women artists whose imaginative designs met an increasing demand for decorative and functional objects. Armantrout won numerous awards from the Kansas State Fair throughout her career. The *Topeka Daily State Journal* praised her sweep of sixteen prizes in nineteen categories at the 1915 Kansas State Fair, though it also noted that criticism had been voiced because Armantrout had received awards at the Oklahoma State Fair as well. Armantrout's career survived the controversy, but porcelain painting fell into relative obscurity, dismissed as a "female domestic craft." This sweet sugar and creamer set exemplifies Armantrout's vibrant approach to color and form. Stylized lime-green cockatoos animate the surfaces, embellished by a border of red flowers on stripes of black.

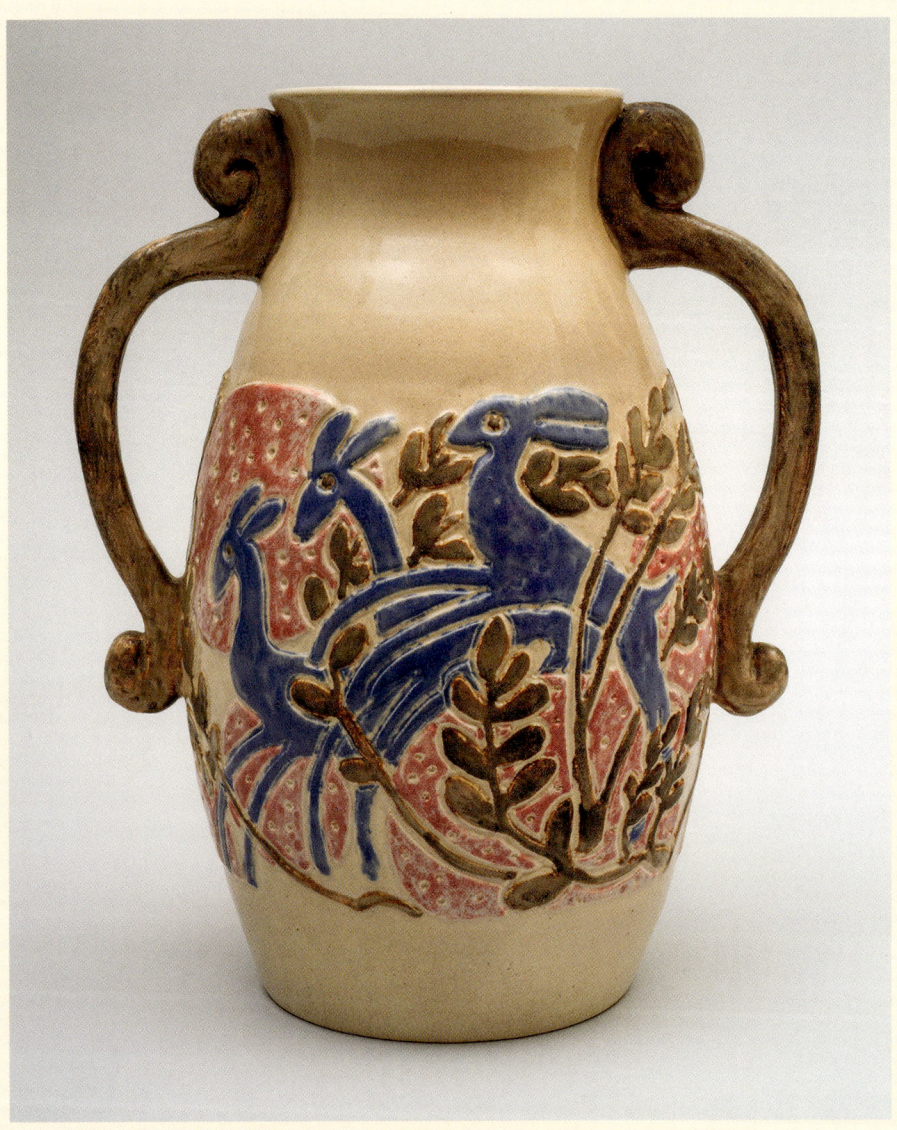

Mary Frances Overbeck, Vase with deer (untitled), ca. 1939

Glazed earthenware, 12 in. high.

The sisters Margaret, Hannah, Elizabeth, and Mary Frances Overbeck established a pottery studio in the small town of Cambridge City, Indiana, in 1911. Although women were often encouraged to paint ready-made porcelain objects rather than create their own, the Overbeck sisters oversaw all aspects of production, including throwing and firing ceramics.

By the 1920s they had earned numerous accolades for their designs. "For a number of years we have taken practically all the first and second premiums for pottery in the applied arts section at the Indiana State Fair," wrote Elizabeth in 1936, shortly before her death. Mary Frances, the last surviving sister, continued to manage the business and to win ribbons at the Indiana State Fair. This vase features one of her signature organic motifs—deer leaping through foliage—and a robin's-egg-blue glaze.

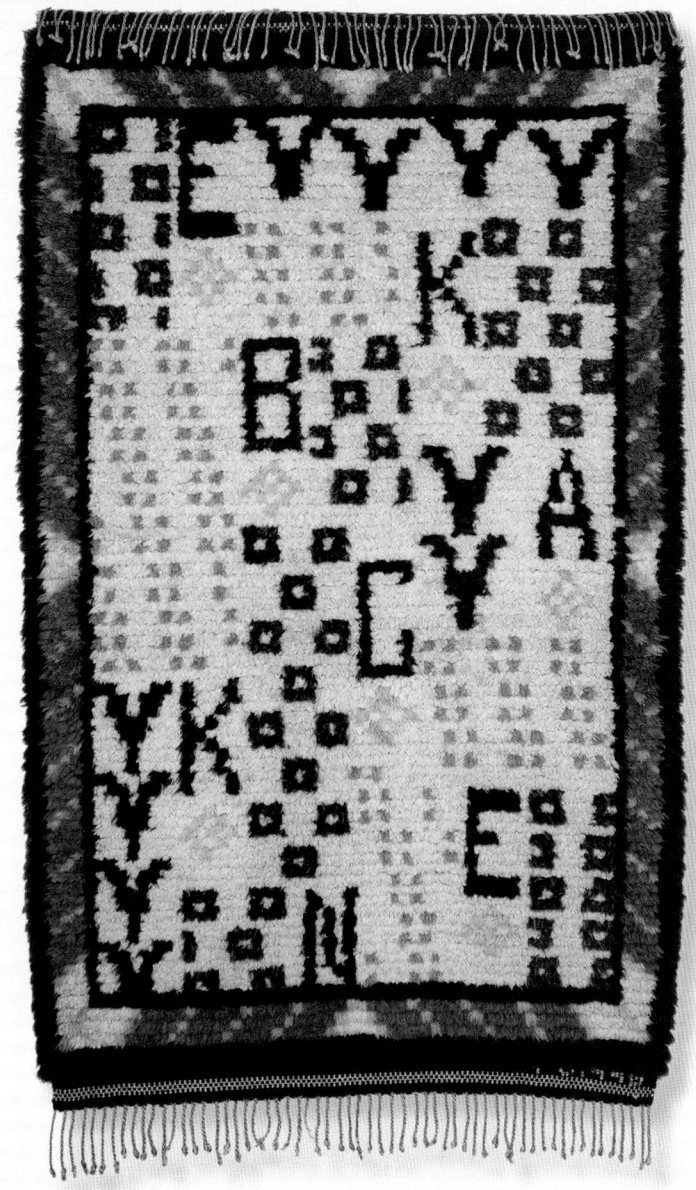

Valborg "Mama" Gravander, Ekbacken Spring, 1948

Wool, linen, 67 × 38 in.

In the 1920s, Axel and Valborg "Mama" Gravander emigrated from Sweden to San Francisco, California, where Valborg began teaching traditional weaving techniques. In the early 1940s, they moved to Mill Valley in nearby Marin County and built a weaving school, Ekbacken (Swedish for "oak hill"). The Gravanders became known for their commitment to Swedish customs: Ekbacken emulated folk architecture, and Valborg wore long peasant skirts and Swedish blouses at her loom.

Both Valborg and Axel competed in the California State Fair as early as 1948 and off and on through the 1950s. Their participation likely helped them attract new students.

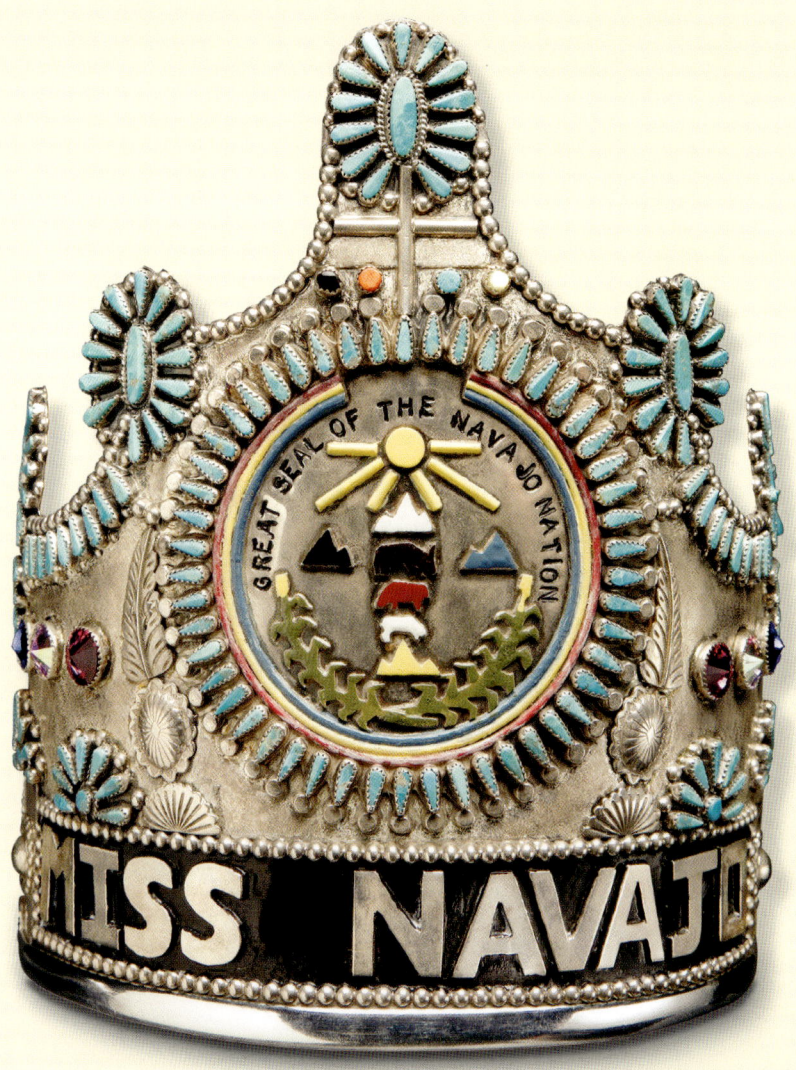

Tommy Lowe (Diné), *Miss Navajo Nation Crown* (2016–2021), 2016

Sterling silver and turquoise, 6¾ × 7¼ × 7½ in.

Every year a Diné (Navajo) woman is crowned Miss Navajo Nation at the pageant of the Navajo Nation Fair in Window Rock, Arizona. Beulah Melvin Allen was crowned the first Miss Navajo Nation in 1952. The pageant requires contestants to demonstrate their knowledge of Navajo skills and traditions such as sheep butchering, fluency in the Navajo language, food preparation, and wool spinning. They also give presentations on history and dress. The winner is seen as a representative of the Navajo Nation and as a role model for young women.

From 2016 to 2021, the reigning Miss Navajo Nation wore this crown, made of sterling silver embellished with turquoise (a sacred stone in Navajo culture, with powers of health and protection). Five winners proudly wore this crown, crafted by the renowned Diné jeweler, Tommy Lowe.

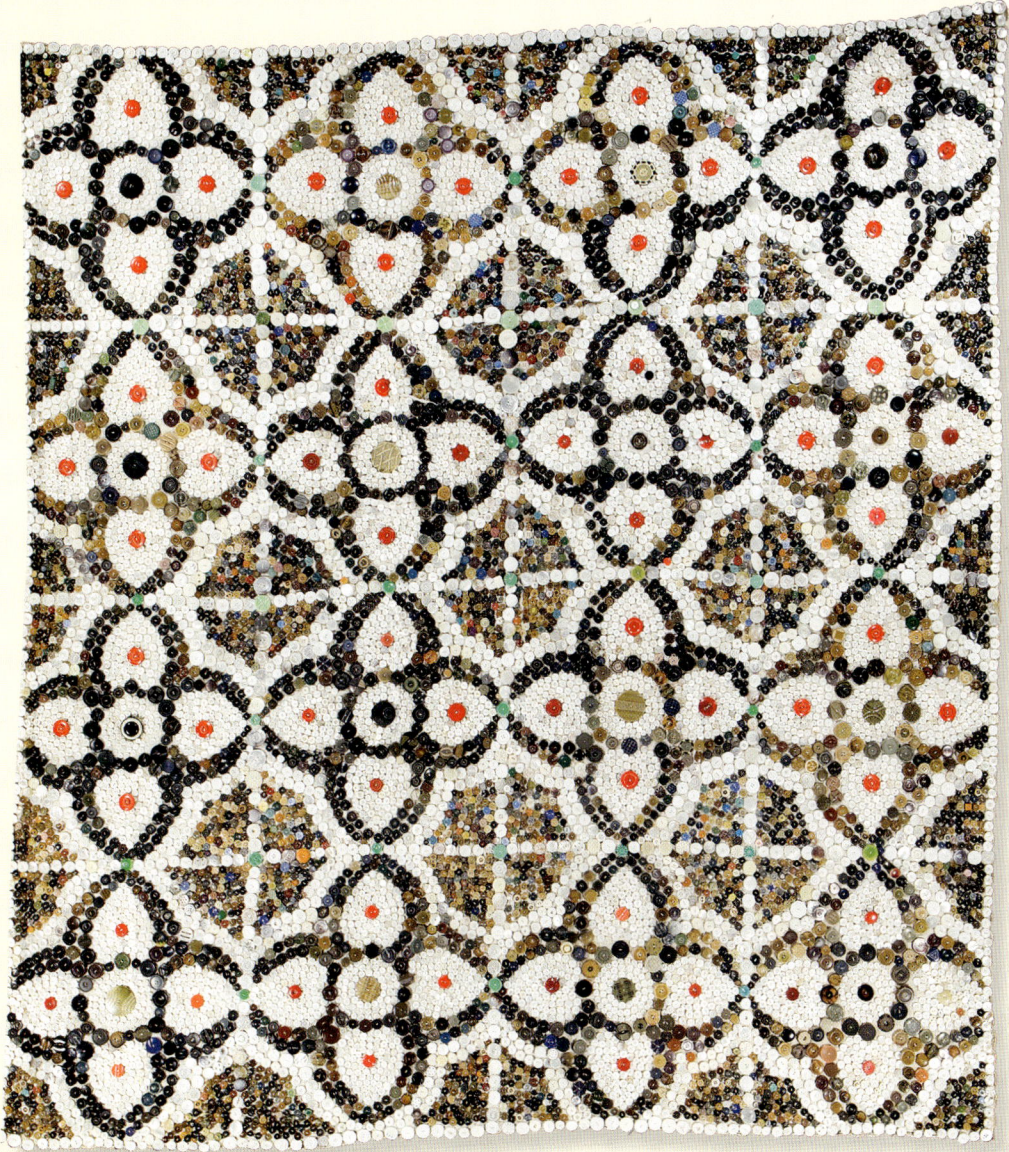

Mary Elizabeth Shelby, *Friendship Quilt*, 1940

Cotton, buttons, 87 × 79 in.

As a child, Mary Elizabeth Shelby loved playing with her mother's button box. Later she assembled her own button collection for various creative pursuits, including picture collages and mosaics. Her *Friendship Quilt* was her most ambitious work. Comprising 11,923 buttons, it weighs approximately sixty pounds. Shelby sewed the buttons onto a tablecloth following a friendship quilt pattern published in the *Kansas City Star* in 1938. The piece highlights the diversity of materials and colors used to make buttons, including celluloids, tagua, and plastics, as well as shimmering pearl, seashell, and abalone. The quilt placed fourth in a novelty quilt contest at the 1938 Missouri State Fair.

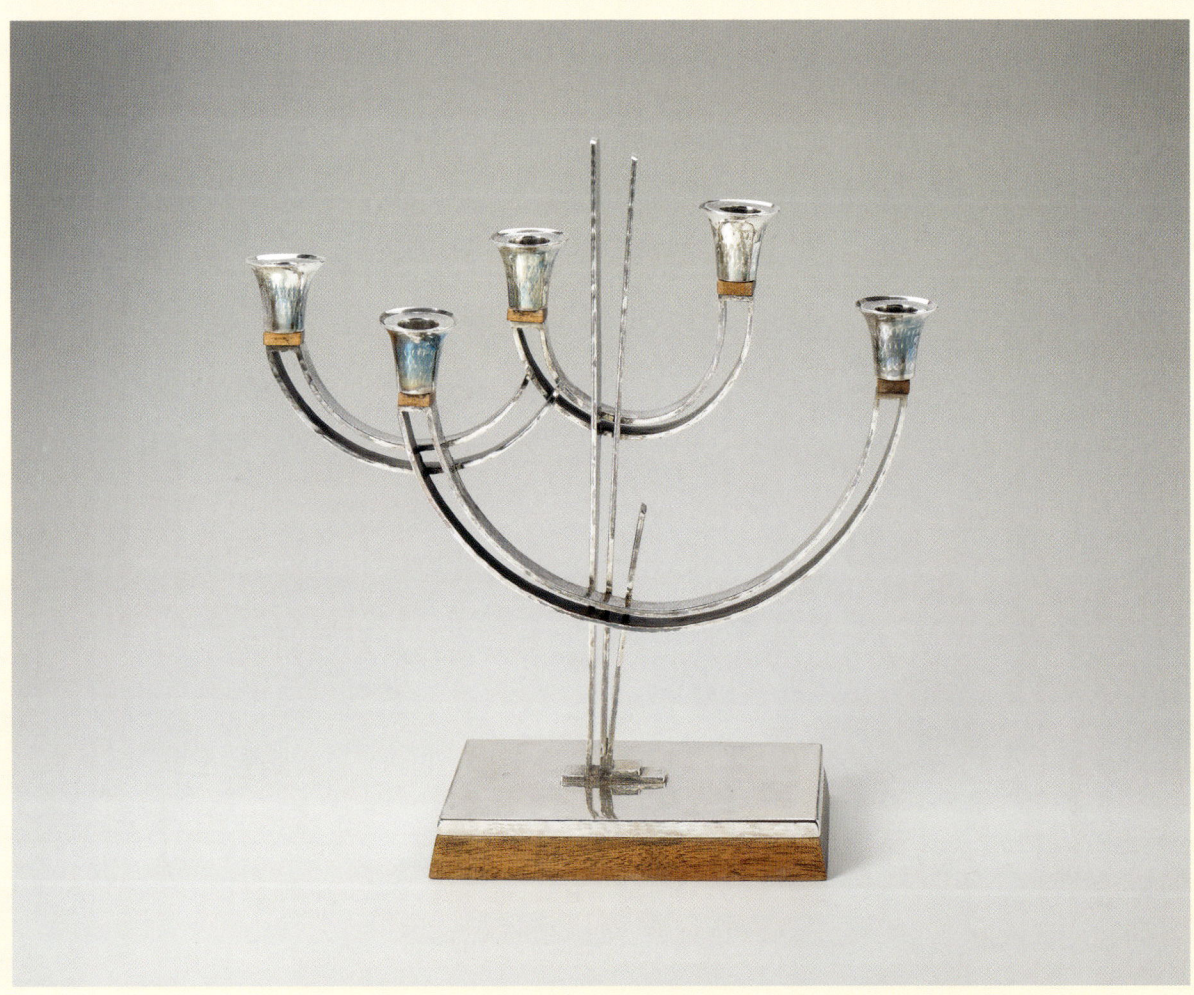

Victor Ries, Candelabra, ca. 1957

Sterling silver, wood base, 14 × 14⅛ in.

Victor Ries was a modernist metalsmith and educator. Forced to flee Nazi Germany in 1933, the young Jewish artist eventually settled in the United States in 1948. He first taught at the Pond Farm artist colony in Guerneville, California, and went on to teach metalsmithing at the California College of Arts and Crafts in Oakland. Ries crafted jewelry, housewares—like this sterling silver candelabra—and liturgical objects for churches and synagogues. Along with many other faculty and students at the California College of Arts and Crafts, Ries competed at the California State Fair, bringing home ribbons every year from 1948 to 1952.

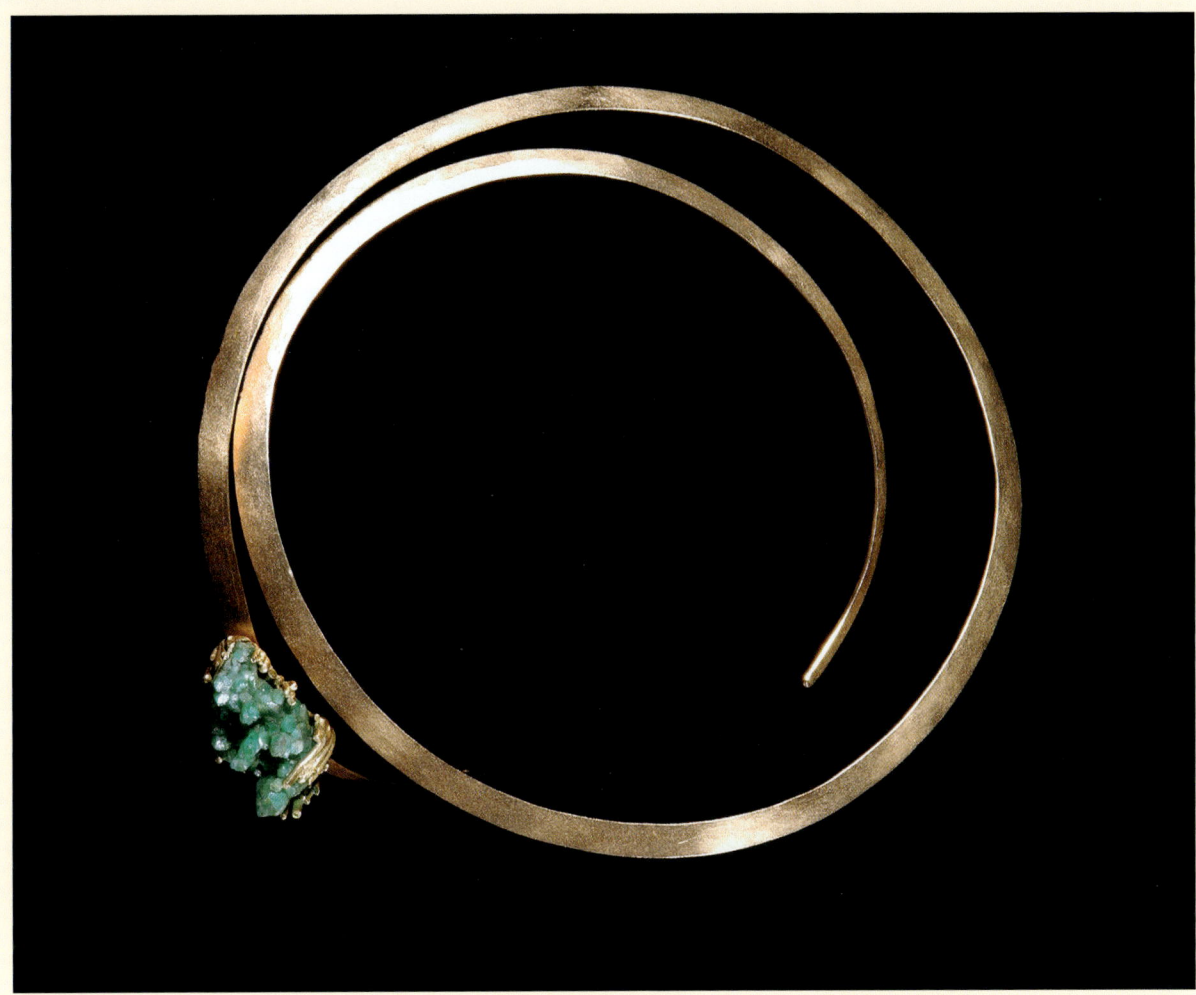

Irena Brynner, *Necklace*, ca. 1965

Forged gold with natural emerald crystal, 6¾ × 5⅝ × 3½ in.

Irena Brynner was a modernist jewelry designer in the Bay Area. Trained as a painter, she approached jewelry as small-scale sculpture activated by the body. She was instrumental in forming the Metal Arts Guild in San Francisco. The guild set up a booth at the California State Fair in the 1950s. They protested proposed artist entry fees at the 1955 fair, seeking to keep the art competition accessible to all artists.

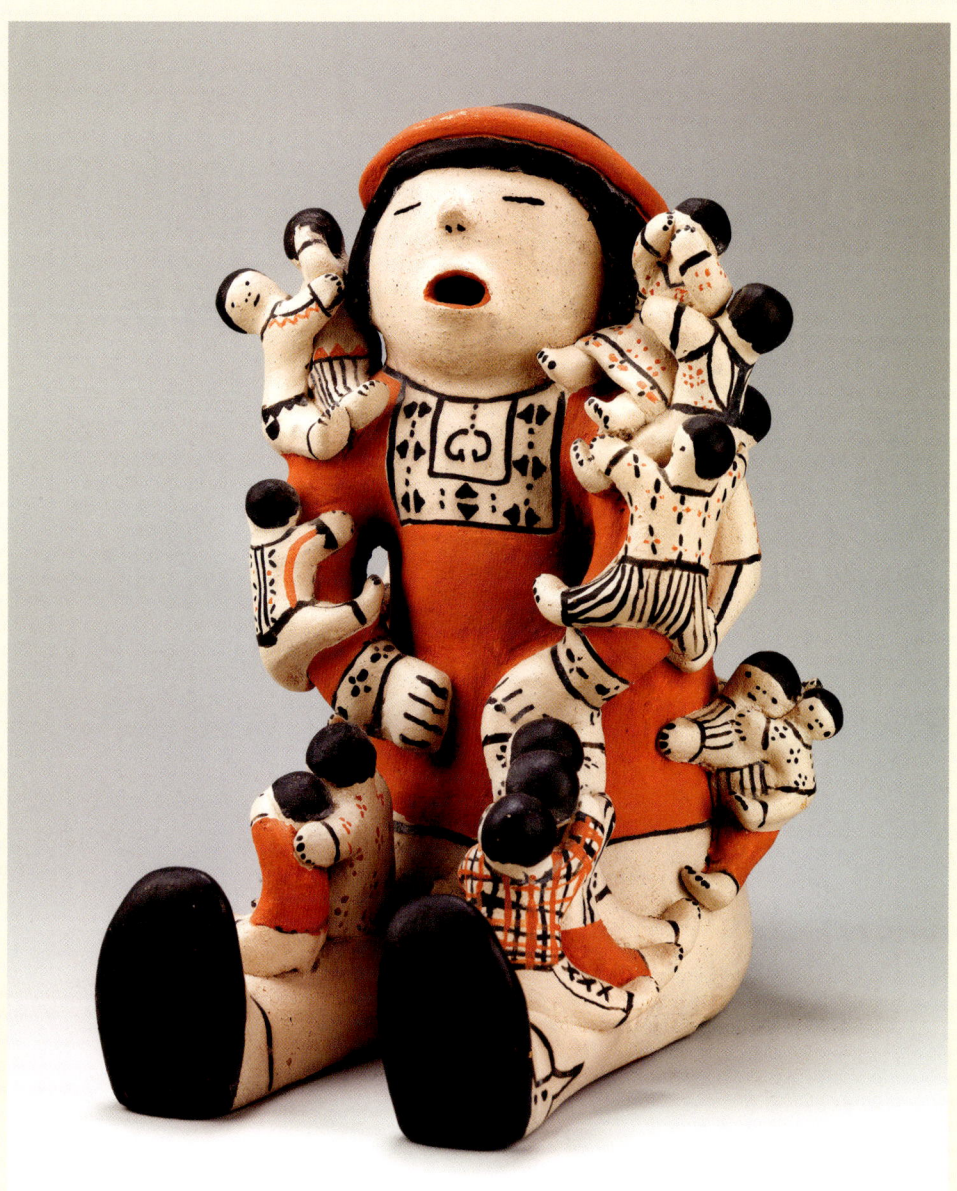

Helen Cordero, *Storyteller with Twenty Figures*, ca. 1985

Fired clay with slip and beeweed, 11⅛ × 7⅞ × 11 in.

Helen Cordero, a potter from Cochiti Pueblo, New Mexico, was best known for her clay "story-tellers," depictions of a male figure singing to a group of enraptured children. Thinking of her grandfather, a Cochiti storyteller, and the Singing Mother motif from traditional Pueblo pottery, she made the first storyteller figurines in 1964 and won first-, second-, and third-place ribbons for them at the New Mexico State Fair that year. She continued sculpting similar but distinct pieces over the next several decades and has inspired other Pueblo potters to create variations on her charismatic concept.

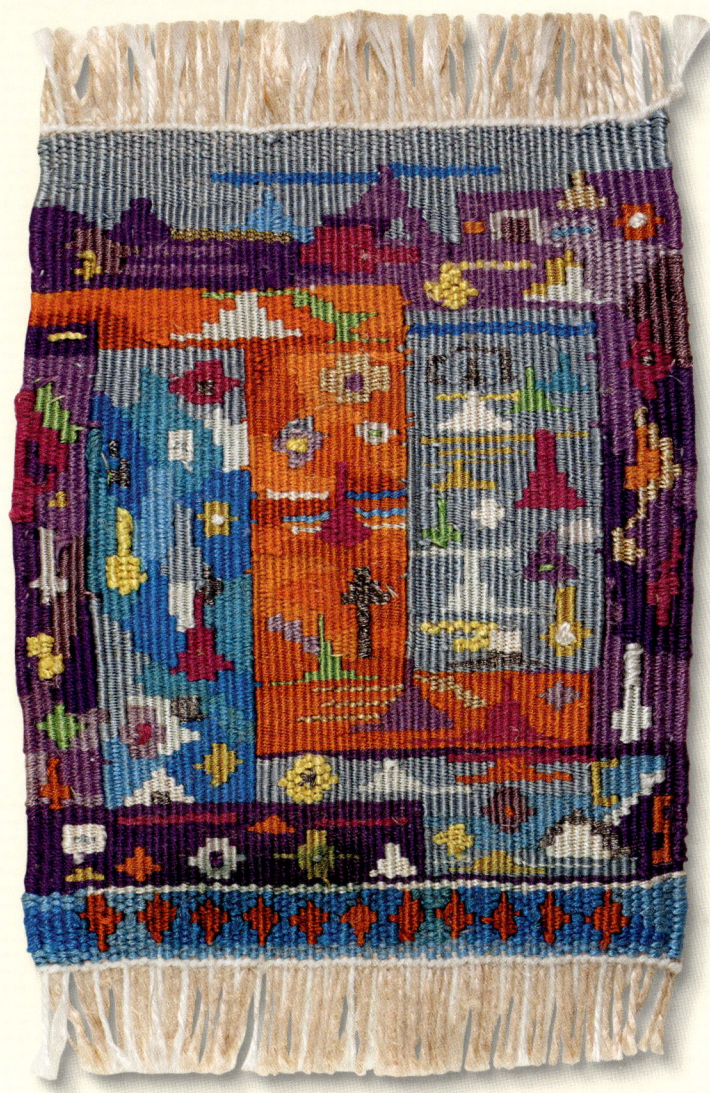

Consuelo Jimenez Underwood, *Me, Sleeping*, 1980

Frame loom tapestry, linen, cotton, and metallic threads, 5 × 3 in.

The renowned weaver Consuelo Jimenez Underwood was raised by agricultural field workers in California and spent her childhood working alongside them. They introduced her to sewing and encouraged her to dream big. She was the first in her family to earn a high school diploma. In the early 1980s, she started a master's program in weaving at San Diego State University.

Her first assignment in her weaving class was to design a miniature Persian rug. In this small tapestry—the size of an index card—Consuelo wove and embroidered abstractions from her dreams. Underwood recalls: "I seized the opportunity to express my subconscious dream worlds with threads. I brought together the expressive embroidery into the new formal structure of the loom. To this day, when challenged by a formal decision in the studio, I refer to my embroidery 'lens.' It works!" Underwood entered *Me, Sleeping* in the 1980 California State Fair, where it earned an honorable mention and validated the young artist's dreams.

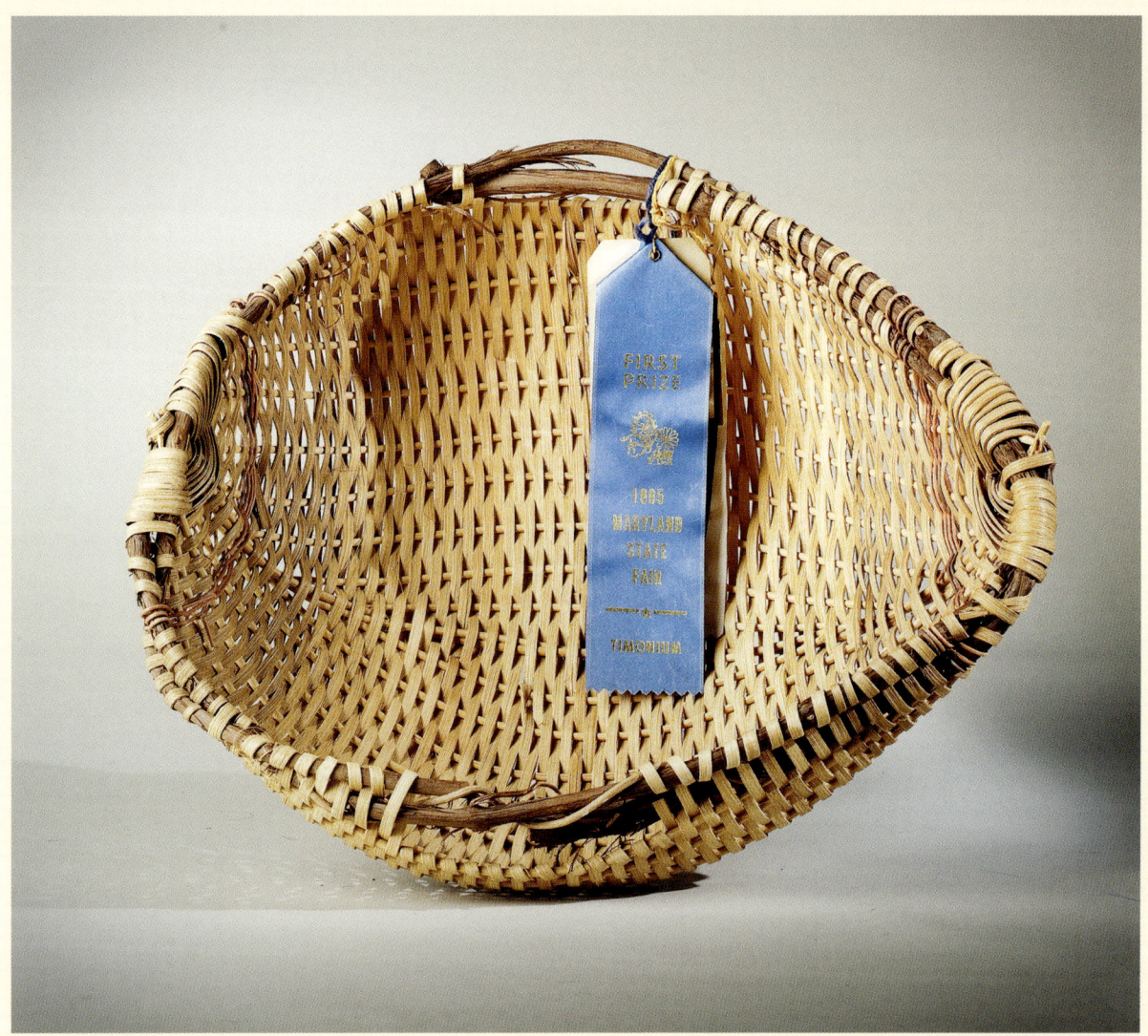

Ira Blount, *Melon-Shaped Basket with Side Handles,* 1995

Wood splint, reed, twigs, 7½ × 18⅜ × 16¼ in.

Basketry was just one of fifteen different crafts that the self-taught artist Ira Blount explored during his lifetime. Blount was born in Memphis, Tennessee, and attended Tuskegee Institute (now Tuskegee University) for two years, until he was drafted into the US Army in 1941. He moved to Washington, DC, in 1950, and began teaching himself numerous crafts. Blount shared his prolific skills in quilting, woodwork, and basketry with his community in Washington, DC, inspiring others—particularly senior citizens—to "create, to challenge themselves."

This basket won first prize at the Maryland State Fair in 1995, introducing Blount's work to a wider audience.

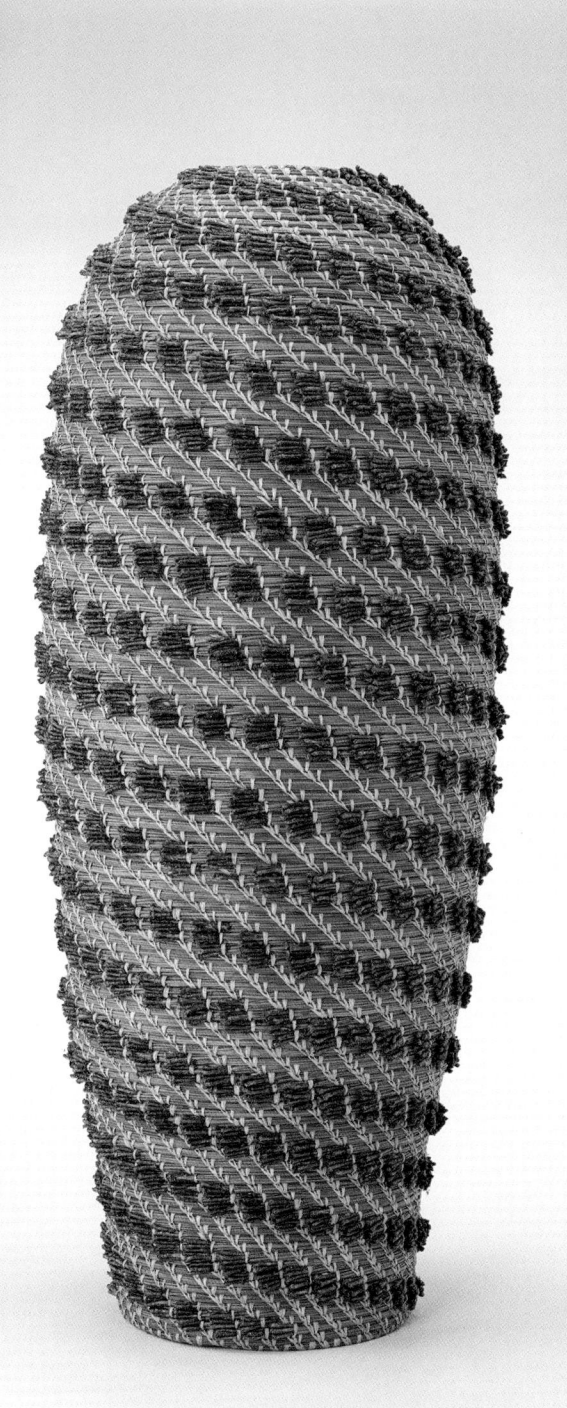

Lee Sipe, *Vessel No. 27*, 1990

Pine needles and raffia,
32 × 13 × 13 in.

Lee Sipe has entered her inventive woven vessels and sculptures into the Professional Division of the South Carolina State Fair Fine Arts Juried Exhibition for several years. She found her way to basketmaking through a course on pine-needle basketry, a thriving tradition in South Carolina.

Sipe combines the pine needles gathered from her yard in Columbia, South Carolina, with raffia stitchwork to create intricate, gestural patterns. Born in Korea, she also draws on her knowledge of Korean ceramics to mimic the shape of large functional storage jars but with unconvential materials. Over the years she has received the "Best in Show" and "Top Purchase Award" at the fair. Of her work, she says, "The thrill of creating unique pieces energizes me. Each new piece gives me ideas for additional new creations."

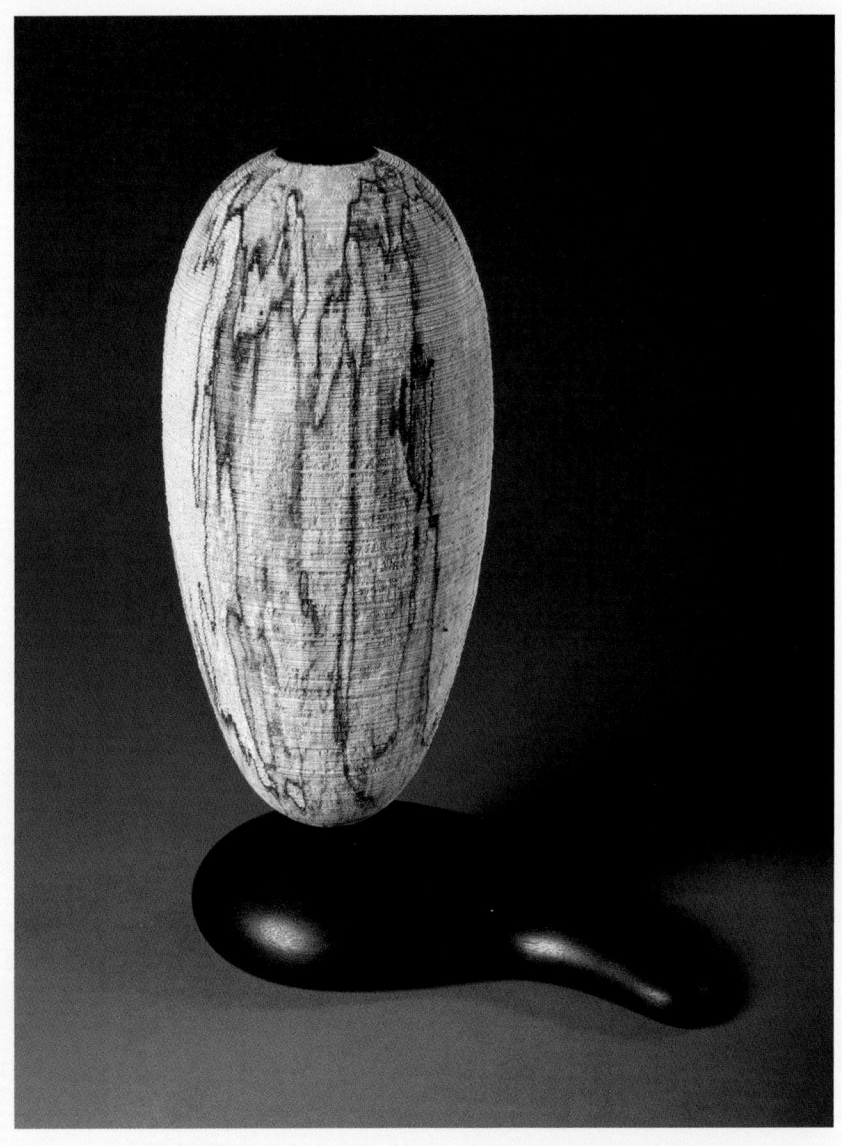

Betty Scarpino, *Not a Hollow Vessel: Full of Herself*, 2018

Spalted maple, 10 × 7 × 4½ in.

Woodturning and carving have long been staple categories of craft displays at state fairs. Betty Scarpino participated in her first state fair in 2023 and took home the blue ribbon in the woodturning division at the Indiana State Fair. Scarpino is nationally recognized for her skillful and metaphorical sculptures in wood. With *Not a Hollow Vessel*, she turned a piece of spalted maple into a simple but subversive form. The title is a play on a much more common form, a hollow vessel. Scarpino's works draw uneasy comparison to designations of the female body as a hollow vessel and the fact that woodturning is still largely dominated by men. Scarpino turns this metaphor around, centering her own feminist politics.

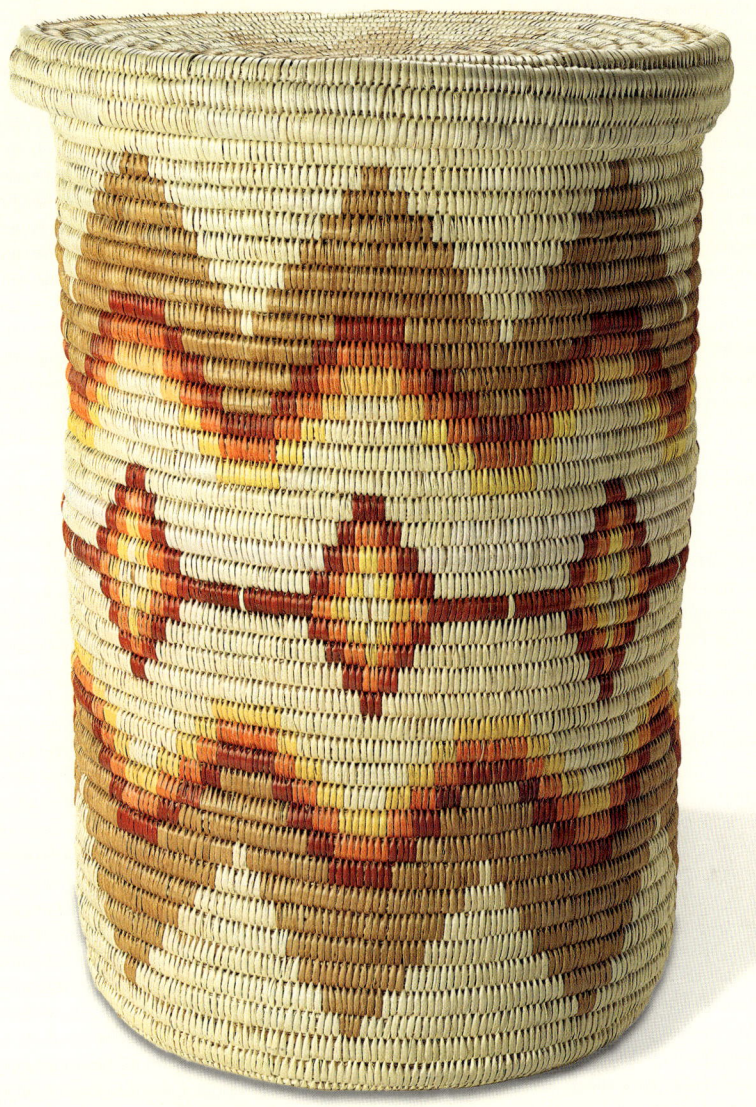

Rowena Mora (Jicarilla Apache), Jicarilla Apache storage basket with lid, 2019

Sumac, willow, basket: 19½ × 13½ in. diameter; lid: 1¼ × 15 in. diameter

Rowena Mora (Jicarilla Apache) lives on the Jicarilla Apache Nation Reservation in northern New Mexico, near the Colorado border. Jicarilla Apache artists have long sold pottery and basketry at state fairs in New Mexico, Arizona, and Colorado. Mora is a renowned weaver and educator who passes traditional knowledge on to younger generations. This elegant basket, featuring one of Mora's signature bold patterns, won "Best in Show" at the 2019 New Mexico State Fair in the Native American Indian Arts Gallery.

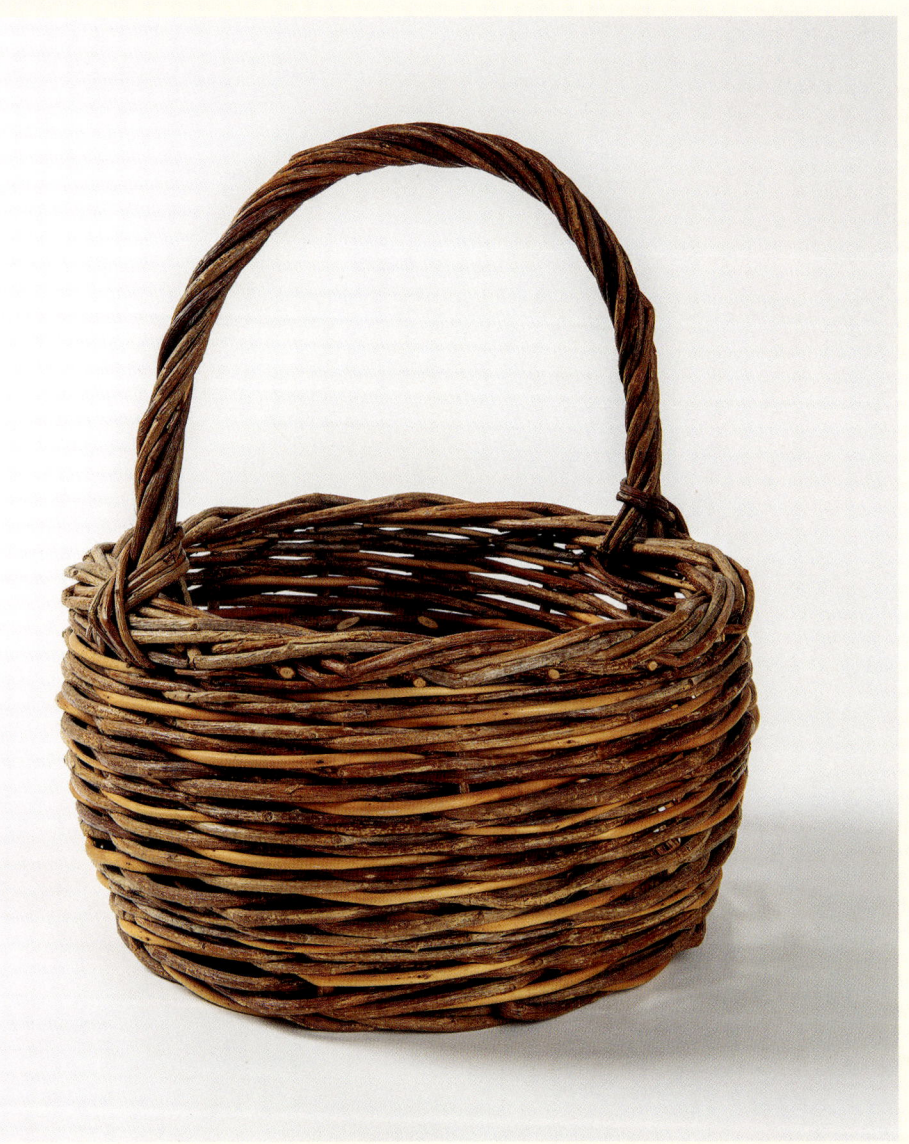

LeRoy Graber, basket, ca. 1985

Willow, 12 in × 11 in × 11 in.

LeRoy Graber learned to weave from his grandfather, Jacob, when he was ten years old. The family tradition began in 1874, when Jacob migrated to the Dakota territories from Russia and taught himself how to make functional baskets from willow, an abundant resource in the prairieland. When LeRoy retired from farming in the 1970s, he committed more time to his craft. He demonstrated weaving techniques at the Sioux Empire Fair in South Dakota, the state's largest county fair.

Viki Graber, LeRoy's daughter, is a fourth-generation willow weaver who has demonstrated at the Pioneer Village at the Indiana State Fair. She reflected, "Weaving a basket is when I feel closest to my great-grandfather and one of the few things we have in common."

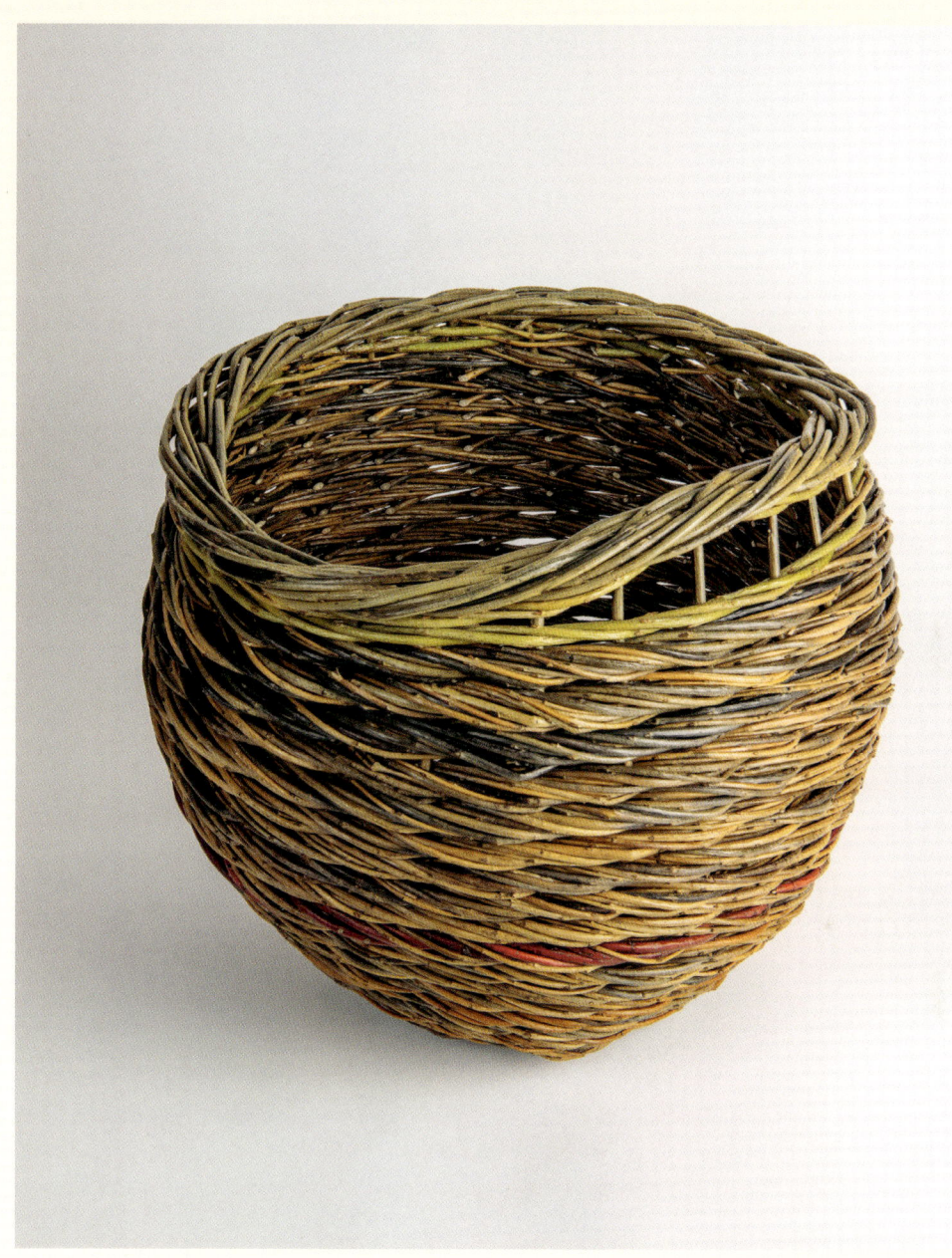

Viki Graber, rope coil basket, 2025

Willow, 12½ × 15 × 15 in.

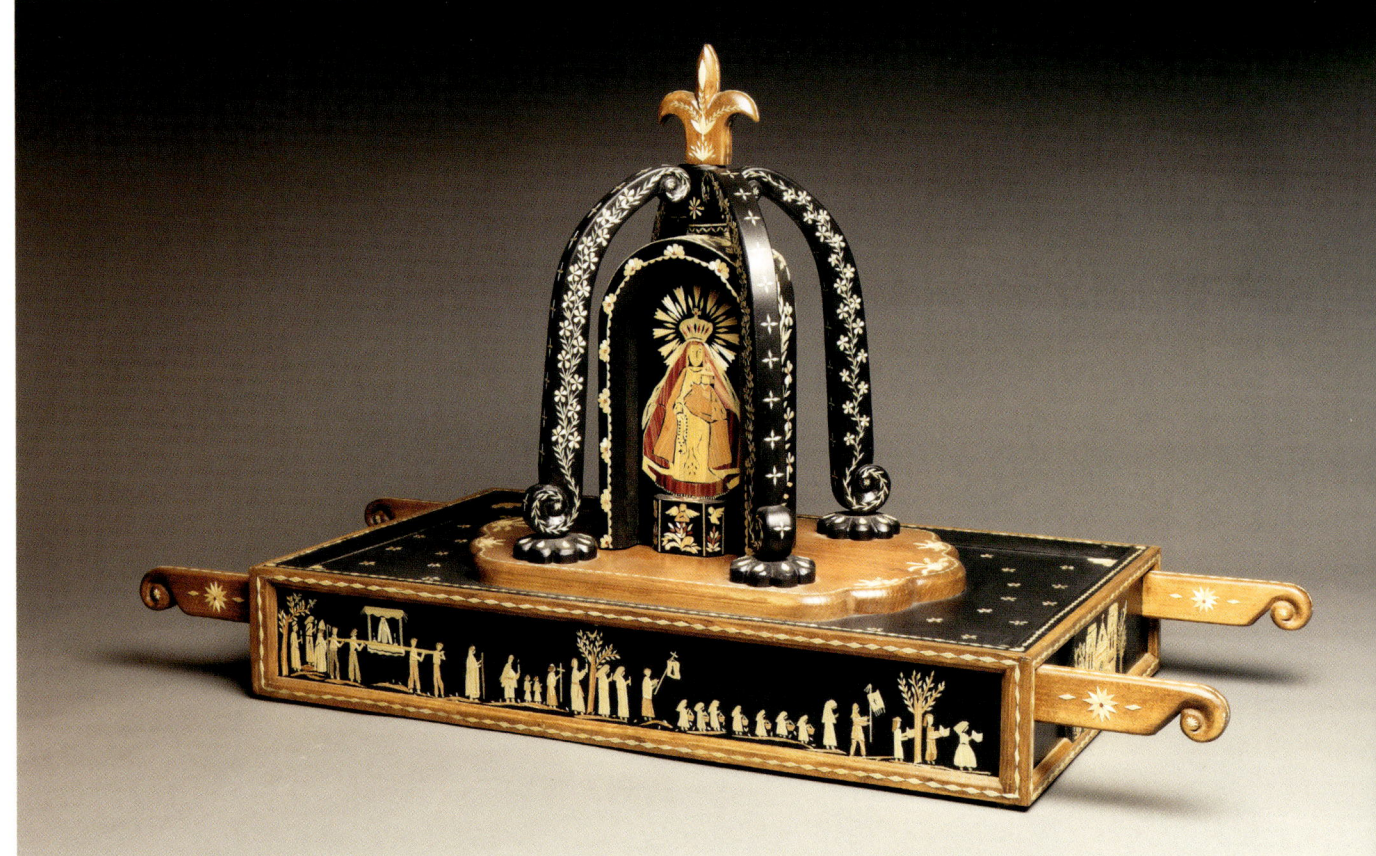

Martha Varoz Ewing, *La Procesión-Novena de Nuestra Senora de la Paz*, 2006

Straw appliqué, wood, straw, paint, 19½ × 14 × 33 in.

Martha Varoz Ewing made this straw-appliqué *anda* (float) to bear witness to both the prayers and the struggles of Hispanic Americans in New Mexico. For centuries, Spanish colonists decorated crosses and other liturgical objects with straw to emulate gold. The practice gained popularity in the 1930s through New Deal public works projects. In New Mexico, the husband-and-wife artists Eliseo Jose and Paula Rodriguez preserved the practice of straw appliqué. Paula Rodriguez later mentored Ewing.

Today straw art is a unique competitive category in the Hispanic Art Gallery at the New Mexico State Fair. Ewing won a blue ribbon at the 2007 fair with this work, which depicts the procession celebrating the statue of Our Lady of Peace, the oldest image of the Virgin Mary in the United States. The statue resides in the Cathedral Basilica of St. Francis of Assisi in Santa Fe. In 1680 the Pueblo people revolted against Spanish colonizers and gained independence for twelve years. At the time of the revolt, a young Hispanic woman saved the statue. When Spanish settlers regained control over the Pueblo people in 1692, they enacted an annual procession to remind the community of their conquest. In 1992, Bishop Robert Sanchez renamed the statue Our Lady of Peace as a gesture of reconciliation towards the Indigenous community. Every year the statue is carried on a float through Santa Fe to the Rosario Chapel. Ewing depicts the procession in straw details along the side of the float. For her, this work is a prayer for peace around the world.

Verne Lucero, *Fireplace Companion*, 2007

Wood spiraling, punched tin, reverse painting on glass, and repoussé on tin, 40 × 24 × 12 in.

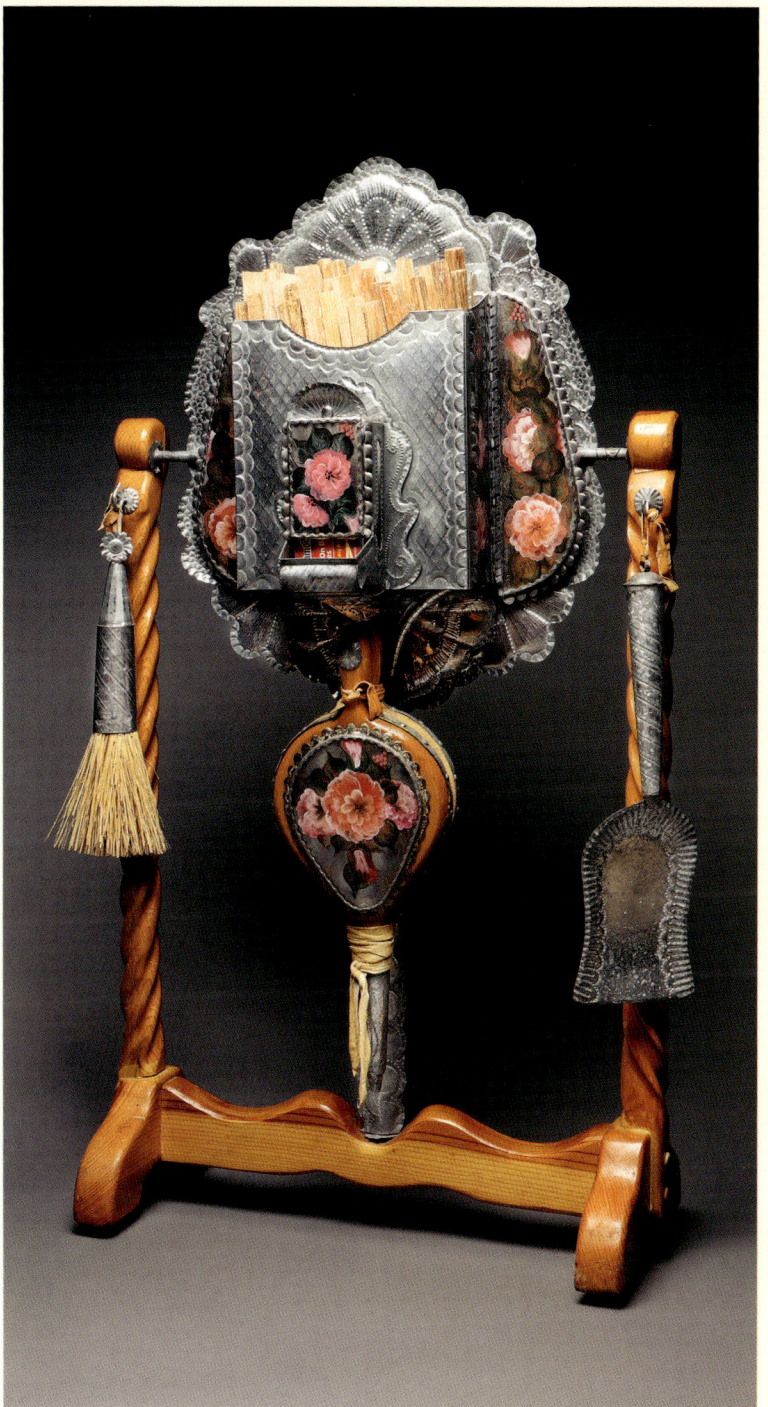

The arts of tinwork and reverse-glass painting were revived in New Deal programs in the Southwest. A few vocational schools taught the techniques of embossing, stamping, and scoring tin to help artists find work. The craft became a vital category in the Hispanic Art Gallery at the New Mexico State Fair. Verne Lucero, a US Army veteran, took it up following his retirement from Española Hospital in 1994, and by 1996 he was winning awards for his works.

Lucero's *Fireplace Companion* won first place at the New Mexico State Fair. The work comprises a matchbox and match safe made of traditional Spanish Colonial punched tin, adorned with two reverse-painted glass panels. It also includes a punched tin shovel, a broom, and bellows with reverse-painted glass panels. Lucero assembled these components in a free-standing, spiral-carved frame. The work earned the Tradición Revista Award at the 2007 New Mexico State Fair.

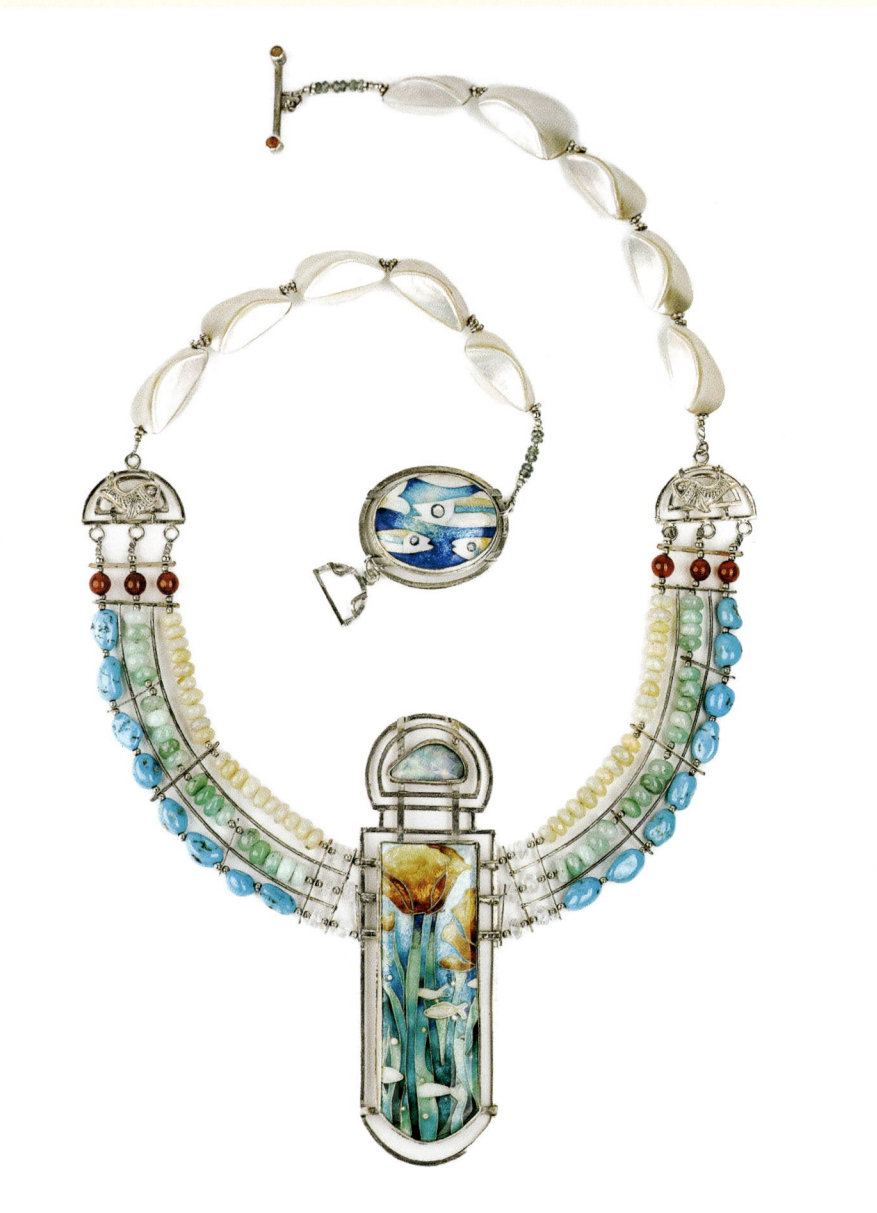

Adriana Griffin, *Delta Smelt with Poppies*, 2022

Fine and sterling silver, opal, turquoise, carnelian, sapphire, moonstone, nautilus shell beads, and chrysoprase, 11 × 7½ in.

Adriana Griffin taught herself enameling techniques from YouTube videos. She entered this necklace in the 2022 California State Fair. The pendant features an orange poppy (the state flower), and the clasp features the Delta smelt, a fish endemic to the Sacramento–San Joaquin River Delta. This necklace scooped awards for "Best in Class" (jewelry) and "Best in Show."

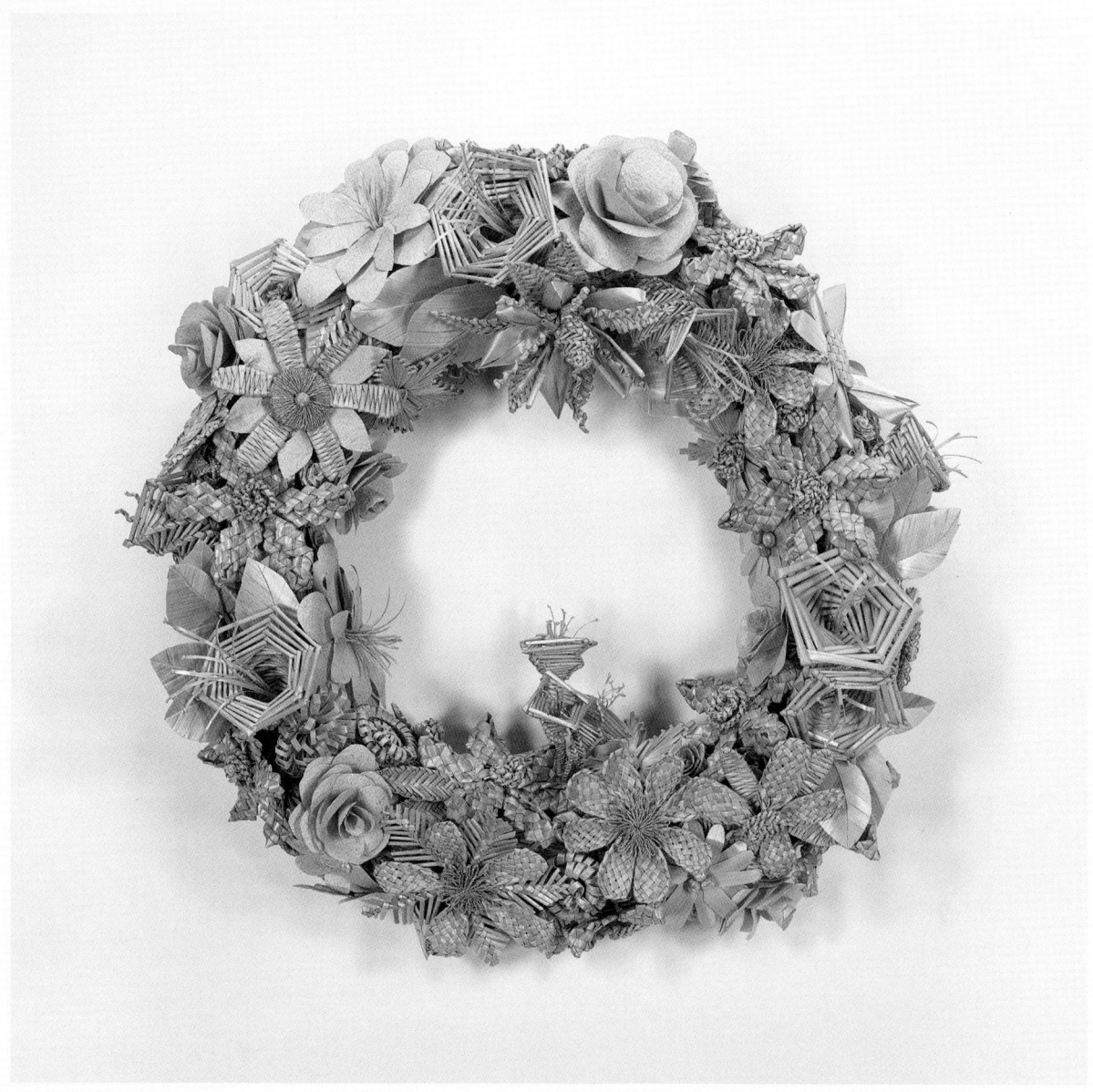

Donna Hall, *Straw Flower Wreath Jubilee,* 2022

Straw, 17 × 18 × 5½ in.

Immigrant farmers from Europe brought the art of straw weaving to North America in the 1700s. According to tradition, creating decorative wreaths out of wheat straw would ensure a bountiful harvest. Growing up on her parents' ranch in Le Grand, California, Donna Hall discovered the craft at a young age and has since become an influential maker and educator in the field. This piece, which illustrates the artist's love of flowers, is one of many straw weavings she has entered in California State Fair competitions since 2002. Created during the COVID-19 pandemic, it won "Best of the Division in Straw Art" at the 2022 fair.

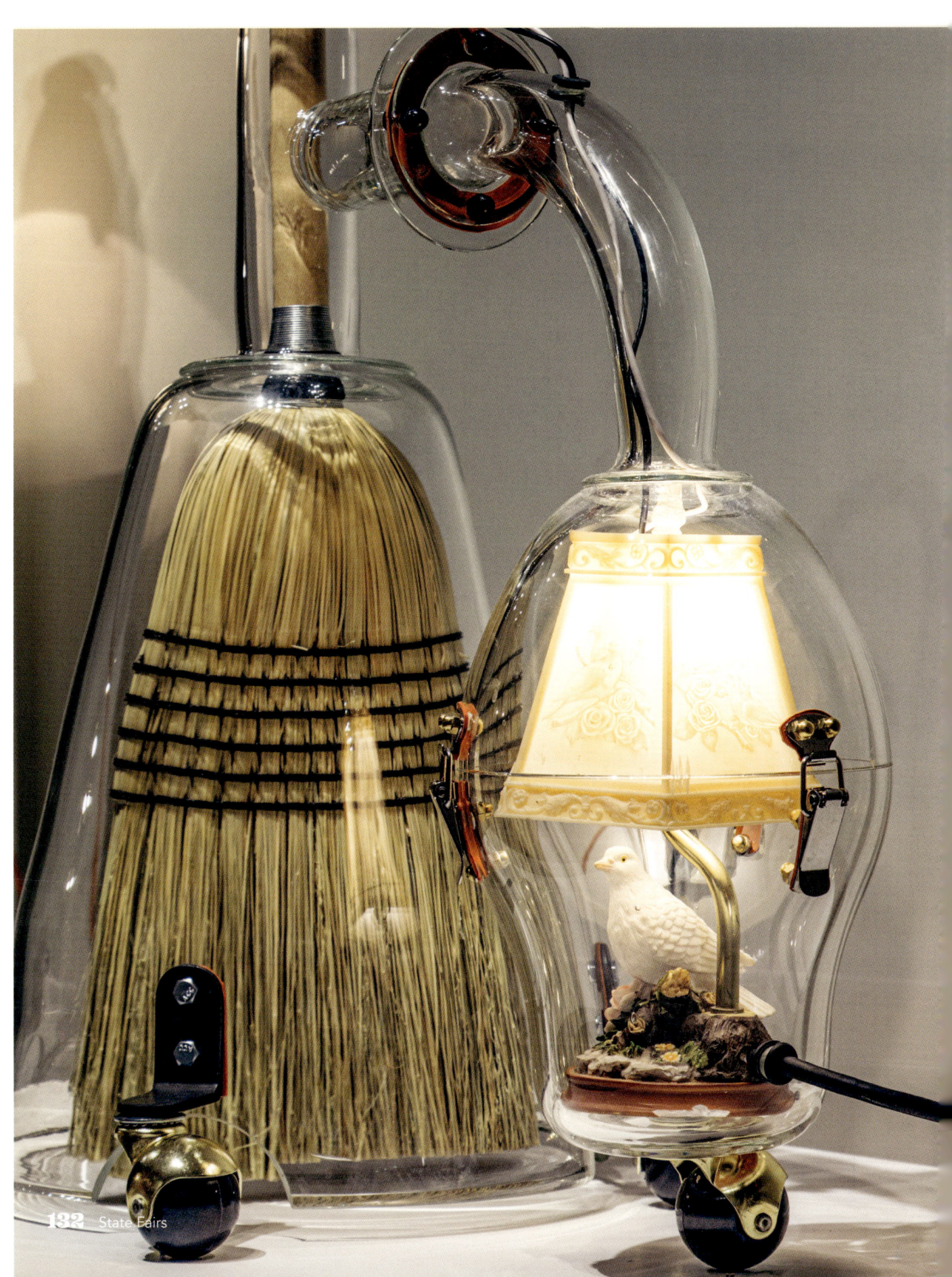

Zac Weinberg, *Kitsch Alchemy*, 2018

Blown, cold-worked glass, broom,
found lamp, electric motor, mixed media,
81 × 36 × 24 in.

Perhaps a bristle broom and a cutesy bird lamp belong not in an art gallery but in a thrift store. At least, that's where artist Zac Weinberg found them. Weinberg transmutes these mundane objects into art. Encasing them in transparent glass fixtures, he makes visible everyday infrastuctures like electrical wiring that often go unnoticed. The broom hovers an inch above the ground and spins in its glass case, always at work but never actually cleaning.

Weinberg loved attending fairs as a child in Maine. He entered *Kitsch Alchemy* at the Ohio State Fair while completing his MA at Ohio State University. It won both the "Juror's Choice" and "New Artist" awards at the fair.

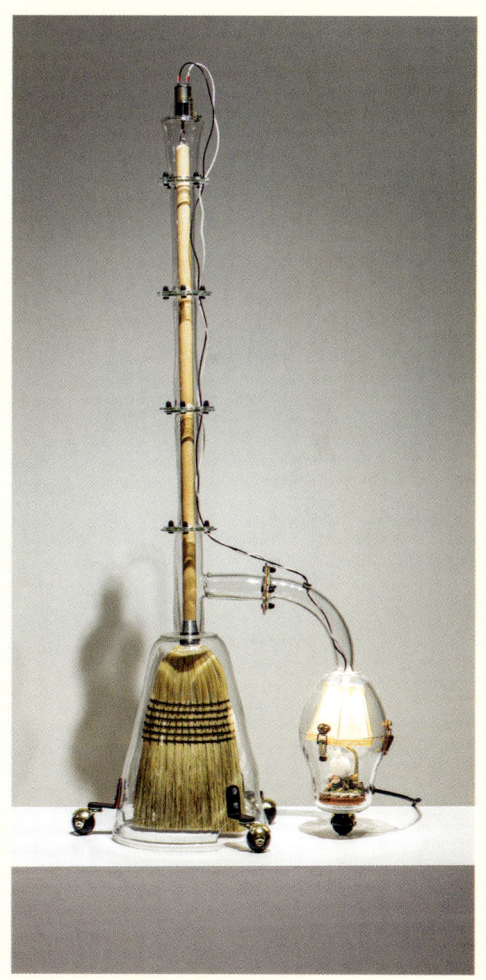

Demonstrations

State fairs offer hands-on learning opportunities through lively public demonstrations of crafts and living cultural traditions. Artists, taking both innovative and time-honored approaches to their work, display and share their varied skills across the fairgrounds, including horse arenas and heritage villages.

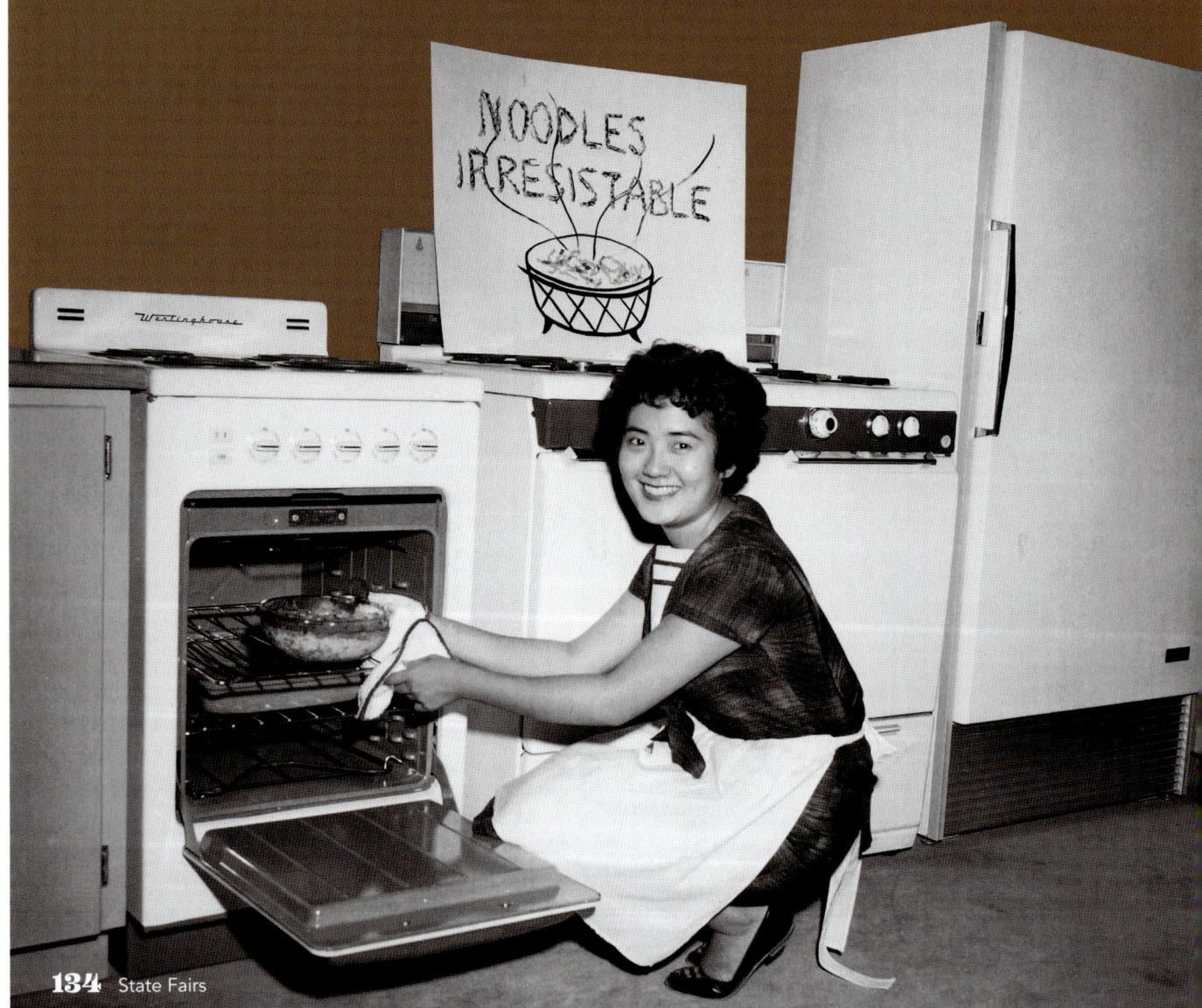

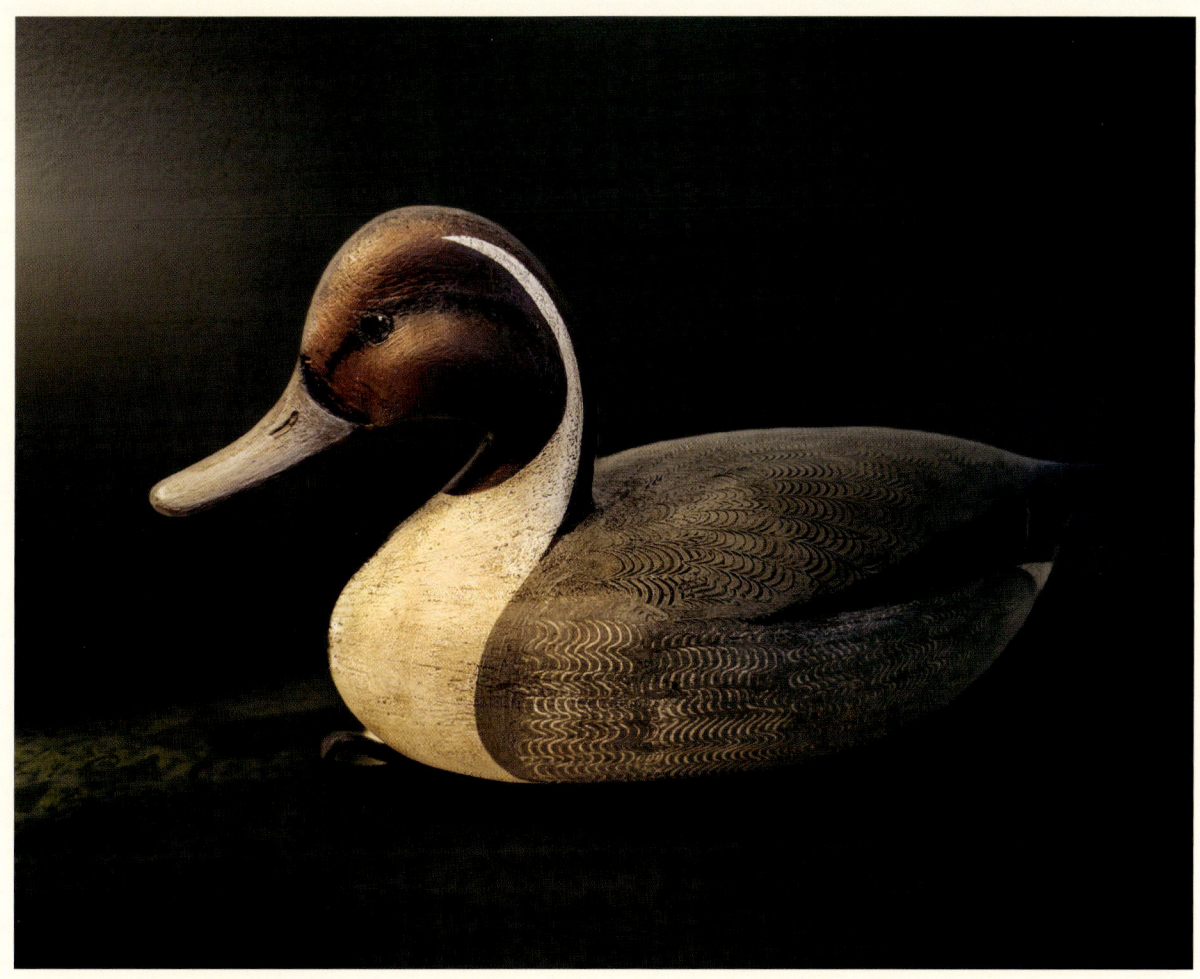

Laurel Dabbs, Pintail, 2019

White cedar, nails, housepaint, 18 × 6 × 6½ in.

Laurel Dabbs has demonstrated traditional decoy carving at the Cracker Country Living History Museum at the Florida State Fair since 1997. First designed by Indigenous people to lure migratory fowl, such decoys were essential to the survival of early colonizers until they could establish successful crops. Over time, decoys have become an art form. Living-history programs enable Dabbs to demonstrate time-honored techniques with hand tools while she exchanges stories with fairgoers, from seniors to students on elementary school field trips.

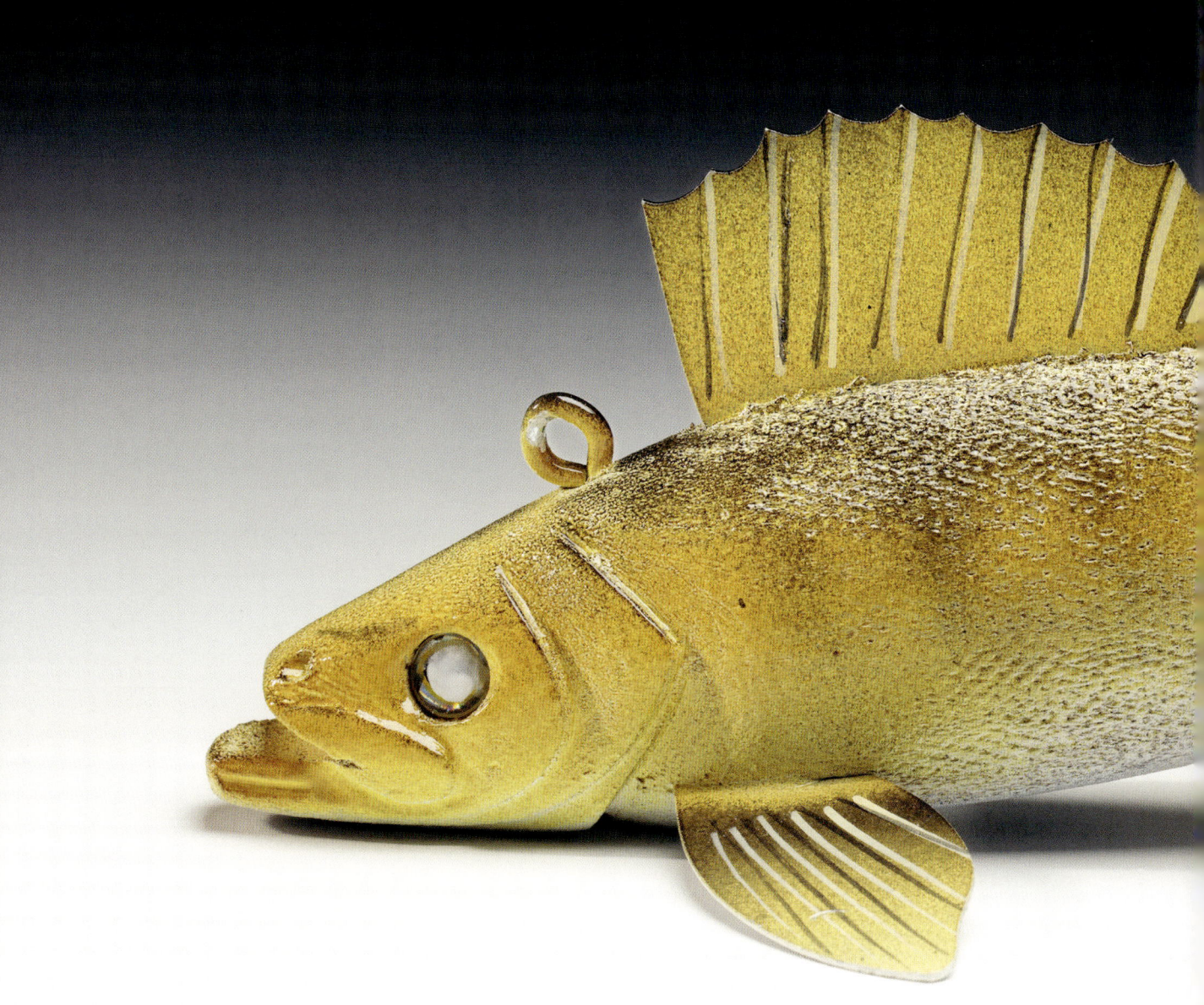

Rick Whittier and Connie Whittier, *Walleye*, 2023

White pine and spray paint, 3 ¼ × 9 in.

Rick Whittier made his first fish decoy in 2004. He and his wife, Connie, had recently retired from careers in law enforcement in Wisconsin and moved to Lidgerwood, North Dakota. Though they did not know many people in the town, a neighbor knocked on their door at 1 a.m. to request an urgent favor: he needed a new decoy before the opening day of ice-fishing season, and he had heard that the Whittiers had some experience with woodworking. They experimented with scrap wood and sheet metal taken from a storm door to assemble a decoy. Since

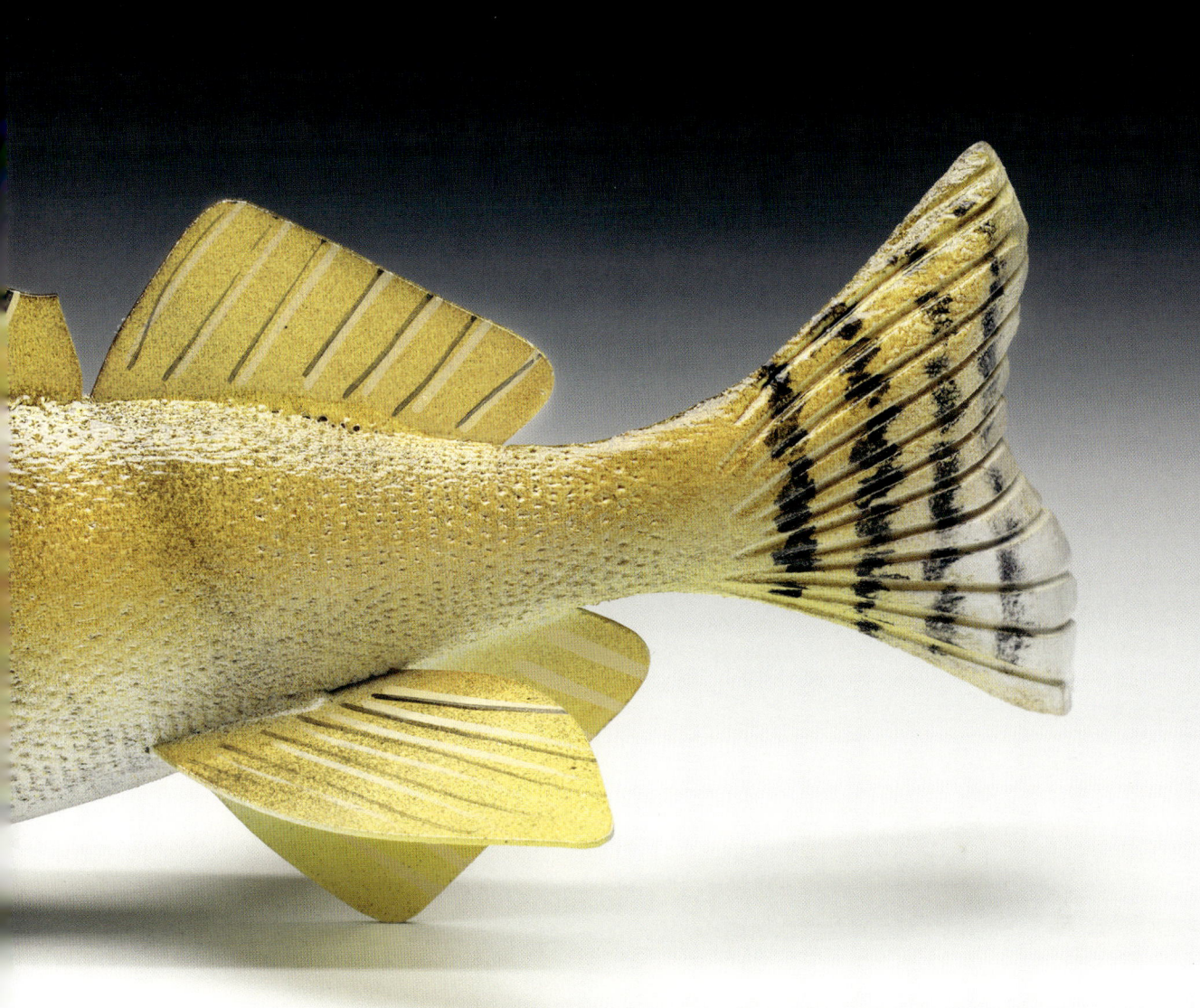

then Rick and Connie have crafted thousands of decoys representing more than four hundred species of fish.

When the Whittiers demonstrated decoy carving at the North Dakota State Fair, the nearby Conservation and Outdoor Skills Park took notice. They acquired some of the Whittiers' decoys to use in an ice-fishing display.

Each decoy is carved by hand and painted to resemble a particular species, like Rock Bass or Walleye. The decoy is designed to enter the water and spiral to the bottom, attracting nearby fish with its natural-looking movements. The Whittiers carry on a tradition of decoy carving rooted in the distinct ecology and Indigenous practices of the Great Lakes region.

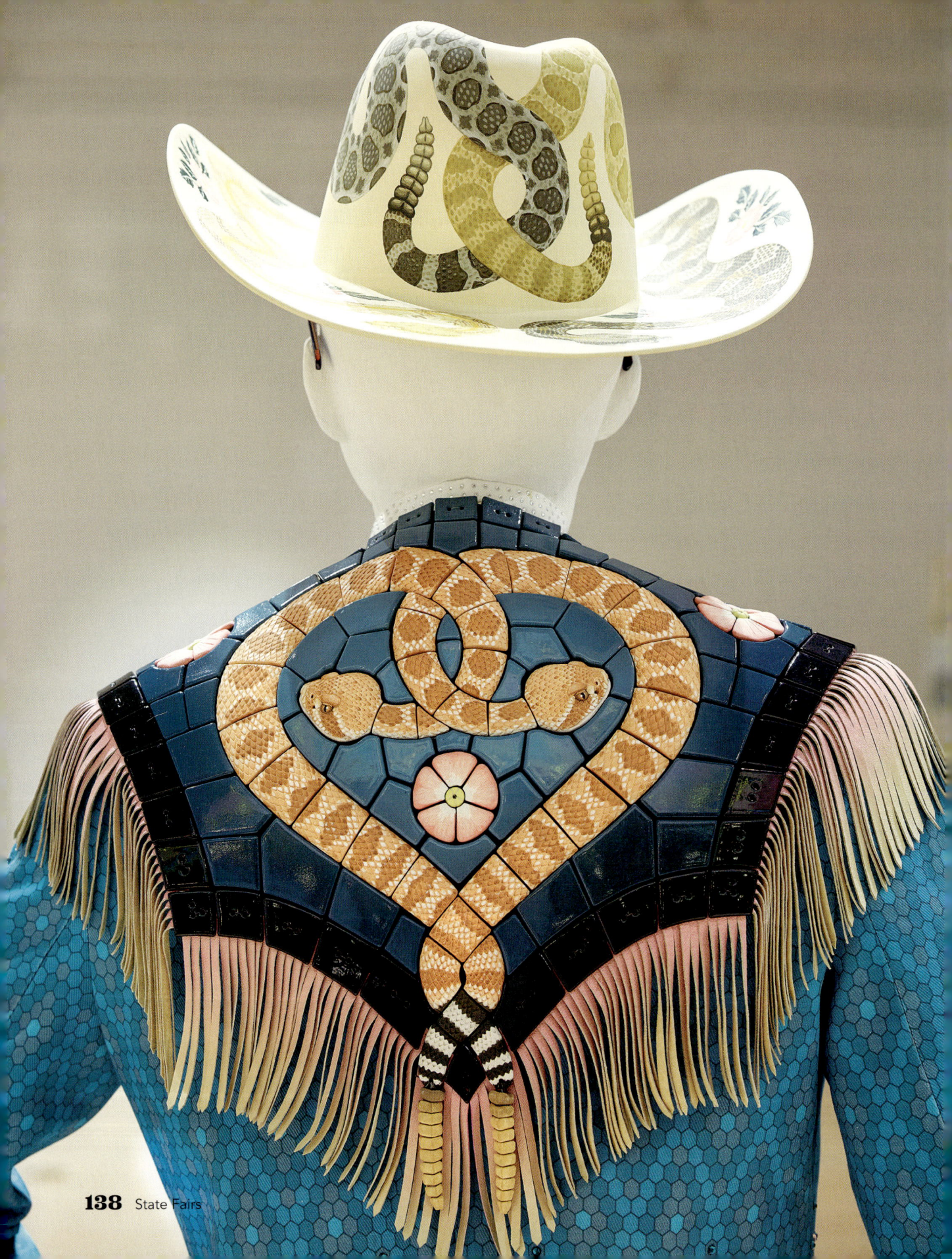

Shae Bishop, *Rhinestone Rattlesnakeboy, Suit and Hat,* 2024

Suit: printed denim fabric, ceramic, leather, and rhinestones; hat: ceramic and underglaze. Suit measurements: 5 ft 9 in. × 24 in. Hat measurements: 16 × 14 × 5 in.

To create his *Rhinestone Rattlesnakeboy* outfit, Shae Bishop merged the themes of cowboy culture, masculinity, and human-animal relationships. Motivated by a commitment to wildlife conservation and the idea that "nature is the original source of all human design," Bishop embellished this suit with ceramic and rhinestone detailing and paired it with a porcelain cowboy hat adorned with a rattlesnake motif. The suit was inspired by the work of the artist Loy Bowlin of Mississippi, known as the Original Rhinestone Cowboy, who often appeared at local fairs. Bishop himself dreams of traveling to fairs as Rattlesnakeboy to promote native snake conservation.

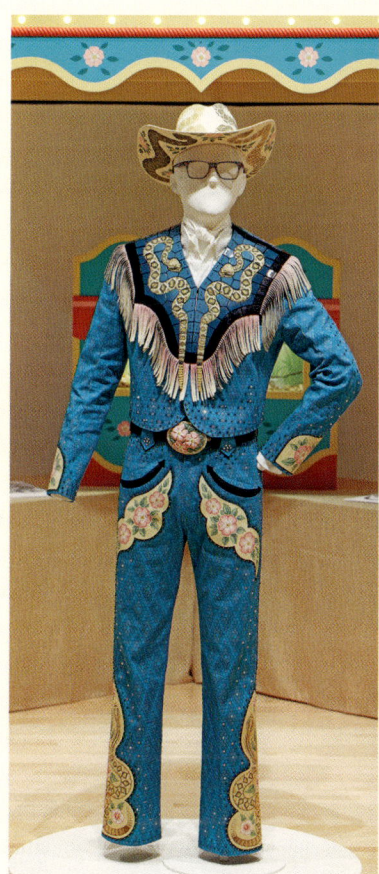
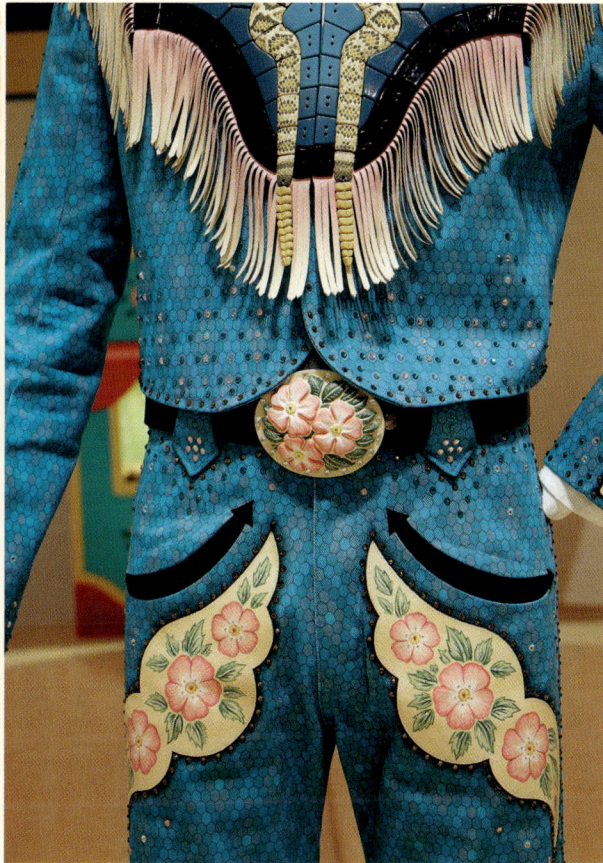

Talabartería la Querencia, Charro Saddle, 1998

Hand-embroidered with maguey cactus fibers and silver inlay, 30 × 21 × 34 in.

Jerry Diaz is a fourth-generation charro cowboy. In seventeenth-century Mexico, charros were country horsemen. Every year at the State Fair of Texas, Diaz and his family produce a rodeo show to highlight charro traditions. As Diaz notes, "To be a cowboy or a charro, it has to come from inside your soul first."

This traditional charro saddle is adorned with *piteado*, a form of decorative embroidery using fiber from the maguey cactus. The saddle horn is worked in silver inlay.

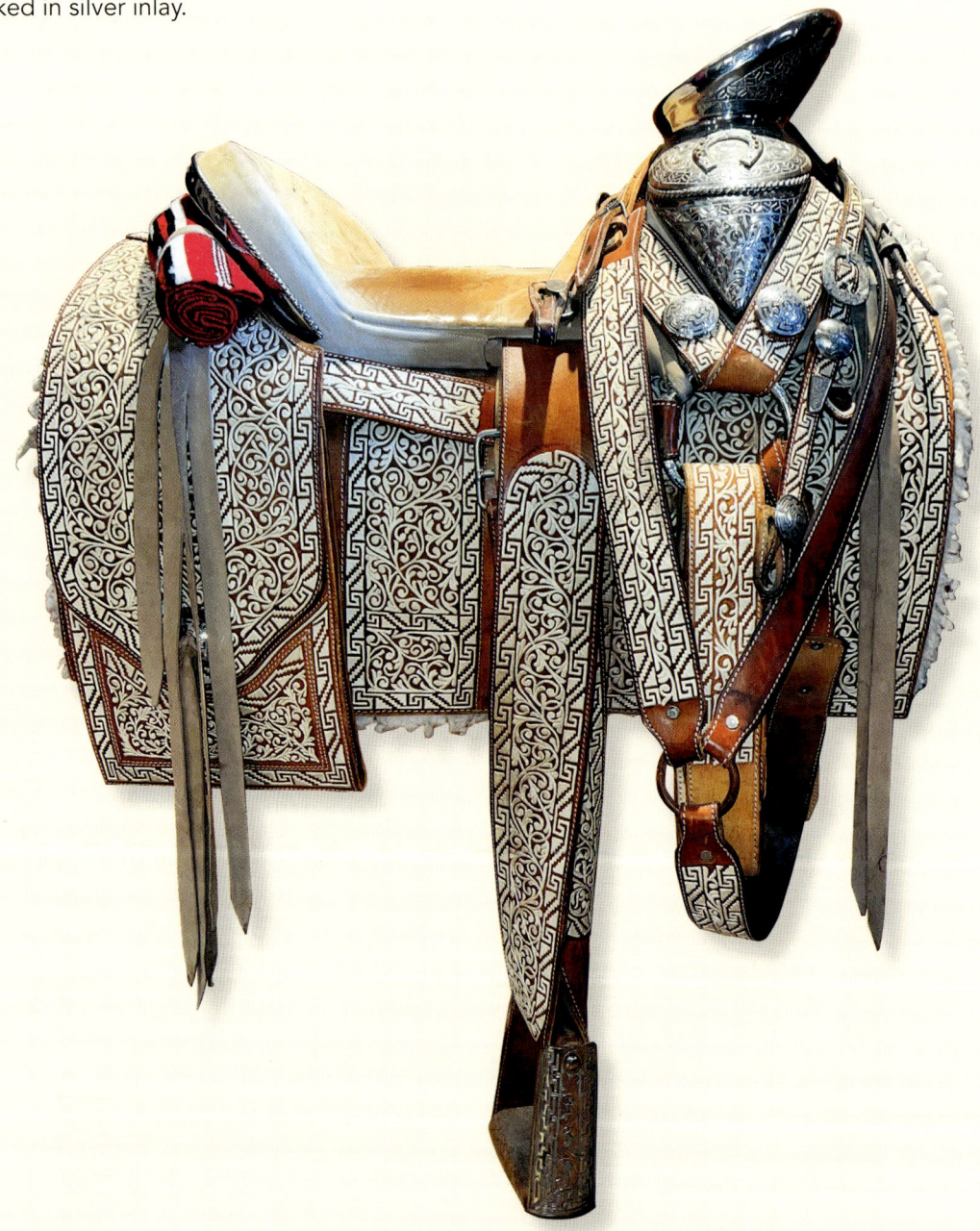

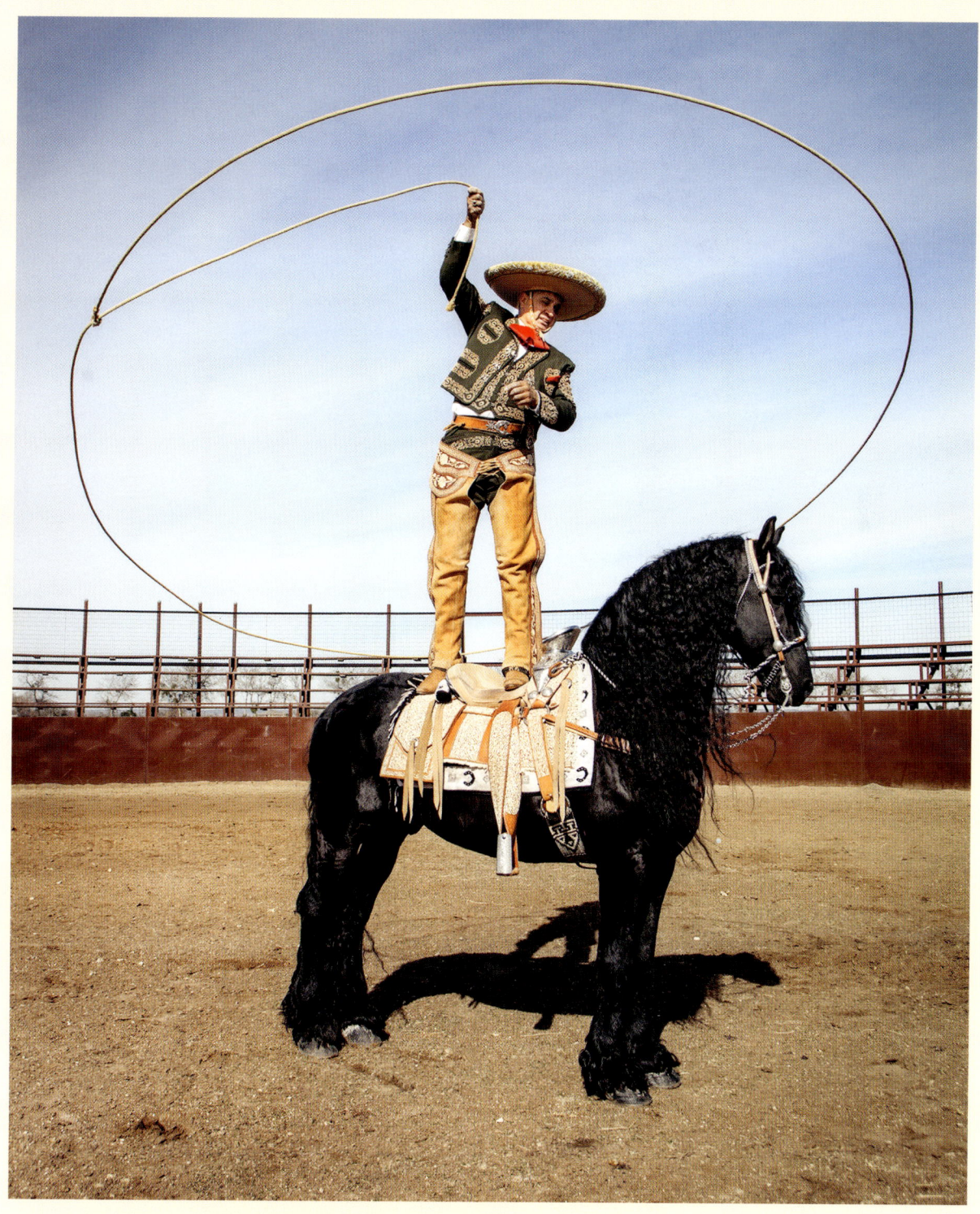

Jerry Diaz and the Big Loop, 2014

Acknowledgments

MARY SAVIG

The first state fair I attended was the Minnesota State Fair, which we called the Great Minnesota Get-Together. The nickname embodies the collective spirit of this catalog. This is a national get-together of extraordinary artists, historians, librarians, princesses, cowboys, and pronto pup vendors.

The Renwick Gallery's team of Elana Hain, Hannah Owh, Elizabeth Routhier, Michael Sperow, and Rebecca Sullesta embraced this project, and together we gave it shape and substance. We were supported by the Smithsonian American Women's History Initiative curatorial researchers Sara Morris, Elizabeth Smith, and Sarah Rogers Morris. Special thanks to the Renwick's former curator-in-charge, Nora Atkinson, who heard my idea and made it happen.

I'm grateful for the insight and expertise provided by our catalog authors and contributing curators: Elana Hain, Sara Morris, Jon Kay, Amber-Dawn Bear Robe, and Wanda Corn. Elizabeth Routhier, Sarah Rogers Morris, Elizabeth Smith, and Sharbreon Plummer also enlivened the Blue Ribbon Gallery with their research and writing.

This project relied on the collaborative and intense work of my dearest colleagues. At the Smithsonian American Art Museum (SAAM), I'm grateful to exhibit designer Meghan O'Loughlin and graphic designer Nathaniel Phillips, interpretation specialist Emily Berg, programs coordinator Mary Lesher, and loans registrar Matt Bacon. At Smithsonian Books, we were led by the brilliant editor Julie Huggins, along with designer Christina Newhard, director Carolyn Gleason, marketing manager Matthew Litts, marketing associate Sarah Fannon, and editor Erika Búky. We are especially thankful to artist Liz Schreiber, who provided the beautiful cover for this book.

The Smithsonian American Art Museum's leadership team—Acting Director Jane Carpenter-Rock, Eric Nastasi, Jean Choi, and Maia Worden—supported and advocated for this project. The advancement team—Donna Rim, Christie Davis, Leigh Hicks, Michelle Atkins, and Elise Pertusati—helped us realize our most ambitious plans. The administration team of Kelly DeFilippis, Marissa Probst, and Krista Aniel Duncan, led by Amma Tabirih, kept this project on track and on budget. My education and interpretation colleagues, Anne Showalter and Gloria Kenyon, led by Carol Wilson, provided helpful advice. The external affairs team

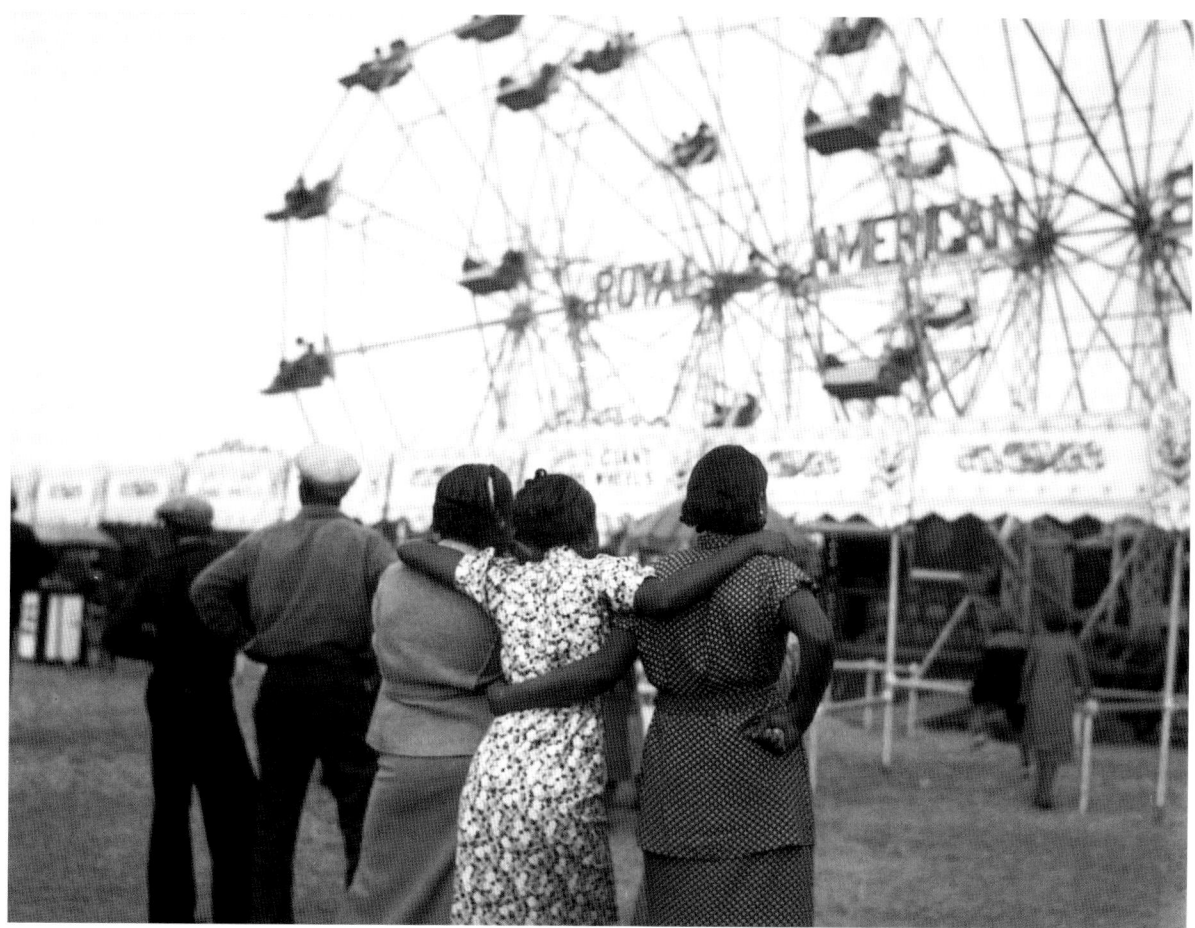

Eudora Welty, The Rides, State Fair / Jackson, *ca. 1930s. Men and women look at Ferris wheels at the Mississippi State Fair.*

of Laura Baptiste, Amy Fox, Amy Hutchins, Howard Kaplan, and Rebekah Mejorado, led by Nina Walia, lent sparkle and perspective to our vision.

The registrars are a blue-ribbon team who helped coordinate artists and artworks from around the nation: Emily Felber, Aubrey Vinson, Edward Bray, Richard Sorensen, Christopher Kirages, Alana McMahan, Claire Denny, Jim Concha, Lucia Martino, and Lynn Putney, all led by Jenni Lee. The conservation team ensured the safe display of our standard fare of quilts and ceramics and embraced unconventional materials like seeds and straw: Leah Bright, Dorothy Chen, and Jenna Gustafson, led by Amber Kerr.

I'm profoundly grateful to the exhibitions team, led by David Gleeson, for exploring the complexities of displaying a butter cow and Big Tex's boots and crafting beautiful displays: Eunice Park Kim, Scott Rosenfield, Tim Nielsen, Nick Primo, Jenna Michael, Harvey Sandler, Andrew Christenberry, and Caleb Plattner.

My fellow SAAM curators and research colleagues brought critical insight to the project: Saisha Grayson, Randy Griffey, Eleanor Harvey, John Jacob, Melissa Ho, Karen Lemmey, Sarah Newman, Dalila Scruggs, Leslie Umberger, Amelia Goerlitz, Avriel Glass, and Lindsay R. Harris.

We got together with Smithsonian colleagues who generously shared their expertise on many subjects: Anya Montiel, National Museum of the American Indian; Anne Evenhaugen and Alexandra Reigle, Smithsonian American Art and Portrait

Gallery Library; Betty Belanus, Smithsonian Center for Folklife and Cultural Heritage; Tey Marianna Nunn, National Museum of the American Latino; Abeer Saha, Peter Liebhold, and John Troutman, National Museum of American History; and Grant Czubinski, Anacostia Community Museum.

The national scope of this project was contingent on generous support from a variety of museums, libraries, and historical societies. I thank these organizations and their staff for sharing their collections and expertise with me, especially when it was not possible for me to travel: Taylor Pulfer, Jason Hays, Karissa Condoianis, State Fair of Texas; Anna Pilcher, Mindy Williamson, Iowa State Fair; Samantha Gilbertson and Keri Huber, Minnesota State Fair; Ramona Vigil-Eastwood, New Mexico State Fair; Alissa Belna-Muhlenkamp and Jessica West, Ohio State Fair; Alex Alcantar, California Exposition & State Fair; Sarah Glover, University of Nebraska—Lincoln; Sophie Pitman, University of Wisconsin; Daniel Davis, Utah State University; Kelley Moulton, University of Idaho; Jordan Miller and Ahnna Matthews, Nebraska State Historical Society; Jonathan M. Olly, New Hampshire Historical Society; Angelica Maier, Ann Frisina, and Todd Topper, Minnesota Historical Society; Tamara Funk, Wisconsin Historical Society; Paul Matheny, South Carolina State Museum; Susannah Koerber, Indiana State Museum and Historic Sites; Matt Renick, Kansas Historical Society; Bobbye Tigerman, Los Angeles County Museum of Art; Jill King, Overbeck Museum; Lana Burgess, McKissick Museum; Carolyn Ducey, International Quilt Museum; Marllyn Zapf, Center for Craft; Diana Pardue, Heard Museum; Mimi Conger and Chloe Autio, Smithsonian Women's Committee; Shana Bushyhead Condill, Evan Mathis, and Lily Wright, Museum of the Cherokee People; Misty D. Brescia, Mississippi Band of Choctaw Indians; Carletta Benally, Office of Miss Navajo Nation; Barry Kern, Kern Studios; Linda Downs and Carol Thompson, California Straw Arts Guild; Beth Puschel Dykstra, Las Arañas Spinners and Weavers Guild; Kaye Whittington and Wanda Nash, Great Lakes African American Quilters' Network.

Numerous artists, art historians, and collectors advised us on specific objects in this project: Teresa Anderson, Blaine Berry, Susie Brandt, Fleur Bresler, Fran Burns, Margarita Cabrera, Diane Charnov, Ellsworth Christmas, Sara Clugage, Ivana Dizdar, Alyssa Erickson, Harriett Green, Consuelo Jimenez-Underwood, Paul Juhl, Forrest L. Merrill, Farrol Mertes, Mary Okin, Karen Smith, Lillian Wilson Szlaga, and Velina Underwood.

This book is possible because of the artists who have participated in state fairs. Thank you to every artist included in this project—I've tremendously enjoyed our time together and learning about your life and practice. This book is dedicated to you.

Finally, I'm grateful to my family. My mom, Patty, grew up on a dairy farm in Minnesota, and her memories of 4-H and fairs inspired this project. I'm thankful to my husband, Will, and our adventurer, John, who visited many fairs with me in the name of research.

Thanks again to everyone who got together to make this project a reality.

NOTES

FOREWORD

1   Chris Rasmussen, *Carnival in the Countryside: The History of the Iowa State Fair* (Iowa City: University of Iowa Press, 2015).

2   Paul C. Juhl, *Grant Wood and the Iowa State Fair* (Iowa City, IA: Brushy Creek Publishing 2020), 19.

INTRODUCTION

1   See Rodger Stroup, *Meet Me at the Rocket: A History of the South Carolina State Fair* (Columbia: University of South Carolina Press, 2019).

2   David Bristow, "150 Nebraska State Fairs," Nebraska State Historical Society Blog, 2019, https://history.nebraska.gov/150-nebraska-state-fairs.

3   Choctaw Indian Fair, "History," Mississippi Band of Choctaw Indians, 2005, https://web.archive.org/web/20050305174238/http://www.choctawindian-fair.com/history.htm.

4   Mark A. Mastromarino, "Fair Visions: Elkanah Watson (1758–1842) and the Modern American Agricultural Fair" (PhD diss., College of William and Mary, 2002), 179.

5   Mastromarino, "Fair Visions," 179–80.

6   Mastromarino, "Fair Visions," 188–92.

7   Elkanah Watson, *History of the Rise, Progress, and Existing State of the Berkshire Agricultural Society, with Practical Directions* (Albany, NY, 1820), 119, https://play.google.com/books/reader?id=CKc-AQAAMAAJ&pg=GBS.PA106&hl=en.

8   Mastromarino, "Fair Visions," 218.

9   Mastromarino, "Fair Visions," 123. See also Wayne Caldwell Neely, *The Agricultural Fair* (New York: Columbia University Press, 1935), 6.

10 Mastromarino, "Fair Visions," 6.

11 Watson, *History of the Rise*, 124–25. Watson claimed to have given up his prize money to the artist.

12 Watson, *History of the Rise*, 129–30. Watson notes, "The women came forth with spirit and animation; producing a fine display of domestic manufactures."

13 Laurel Thatcher Ulrich, "Wheels, Looms, and the Gender Division of Labor in Eighteenth-Century New England," *William and Mary Quarterly* 55, no. 1 (January 1998): 22.

14 Watson noted that "many excellent articles of domestic manufacturers (especially woolens and linens) were exhibited to a considerable extent; but no female was seen to claim premiums." With the help of his wife, Watson went to a great effort to gather and reward the "ladies of the village." Watson, *History of the Rise*, 127–28.

15 Mastromarino, "Fair Visions," 227; see also Watson, *History of the Rise*, 131–32.

16 Neely, *The Agricultural Fair*, 52.

17 Henry W. Schramm, *Empire Showcase: A History of the New York State Fair* (Utica, NY: North Country Books, 1993), 3.

18 Chris Rasmussen, *Carnival in the Countryside: The History of the Iowa State Fair* (Iowa City: University of Iowa Press, 2015), 3.

19 Carol E. Sachs, *Gendered Fields: Rural Women, Agriculture, and Environment* (New York: Routledge, 1996), 11–12. Sachs notes that "studies of farm women in the United States revealed that women participate in farming activities to a greater extent than typically assumed; they do the abundance of both household labor and subsistence production, and they often keep the farm financially afloat through off-farm work."

20 Karen E. Smith, "Framing Quilts/Framing Culture: Women's Work and the Politics of Display" (PhD diss., University of Iowa, 2011), 27–28.

21 Smith, "Framing Quilts/Framing Culture," 15. See also Iowa State Agricultural Society, *Report and Proceedings of the Iowa State Agricultural Society* (Keokuk, IA: Ben Franklin Book and Job Office, 1854), 5.

22 Rasmussen, *Carnival in the Countryside*, 19. See also *Report of the Agricultural Meeting Held in Boston, January 13, 1840, Containing Remarks on That Occasion by Hon. Daniel Webster of the U.S. Senate and of Professor Silliman, M.C., L.L.D. of Yale College* (Salem, MA: Salem Power Press, 1840).

23 Rasmussen, *Carnival in the Countryside*, 19.

24 Karal Ann Marling, *Blue Ribbon: A Social and Pictorial History of the Minnesota State Fair* (St. Paul: Minnesota Historical Society Press, 1990), 96. See also Smith, "Framing Quilts/Framing Culture," 21–56.

25 Marling, *Blue Ribbon*, 95.

26 Land speculators like Elkanah Watson grew rich from selling this land to farmers and laborers who migrated from the Northeast. See Mastromarino, "Fair Visions," 37–89.

27 Neely, *The Agricultural Fair*, 101. In 1862 Congress established the United States Department of Agriculture and passed the Morrill Act providing for land-grant colleges.

28 Pamela H. Simpson, *Corn Palaces and Butter Queens: A History of Crop Art and Dairy Sculpture* (Minneapolis: University of Minnesota Press, 2012), xv.

29 Neely, *The Agricultural Fair*, 102.

30 Neely, *The Agricultural Fair*, 112.

31 Neil Dahlstrom and Jeremy Dahlstrom, *The John Deere Story: A Biography of Plowmakers John and Charles Deere* (DeKalb: Northern Illinois University Press, 2005), xvii.

32 Marling, *Blue Ribbon*, 96.

33 Marling, *Blue Ribbon*, 97.

34 Allen H. Eaton, *Handicrafts of the Southern Highlands* (New York: Dover Publications, 1973), 80.

35 Lucy Morgan with LeGette Blythe, *Gift from the Hills: Miss Lucy Morgan's Story of Her Unique Penland School* (Penland, NC: Penland School of Craft, 2005), 67.

36 Special thanks to Keri Huber, archivist at the Minnesota State Fair, for her research on the history of the folk categories at the fair. "Decorative painted designs," a category from 1937 to 1944, was replaced by "peasant painting or stenciling" from 1947 to 1964 (no fair was held in 1945 and 1946). Then it became "freehand painting or stenciling." Currently, categories for freehand painting styles include folk, peasant, early American, Pennsylvania Dutch, and rosemåling.

37 Lillian Wilson Szlaga, "The Scandinavian Folk Art of Rosemåling: Gender and Revival in America," paper presented at the Fifth Annual Feminist Art Conference, American University, Washington, DC, October 31, 2014, 13.

38 "State Fair Casts Its Colors over National TV Network," *Milwaukee Journal Sentinel*, ca. 1954.

39 The Eastern Band of the Cherokee Indians is descended from Cherokee who survived in North Carolina following the Indian Removal Act. In 1866, Eastern Cherokee land was incorporated under a North Carolina charter, and in 1868, the Eastern Band of Cherokee Indians received federal recognition. See "Cherokee History," Museum of the Cherokee people, https://motcp.org/learn/cherokee-history, n.d.

40 Cherokee Indian Fair and Folk Festival Program, Cherokee Indian Fair Association, 1935, Southern Appalachian Collections, Western Carolina University, https://southernappalachiandigitalcollections.org/object/10577.

41 Ana Fota, "Amanda Swimmer, Potter and Keeper of Cherokee Traditions, Dies at 97," *New York Times*, December 6, 2018.

42 "Amanda Swimmer," in "The 1994 Folk Heritage Awards," *North Carolina Folklore Journal* 44, nos. 1–2 (1997): 95.

43 Oral history interviews with Peggie L. Hartwell, June 3 and July 10, 2002, Archives of American Art, Smithsonian Institution.

44 Thanks to Anya Montiel, curator at the Smithsonian National Museum of the American Indian, for recent research on this artwork.

45 Krista Anderson-McCoon, Dwayne Cartmell, and Robert Terry Jr., "Fairgoers' Attitudes toward Youth Livestock Exhibits at the California State Fair," *Journal of Applied Communications* 100, no. 3 (2016): 22.

46 Anderson-McCoon, Cartmell, and Terry, "Fairgoers' Attitudes," 22.

CREATIVE ARTS COMPETITIONS AND WOMEN'S COLLECTIVITY

1 See Karal Ann Marling, "Women's Work," in *Blue Ribbon: A Social and Pictorial History of the Minnesota State Fair* (St. Paul: Minnesota Historical Society Press, 1990), 94–111.

2 Patricia Mainardi, "Quilts: The Great American Art," *Feminist Art Journal* 2, no. 1 (1973), doi: https://jstor.org/stable/community.28036282.

3 Wisconsin Historical Society, "Intro to Online Museum Collections," January 17, 2005, https://5049.sydneyplus.com/WisconsinHistorical-Society_ArgusNET/Portal/Online-Museum-Collections.aspx?lang=en-US.

4 Roger E. Stroup, "The Colored State Fair," in *Meet Me at the Rocket: A History of the South Carolina State Fair* (Columbia: University of South Carolina Press, 2019), 40–48.

5 Juanita Craft, *a child, the earth, and a tree of many seasons: The Voice of Juanita Craft,* ed. Chandler Vaughan (Dallas: Halifax Publishing, 1982).

6 "History Quilt Club Prepares Unique Display." *Negro History Bulletin* 16, no. 7 (1953): 150–51, doi: http://www.jstor.org/stable/44214555.

7 "Quilt," Kentucky Historical Society, https://kyhistory.pastperfectonline.com/Webobject/9B7FCEC6-0598-4D42-B462-318052352150, accessed October 12, 2022.

8 National quilting trends charted in the writing of Barbara Brackman and Kari Ronning are discussed in Patricia Cox Crews and Wendelin Rich, "Nebraska Quilts, 1870–1989: Perspectives on Traditions and Change," *Great Plains Research* 5, no. 2 (1995):

211–39. See also Barbara Brackman et al., "Rocky Road to Kansas," in *Kansas Quilts and Quilters* (Lawrence: University Press of Kansas, 1993), 17–65; Kari Ronning, "The Contemporary Quilt Revival: 1970–1990," in *Nebraska Quilts and Quiltmakers,* ed. P. C. Crews and R. C. Naugle, 167–208 (Lincoln: University of Nebraska Press, 1991).

STUDIO CRAFT COMPETITIONS AND WORKSHOPS

1 See Richard Petterson, "A Climate for Craft," *Craft Horizons* 16, no. 5 (October 1956): 11.

2 The California State Fair established purchase awards in 1948. From 1948 to 1968 and 1977 to 1978, the fair purchased prize-winning works for its permanent art collection. For more information on the fair's competitions and collections, see *California Visions: California State Fair Art Collection, 1948–1978* (Sacramento: Senate Rules Committee, California State Legislature, 1996).

3 Daniel Defenbacher et al., "Jurying Forum," in American Craftsmen's Council, *Asilomar: First Annual Conference of American Craftsmen* (June 1957), https://digital.craftcouncil.org/digital/collection/p15785coll5/id/3937. This transcript of the forum includes the remarks of Grant Duggins, the California State Fair's exhibit supervisor, who touched on the importance of the juried exhibitions at state fairs.

4 Peter Howard Selz papers, 1929–2014, bulk 1950–2005, Archives of American Art, Smithsonian Institution.

4-H AND YOUTH PARTICIPATION

1 "What Is 4-H?," 4-H, https://4-h.org/about/, accessed August 27, 2024.

2 "History of 4-H," 4-H History Preservation, https://4-hhistorypreservation.com/History/Hist_Nat/, accessed August 5, 2024.

3 Darin Nelson, "4-H and the 1928 State Fair of Oklahoma: Making the Best Better," *Chronicles of Oklahoma* 94, no. 2 (Summer 2016): 212.

4 Karal Ann Marling, *Blue Ribbon: A Social and Pictorial History of the Minnesota State Fair* (St. Paul: Minnesota Historical Society Press, 1990), 169.

5 "'Broken Star' 4-H State Fair Quilt," Wisconsin Historical Society, August 4, 2005, www.wisconsinhistory.org/Records/Article/CS2784.

6 Gabriel N. Rosenberg, *The 4-H Harvest: Sexuality and the State in Rural America* (Philadelphia: University of Pennsylvania Press, 2016), 8–9.

7 Kiera Butler and Rafael Roy, *Raise: What 4-H Teaches Seven Million Kids and How Its Lessons Could Change Food and Farming Forever* (Oakland: University of California Press, 2014), 27.

8 Sarah Z. Barnes, "Each Stitch Soothes Away the Pain," in Susie Brandt et al., *Quilting in the Age of the Pandemic* (Baltimore: Maryland Institute College of Art, 2023), 68.

THE INDIANA STATE FAIR PIONEER VILLAGE AND FOLKLIFE

1 See "Pioneer Hall," n.d., Iowa State Fair Blue Ribbon Foundation, www.blueribbonfoundation.org/renovations/pioneer-hall.

2 Ray Cashman, "Critical Nostalgia and Material Culture in Northern Ireland," *Journal of American Folklore* 119, no. 472 (2006): 137–60.

3 In the early 1960s, the civil rights movement amplified the stories of the oppression and abuse that Black sharecroppers faced, even as the history of the Black farmers was being erased, and their farms were being lost (Hinson 2008).

4 Jon Kay and Shaun Williams, *2015 Indiana State Fair Master: Mauri Williamson*, video, August 2015, Indiana University Media Collections Online, https://media.dlib.indiana.edu/media_objects/8336hp85n.

5 Maurice L. Williamson, "Old Time Farming for the City Folks," *Farm Collector: Dedicated to the Preservation of Vintage Farm Equipment*, July 1, 1996, www.farmcollector.com/steam-traction/old-time-farming-for-the-city-folks/.

6 Erica Quinlan, "A Stroll through Pioneer Village," *AgriNews*, August 31, 2021.

7 Jon Kay, *2019 Indiana State Fair Master: Ellsworth Christmas (Pioneer Arts Demonstrator)*, video, July 2019, Indiana University Media Collections Online, https://media.dlib.indiana.edu/media_objects/th83mm084.

8 Jon Kay, *Art of the Adze: Bowl Hewing in Indiana*. (Terre Haute, IN: Swope Museum of Art, 2023).

9 Jon Kay and Anders Lund, *The Piecemakers: Master Quilters from Vanderburgh County*, video, January 2016, Indiana University Media Collections Online, https://media.dlib.indiana.edu/media_objects/dz011b851.

10 Jon Kay, *Harold Stark, Indiana State Fair Master, 2011—Steam Engineer and Repairman*, video, July 2011, Indiana University Media Collections Online. https://media.dlib.indiana.edu/media_objects/3r075g62b.

INDIGENOUS FASHION AND CULTURAL EXCHANGE IN NATIVE GATHERINGS

1 Wild West Shows, popular in the early twentieth century, were traveling performances that dramatized life on the US frontier, showcasing staged battles, rodeo stunts, and depictions of cowboys, Native Americans, and lawmen. Often led by figures like Buffalo Bill Cody, these shows romanticized the West, but they also reduced Indigenous cultures to adversaries and stereotypical figures, failing to capture the reality, complexity, and diversity of the American West. The genre of Western films perpetuates this image of the Indian to the present day.

2 Bruce Bernstein, *Santa Fe Indian Market: A History of Native Arts in the Marketplace* (Santa Fe: Museum of New Mexico Press, 2012), 10.

3 Bruce Bernstein, "The Passion of Santa Fe Indian Market: Camping Out, Booth Sitting, and Other Curious Phenomena," *El Palacio*, 112(2): 56-62.

4 "The History of Santa Fe Indian Market and the Southwestern Association for Indian Arts," Artspan, https://www.artspan.com/article/766/the-history-of-santa-fe-indian-market-and-the-southwestern-association-for-indian-arts

5 Teri Greeves, phone conversation, September 23, 2024.

6 Virginia Ballenger, phone conversation, September 11, 2024.

7   Sally Euclaire, "Clothing Show Shows the Finest," *Santa Fe New Mexican*, August 19, 1993, 68.

8   Teri Greeves, phone conversation, September 23, 2024.

9   Amanda Schoenberg, "Fashion Here and Now: Contest Draws Contemporary Takes on Traditional Clothing," *Albuquerque Journal*, August 5, 2012, 28.

10 Schoenberg, "Fashion Here and Now."

11 Maureen E. Reed. "Mixed Messages: Pablita Velarde, Kay Bennett, and the Changing Meaning of Anglo-Indian Intermarriage in Twentieth-Century New Mexico," *Frontiers* 26, no. 3 (2005): 116.

12 Wheeler noted that once she became a SWAIA artist, her fashion production shifted from couture to weaving. "I started doing more blouses, jackets that were my bread and butter. The Indian Market changed my style." She considers her fashion collections as art pieces and her SWAIA sales as a reliable source of income.

13 See Jessica Metcalfe, "Native Designers of High Fashion: Expressing Identity, Creativity, and Tradition in Contemporary Fashion" (PhD diss., University of Arizona, 2010).

14 Formline design is found among Northwest Coast groups such as the Haida, Tlingit, and Kwakwaka'wakw. It typically incorporates stylized representations of animals, humans, and supernatural beings rendered in bold, flowing curves and shapes that create a sense of movement and depth. Formline is not only an aesthetic choice but also a means of storytelling, with the elements of the design conveying cultural narratives and symbolism unique to the artist's community.

15 For more information on the exhibition, see "Dorothy Grant: Raven Comes Full Circle," Haida Gwaii Museum, accessed October 2, 2024, https://haidagwaiimuseum.ca/exhibitions/dorothy-grant-raven-comes-full-circle/.

BLUE RIBBON GALLERY

1   Pamela Hemenway Simpson, *Corn Palaces and Butter Queens: A History of Crop Art and Dairy Sculpture* (Minneapolis: University of Minnesota Press, 2012), 16.

IMAGE CREDITS

Cover: Seed art cover, front and back, handmade by Liz Schreiber. Courtesy the artist. **iv:** Seed map created by Liz Schreiber. Courtesy the artist. **3:** The Art Institute of Chicago / Art Resource, NY. **4:** Photograph by Carol Highsmith. Carol M. Highsmith Archive, Library of Congress Prints and Photographs Division Washington, DC. **5t:** Iowa State Fair. **5b:** Iowa State Fair. **6:** Library of Congress Prints and Photographs Division, Washington, DC. **7t:** Onondaga Historical Association. **7b:** Onondaga Historical Association. **8:** Photograph by Carol Highsmith. Carol M. Highsmith Archive, Prints & Photographs Division, Library of Congress. **9:** © Rodney White/The Register **10:** Copyright © The State Media Company. All rights reserved. Richland Library, Columbia, SC. **11:** "New Mexicans bring their Prize Winners to the State Fair," Albuquerque Progress 11, no. 6, 1944. Albuquerque and Bernalillo County Library. **12:** Minnesota Historical Society Collections. **15:** Oregon Historical Society Museum, 2018-31.1.1.2. **17:** Library of Congress Prints and Photographs Division Washington, DC. **18:** Library of Congress Prints and Photographs Division Washington, DC. **19:** Library of Congress Prints and Photographs Division Washington, DC. **20:** Courtesy of the Minnesota State Fair Archives. **21:** Liz Crowe Collection, Museum of the Cherokee People, 2013.372.0068.1. **22:** McKissick Museum, University of South Carolina, Columbia, South Carolina. **23:** Alcoa Collection, Museum of the Cherokee People, 10/93.8. **24:** Smithsonian American Art Museum, gift of Carolyn L. Mazloomi, 2022.6. **25:** Smithsonian American Art Museum, museum purchase through the Smithsonian Latino Initiatives Pool and the Smithsonian Institution Collections Acquisition Program, 1995.46. **26:** Smithsonian

American Art Museum, gift of Chuck and Jan Rosenak and museum purchase made possible by Ralph Cross Johnson, 1997.124.188. **27:** Photograph by Ruth Ronan. Courtesy Las Arañas Spinners and Weavers Guild. **29:** Minnesota Historical Society Collections Online, FM6.55D. Minnesota Historical Society. **30:** Courtesy Tampa-Hillsborough County Public Library System. **31:** Wisconsin Historical Society, 2004.12.1. **32:** Courtesy Hickman (R.C.) Photographic Archive, The Dolph Briscoe Center for American History, The University of Texas at Austin. **33:** Atlanta University Center, Robert W. Woodruff Library. **34:** Kansas State Historical Society. **35:** Museum of Arts and Design, New York; gift of the Johnson Wax Cmopany, through the American Craft Council, 1977. 1977.2.50. **36–37:** Wisconsin Historical Society. **39:** Image from the 1957 California State Fair and Exposition Catalog. **40:** Image courtesy of Cal Expo. **41:** Gift of Margaret and Joel Chen through the 2020 Decorative Arts and Design Acquisitions Committee (DA²) in memory of Peter Loughrey, Los Angeles County Museum of Art © Kay Sekimachi. **42:** California State Fair Art Collection. **43t:** Image from the 1957 California State Fair and Exposition Catalog. **43b:** Fred Uhl Ball papers, 1936-2002. Archives of American Art, Smithsonian Institution. **44:** Los Angeles County Museum of Art, Smits Ceramics Purchase Fund, Modern Art Deaccession Fund and the Decorative Arts Council Acquisition Fund (M.91.245). **45:** Krannert Art Museum, Bequest of George M. Irwin (2021.12.28). **47t:** University Archives Photograph Collection. Oversize photographs (UA023.030), Special Collections Research Center at NC State University Libraries. **47b:** 4-H Club photograph collection, 1900-1990. (P0114). Utah State University. Special Collections & Archives Department. **48:** 4-H Quilt made with the participation of 4-H members. **49:** Utah State University, Special Collections & Archives Department. **50:** Photograph by University of Minnesota, Photographic Laboratory. **51:** Photograph by J.C. Allen and Son. Indiana Historical Society. **52:** Nebraska State Historical Society, 9530-1. **55:** Photograph courtesy of Indiana State Fair. **56:** Photograph courtesy of Indiana State Fair. **57:** Courtesy of Indiana University's Traditional Arts Indiana. **58:** Courtesy of Materials at Hand: Indiana Folk Crafts Today. **59l:** Photograph by Jon Kay. Courtesy of Indiana University's Traditional Arts Indiana. **59r:** Photograph by Jon Kay. Courtesy of Indiana University's Traditional Arts Indiana. **60:** Photograph by Jon Kay. Courtesy of Indiana University's Traditional Art's Indiana. **61bl:** Photography by John Kay. **61tr:** Photograph by Jon Kay. Courtesy of Indiana

University's Traditional Arts Indiana. **63:** Photo by Phil Karshis. **64:** Photo by Kitty Leaken **65:** Santa Fe Plaza. Photo by Gabrielle Marks. **66:** Image courtesy the Choctaw Indian Fair. **68:** Photo by Gabrielle Marks. **69:** Photo by Stephen Lang Photography. **70:** Photo by Tira Howard. **72:** Photograph by International Harvester Company. Wisconsin Historical Society. **73:** National Museum of American History, Gift of Deere and Company, AG.38A04. **74:** McCormick Harvesting Machine Company. Photograph by John Newhouse, 1951. McCormick Historical Association Collections, Wisconsin Historical Society. **75:** Photograph by International Harvester Company. Wisconsin Historical Society. **76–77:** Images courtesy the artist. **78:** Courtesy of the Minnesota State Fair Archives. **79:** Photographed by D.A. Cline. Nebraska State Historical Society. **80:** Montana State University Uhistorical Photos, Montana State University (MSU) Library, Bozeman, Montana. **81:** Photograph by J.C. Allen and Son. Indiana Historical Society. **82–83:** Images courtesy the artists. **84:** Image courtesy the artist. **85:** Image courtesy the artist. **86–87:** Image courtesy the artist. **88:** Photograph by the Columbus Free Press, 1985. Ohio History Connection. **89:** Collections of Maine Historical Society, MaineMemory.net #152043. **90:** Photograph by the International Harvester Company. Wisconsin Historical Society. **91t:** Sponsored by Beatrice Creamery Co. **91b:** Indiana Historical Society. **92:** Photographed by Howard Ryan, Minnesota Historical Society. **93:** Gale Family Library, Minnesota Historical Society. **94t:** Courtesy of the Minnesota State Fair Archives. **94b:** Courtesy of the Minnesota State Fair Archives. **96–97:** Photographs by Matthew Putney, courtesy Iowa State Fair. **98:** Photograph by State Fair of Texas. **99:** Nebraska History Museum. **100:** New Hampshire Historical Society. **101:** Collection of Nebraska State Historical Society, Museum of Nebraska History, Lincoln. **102:** Courtesy of the artist. **103:** Courtesy of the artist. **104:** Courtesy of the artist. **105:** Collection of the Heard Museum, Phoenix, Arizona. **106–107:** Courtesy of the artist. **108:** Photo Addison Doty, Santa Fe, New Mexico. **109:** Courtesy of Weston Klug. **110:** Courtesy of the artist. **111:** Photograph by State Fair of Texas. **112:** Indiana Historical Society. **113:** Collection of the Kansas Historical Society. **114:** Overbeck Museum, Cambridge City Public Library, Cambridge, Indiana. Photograph by Matthew Pevear. **115:** Collection of Forrest Merrill. **116:** Photo Addison Doty, Santa Fe, New Mexico. **117:** International Quilt Museum, Lincoln, Nebraska, Donated in memory of Mrs. Mary Elizabeth Shelby by the William J. Shelby family, 2014.022.0001.

CONTRIBUTORS

MARY SAVIG is the Lloyd Herman Curator of Craft at the Renwick Gallery of the Smithsonian American Art Museum. She currently oversees the Renwick's acquisition and exhibition programs. Sadly, she was never a dairy queen.

WANDA M. CORN is the Robert and Ruth Halperin Professor Emerita in Art History at Stanford University. She looks forward to publishing her new study, *The Couple with the Pitchfork: From Local Folk to Global Icon,* in 2026.

SARA MORRIS is the Ruth Rippon Curator of Ceramics at the Crocker Art Museum. She is also a PhD candidate in art history with a focus on feminist studies at the University of California, Santa Barbara.

ELANA HAIN has worked at the Renwick Gallery since 2017, first as a curatorial assistant and now as the Renwick's collection manager. In addition to overseeing the permanent collection, she has assisted in organizing around a dozen exhibitions (though this is her first involving butter).

JON KAY is an associate professor of folklore at Indiana University, where he directs Traditional Arts Indiana, the state folk arts program. A public scholar, Kay curates exhibitions, facilitates programs, and produces documentaries.

AMBER-DAWN BEAR ROBE is a fashion curator and art historian specializing in Indigenous fashion arts. She curates exhibitions and runway shows across Canada and the United States.

INDEX

THANK YOU TO OUR SUPPORTERS

State Fairs: Growing American Craft is organized by the Smithsonian American Art Museum.

Support is provided by the Smithsonian's Our Shared Future: 250, a Smithsonian-wide initiative commemorating the nation's 250th. Signature support for Smithsonian's Our Shared Future: 250 has been provided by Lilly Endowment Inc.

MAJOR SUPPORT IS PROVIDED BY:
Altria Group

GENEROUS SUPPORT IS PROVIDED BY:
Sheila Duignan and Mike Wilkins
The James Renwick Alliance for Craft

ADDITIONAL SUPPORT IS PROVIDED BY:
Brenda Erickson
Tania and Tom Evans Curatorial Endowment
Mrs. M. Kathleen Manatt and Michele A. Manatt
Jacqueline B. Mars Endowment
Smithsonian Women's Committee

This project received federal support from the Smithsonian American Women's History Initiative Pool, administered by the Smithsonian American Women's History Museum.

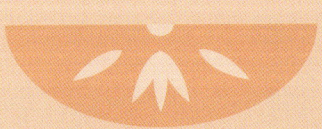